T0244220

ROBERT LORD DIARIES

ROBERT LORD

DIARIES

EDITED BY
**CHRIS BRICKELL,
VANESSA MANHIRE
& NONNITA REES**

OTAGO UNIVERSITY PRESS
Te Whare Tā o Te Wānanga o Ōtākou

CONTENTS

Robert in 1973 when he stayed in Tauranga to stage *It Isn't Cricket* and *Balance of Payments*. MS-1907/006/003, Hocken Collections

INTRODUCTION

ROBERT NEEDHAM LORD wrote over 20 plays for radio and stage, multiple episodes of television series, dialogue for several films and screenplays, and a set of eight lively diaries that describe his life in New Zealand and New York during the 1970s and 1980s. Phillip Mann, who taught Lord at university in 1970, described him as 'an imposingly tall man – well over six feet, with light brown hair, a slight stoop and a manner that could switch from being serious and earnest to riotously funny in the course of a single sentence'.[1] In life and art, 'like all satirical writers, he had a sharp eye for the foibles of those about him'.[2]

Born in Rotorua in 1945, Robert grew up in several provincial cities and attended school in Auckland, Hamilton and Invercargill. His father Dick was a bank manager, his mother Bebe a housewife.[3] Robert's young life had its share of idyllic moments. Recalling his years in Hamilton, he wrote, 'We'd spend most of the summer at the MacFarlane Street beach with its steep white pumice sand ... We'd clamber upstream on the riverbank and float happily down on the current.'[4] Hamilton Boys' High School, though, 'with its quasi-military underpinnings failed to make any sense at all ... So incomprehensible and irrelevant were the activities that surrounded me that I frequently retreated to a fantasy world where I wrote my own reality.'[5]

---

* Notes for the Introduction begin on page 34.

9

Robert discovered an aptitude for writing at primary school, where he penned his first tale, 'The Story of the Sad Sandcastle': 'It was washed away by the tide – how like my life.'[6] At 12, he wrote a short book, 'Two Years in a Wilderness', consisting of a dozen typewritten pages. The protagonist parachutes out of a faltering plane over dense Amazon rainforest, hacks off his own gangrenous leg with a pocketknife, and hops through the heavy vegetation to emerge two years later.[7] A sense of the absurd would stay with Robert through his entire writing career. He wrote his very first play at high school, a short piece 'about a dying man during which a clock ticked dramatically away and very little else actually happened', but it was never staged. He sent the script to the New Zealand Players and they rejected it 'with a note suggesting it wasn't "quite what they were looking for"'.[8]

Steve Dakin befriended Robert in the sixth form at Southland Boys' High School in 1962. He recalled that Robert already felt certain of his literary

Robert (far left in front row) in a rugby team at Southland Boys' High School, 1961. Rugby players would feature in a number of his plays, including *Blood On My Sprigs* and *The Affair*. MS-1907/007/003, Hocken Collections

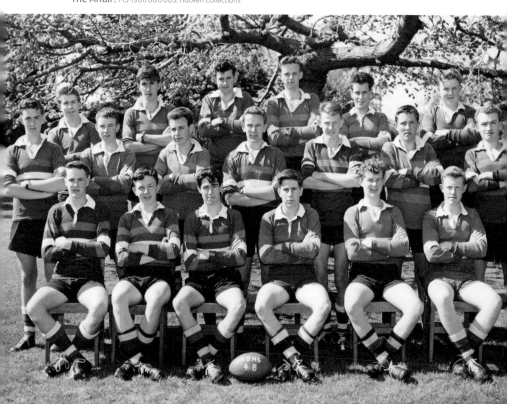

destiny and he 'inhabited characters and puzzled about others' characters'. Oscar Wilde provided creative inspiration, as did Truman Capote. The boys were entranced by Audrey Hepburn when they watched the movie *Breakfast at Tiffany's*, adapted from a Capote novella. 'The full moon was coming and going through scudding clouds and Bob danced around me in his infatuation,' Steve later wrote. 'In his eyes I had achieved an unlikely transformation into Audrey.' That summer, Steve and Robert hitchhiked from Invercargill to Dunedin and went on to Auckland. Robert's legs 'had a momentum of their own, independent of his upper body. His arms, like an Irish dancer, were still by his sides, long legs striding down the road', and he had a knack for securing a lift. 'Bob insisted we would be more likely to get picked up if we were on the move rather than idly loitering by the side of the road with our thumbs out. Every time a car came by we had an act, scripted by Bob – we would turn, thumbs out, smile, wave cheerfully as they passed. We rarely had more than 20 minutes waiting for a ride.'[9] They stayed in Auckland for several days, camping on Steve's future in-laws' lawn in Remuera, 'two 16-year-olds experiencing the first tastes of freedom'.

Robert began a Bachelor of Arts in English Literature and Political Science at the University of Otago and finished it at Victoria University.[10] In 1969, while studying at Wellington Teachers' College, he won the Katherine Mansfield Young Writers' Award for 'Mrs Weeve', an atmospheric short story about a 68-year-old woman's lonely life in the country, her home help who goes mad and is taken away, and a visit from a much younger man whom Mrs Weeve briefly desires.[11] Robert enrolled in New Zealand's first university drama course at Victoria University, where he became Mann's student in 1970. He taught for a year at Petone Central School and in 1971 some of his pupils took part in *The Day We Landed on the Most Perfect Planet in the Universe*, an experimental Pacific Films/NZBC documentary for which Robert had written the dialogue.[12] Producer John O'Shea described it as 'an unusual and strange juvenile hymn to freedom'.[13]

Wellington's Downstage Theatre opened in 1964 with a mission to attract 'new and controversial playwrights', and Robert fitted right in during the early 1970s.[14] He took up the role of stage manager, directed, and acted in children's plays: he was Eeyore in a production of *Winnie the Pooh*. He picked

The cast of *Winnie the Pooh* at Downstage in Wellington, 1971.
From left: Janice Finn, Robert Lord, Susan Wilson, Paul Holmes
and Craig Ashley. Photograph by Terence Taylor. Nonnita Rees collection

up a hammer and a paintbrush to work on stage sets, did part-time publicity, sat on the programme advisory committee, and named the first theatre cat, Fucky.[15] Robert also helped to edit and write for *Act*, a theatre magazine established in 1966.[16]

Bruce Mason's work paved the way in local theatre, but New Zealand plays were still a novelty in 1970 when Robert wrote *It Isn't Cricket*. This, his first successful play, was put on in July 1971 as a Sunday night reading directed by Downstage's artistic director Sunny Amey. It received a standing ovation. *It Isn't Cricket* consists of 17 scenes that depict a series of conversations between six characters in a range of different combinations. It explores

The programme for Unity Theatre's double bill of *It Isn't Cricket* and Christchurch playwright Eve Hughes' *The House That Jack Bought*, a play about the futility of mortgage payments and home maintenance. MS-1907/032, Hocken Collections

themes of relationships, fair play, deceit and distrust, drawing from Lord's interest in 'the way people delude and misguide each other, and come to false perceptions of themselves'.[17] The play also evokes the feeling of being trapped in life: one character refers to the 'small bird that is flying around' inside his chest, trying to escape.[18] Amey recalled that the audience, many of whom knew Robert, were stunned by the work's originality; they had no idea he had been writing a play while making the theatre's wheels turn. Downstage did not offer a season of *It Isn't Cricket*, but Unity Theatre, a left-wing Wellington group formed during the 1940s, staged the play as part of a double bill.[19] In 1973, *It Isn't Cricket* was workshopped at the inaugural

Australian Playwrights Conference in Canberra during a trans-Tasman visit that Robert greatly enjoyed.[20]

In 1973, along with Nonnita Rees, Judy Russell and Ian Fraser, Robert founded Playmarket, New Zealand's playwrights' agency and publisher. The first meeting took place in Wellington, 'on the bed in his tiny Clifton Terrace bedsit'.[21] He and the others worked hard to get New Zealand writing into the country's theatres.[22] Lord wrote *Well Hung*, a farce partially based on the unsolved Crewe murders of 1970. The play is set in a country police station where officers investigate a murder that turns out to have been committed by the station sergeant. The guilty officer hangs himself at the end.[23] *Well Hung* was first up at Downstage in 1974 when Amey chose four new New Zealand plays as part of a wider programme.

That year, too, Robert received a Queen Elizabeth II Arts Council travel bursary and spent six months in the USA, Canada and Britain. He left in July, travelling first to Australia.[24] Once again he was inspired by the vibrant, high-energy Australian scene, enthusing about 'the tremendous life of it – the activity – there is so much of it'.[25] In America he attended his first Eugene O'Neill Playwrights Conference and visited Providence, Rhode Island, where *Well Hung* was being performed. He met Gilbert Parker from the Curtis Brown agency, who worked to have another Lord play, *Meeting Place*, staged at the Phoenix Company in New York. Robert returned to New Zealand for a year and worked as writer-in-residence at Auckland's Mercury Theatre, where he wrote *Heroes and Butterflies*. Buoyed by his professional relationship with Parker, he flew back to New York in 1975.[26] He went on to have works programmed by major off-Broadway and regional American repertory companies.[27]

Lord began his first diary in August 1974, the day he visited the small Connecticut town of East Haddam. He describes the theatre there, 'quite marvellous with an elegant appearance – beautiful bars & so forth & the theatre on the top floor'. The people he met, the dress rehearsal he went to, and lunch with a view of the river also appear in his first diary entry. Lord's jottings remind us that diaries serve a variety of functions. Their writers may see them as a pleasurable diversion from everyday tasks, a companion of sorts, or an opportunity for literary expression and self-memorialisation.[28] Private journals record experiences and relationships and, at their most

Robert in 1974. Russell Craig collection

profound, reflect their writers' progress in emotional, economic or spiritual terms.[29] Lord's diaries do each of these things. Together they offer up a treasure trove of information about the author's approach to writing, his rich social life in New Zealand and New York, his abiding ambivalence about being a New Zealander, and his being gay. More broadly, they tell of the many ways his intimate and intellectual experiences reflected a changing world.

Life in New York was both pleasurable and difficult. Robert and his cherished beagle Becky walked around Riverside Park every day.[30] She rolled in dead squirrels and once had her paw injured in the door of a taxi. Gilbert Parker was so taken with Becky that Robert wondered if Gilbert found the dog more captivating than his plays. Robert took a range of jobs to make ends meet. He was a typesetter for pornographic magazines, a realtor, and a 'shop girl' at news store Le Magasin, where men came in to read porn and cruise.[31] The real estate gig turned up when he cleaned summer rental houses on Fire Island and met Cappy, an enthusiastic realtor. Robert's income was never secure, though, and sometimes the $20 in his wallet was all he had.

Lord's diaries offer a saltier, more explicit and occasionally darker New York version of Armistead Maupin's popular *Tales of the City* books that describe the gay world of San Francisco between 1978 and 1989. Robert was a huge fan of Maupin's writing and, like Maupin, he describes sex and relationships in all their kaleidoscopic colour. There are gay characters, straight ones and those in between. He tells of diners, drag queens, the baths, wet Jockey Shorts contests and smoking hash in the streets at 4am; 'the Saturday night ritual, the coke & quaaludes, The Saint, the high-powered nonsense of that world'. The Saint was a gay megaclub in Manhattan with a circular dancefloor beneath a planetarium dome, and he mentions 'speeding my tits off' on the balcony there. 'New York is the easiest city in the world to do nothing in – and not notice it,' he adds. 'And being gay accentuates this. One is trapped in a ghetto of parties & hunts.'

Robert mingled with New York's actors, directors, designers, writers and dancers. He partied with Broadway and ballet stars – and David Bowie – while Kevin Bacon took part in a staged reading of one of his plays that Bob Balaban directed. Fellow New Zealand playwright Roger Hall recalled that Robert 'seemed to know everyone there: actors, directors, critics, agents'.[32] Meryl

Streep, Christopher Lloyd and Jill Eikenberry were all on the 'brink of fame', and they acted in his plays. He found professional life highly stimulating, and in 1975 he said he liked working with the city's 'major talents'. 'I felt at ease, I felt I had new opportunities to develop and so I wanted to stay.'[33] He became involved with the New Dramatists, an organisation that helped novice playwrights develop their careers. His friends included theatre and film director Jack Hofsiss; Jay Funk, a sometime lover who turned to Christianity; the costume designer Gary ('Granny') Lisz, with whom Robert had a standing lunch appointment every Friday; and actress Joyce Reehling, who later visited him in New Zealand.

A few years after Robert arrived in New York, the emerging AIDS epidemic cast a dark shadow over gay life. In 1981, the year the strange new disease appeared, Robert returned home from a rowdy night out and learned that one friend 'had died of gay cancer' and another was in hospital. 'All this is quite depressing & causes one to have healthy/unhealthy moments of introspection,' he wrote in his diary. Sex lost its appeal for a while. 'One dreads having it – the plague being forever in the spotlight.' Robert worried about the social and political impact of AIDS. He wondered if there might be a 'hideous backlash' against gay men, having read a newspaper opinion piece 'going on about homosexuals turning their back on nature & now nature is getting back at them!' Such hostile views appeared over and over again.[34] Gallows humour provided a little respite: 'Peter Buckley is worried about his health – glands swollen etc & fears he has gay cancer & if he does will not get his teeth fixed – waste of money. I told him to have his teeth out & give the best blowjobs in town.'

Long-distance travel is an endurance test for a nervous flyer, but Robert flew between New York and New Zealand with regularity. He wrote notes in his diary along the way, his thoughts punctuated by bouts of turbulence and views out the window: cities, cloud, snow. A long flight offered an opportunity to ponder a transnational double life and the divided loyalties of the expatriate writer. Where did he belong, and how might he reconcile his wildly different experiences of place and cultural scene? 'There is so much to write & I know I'm going into a time-warp where my Fire Island/New York life with its discos, drugs, spiritualism, enthusiasms & speeches will seem unreal, a dream, just as New Zealand at this moment seems an absurdity.' But he keenly felt his New Zealand origins: 'I could be blind & know I was in NZ. Those strange vowels! It is a voice that sounds to me homely & naïve. It gives me a warm feeling & it puts me on edge all at once.' In a creative sense, Robert's new American life left him stranded on an awkward middle ground:

> I am not now & never will be an American but I have ceased to be a New Zealander. I exist in a limbo. It is very hard to write plays of weight that do not come out of a real world. I still can write with ease about New Zealand. I find it very hard to write about America. A gut understanding is missing. But there is my impression of America & that is probably where I should work.

He had to learn, in his words, 'how to write American'.[35] Several of his later plays, including *China Wars*, *Glorious Ruins* and *The Travelling Squirrel*, were set in the US. Conversely, life in New York, a diverse city of around 7 million people, gave him a fresh perspective on the 'small, contained culture' of New Zealand.[36] 'I do want to write about New Zealand & my life, I want to find out if I ever could live there again & how that country has shaped this 36-year-old penniless writer, typesetter, realtor.' Ambivalence towards his homeland appeared during a visit to the North Island in 1981: 'We then arrive in Raetihi, the carrot capital of NZ, a town with 2 collapsing shops & an abandoned opera house surrounded by dirty fields of carrots. What was an opera house doing here? Was *Tristan* ever performed? A terrible anomaly lost in a world of carrots. It was all too much. We drove home.' He often pondered the relationships between social climate, place and identity: 'Of course being gay & effeminate in a country which above all prizes rude masculinity doesn't make life simple & maybe explains my need for arrogance.'

Some of those who knew Robert well seemed not to recognise the fact he was gay. One family member expressed a reluctance to throw out her children's pram in case Robert decided to get married and have offspring of his own ('can you believe it?'), while another described a local man to him 'with a sashay as gay as if I were some acclaimed heterosexual. It is too bizarre.' One evening, when drinking in a pub at Lake Ōhau, he took part in a very New Zealand conversation about sex and sheep, becoming both participant and observer:

October 27

Sitting in the restaurant of the Northwestern terminal of JFK & feeling somewhat queasy about flying. Had a busy night's sleep after exhausting myself packing & writing notes & paying bills. So I'm leaving N.Y. with $15 and $20 in the bank. Here I am, 36 & penniless which is not exactly how I thought I would be in younger & more ambitious days. I'm wondering if I can actually do what I'm planning. If I can write the book I want to write. Passages of it have formed in my mind over the last several months & then been lost in the shuffle of my rather pointless daily life. But I do want to write the book. I do want to write about New Zealand & my life, I want to find out if I ever could live there again & how that country has shaped this 36 year old penniless writer, typesetter, realtor. Left Fire Island about three weeks ago & reentered the village of Manhattan. Left that strip of sand for the city. Went back again to say goodbye on a glorious autumn day. Pastel shades. Pale reds & yellows & the sun casting pink over the beach. Enormous clarity. Clear. Wandered along the beach. A few clusters of people casting long shadows. Looking posed. Posed by who? Did a larger group surrounding a prone young man. His girl stroking his forehead. What happened? He dove into a wave & hit his head on the sand. Unable to move now & lying with clothes piled over him. A Hilo van parked on the sand next to him. And then a police car. And then a helicopter to take him to the mainland. Later that night I said a prayer for him — whoever he was. And the next day grey & damp as I tidy the 3 bedroom shack that had been home for 6 months. The shack with a ill-shaped swordfish cut out of plywood & tacked

A page from Robert Lord's handwritten diary for 1981–83. MS-2438/109, Hocken Collections

Was grilled about my life & there were a few veiled comments about my sexuality but it was amusing & became hilarious when we were joined by 2 shearers & a carpenter. A variety of stories, mostly lewd, a demonstration of how they shear – one shearer using the other as a sheep & the two bus drivers doing the same & one pulling the other's trousers down – which everyone else overlooked ... The two shearers, good mates, flirt with each other almost. Egg each other on. One of them, Noel, keeps staring at me hard, asks all sorts of questions about New York, wants to show me how to shear. Strange. He takes my address.

Lord's worlds often intersected. During the years he based himself in New York, he developed and maintained rich professional and social networks in New Zealand. His plays continued to be performed here, and he wrote for New Zealand radio and television. Anthony Taylor, director of *Meeting Place*, commissioned and directed Lord's plays for Radio New Zealand and continued to champion his work when he was artistic director at Downstage between 1977 and 1982. Robert cultivated friendships at Downstage, at the newly founded Circa Theatre in Wellington, and in the television and film worlds. He encouraged Sunny Amey to try marijuana, something she did only once.[37] He showed off New York to countless visiting New Zealand and Australian friends and colleagues, organising tickets and invitations for them. George Webby remembered, 'In his jaunty manner, Robert threaded me through everything he could find in New York that would get me through an astonishing lack of sleep.' [38]

In recalling their times with Robert over the years, many friends remember his generosity, energy, warmth and constant humour. One described his 'laugh, walk and presence, his exotic ordinariness'; another said he could be 'wickedly fun' to be around. They listened to him read from his work, 'screeds of pages printed on a dot matrix printer', laughing so hard he could barely get the words out.[39] A talented host, Robert often entertained at home in his tiny New York apartment or his place in Dunedin. He enjoyed domesticity, and his diaries include a recipe for salmon and references to poaching fruit and baking bread. In 1970 he stage-managed Amey's Downstage production of DH Lawrence's *The Daughter-in-Law* and devised the on-stage baking. He had the raw ingredients ready for actor Jeanette Lewis to mix, knead, shape and put into the oven. He also had a real loaf underway in the Downstage

Robert set up his office in the living room and this 1986 iteration includes an Atari computer. MS-1907/002/001, Hocken Collections

kitchen and, at the appropriate point in the performance, discreetly switched the uncooked mixture for the delicious-smelling, freshly baked version.[40]

Lord was an innovative stage manager, no doubt, but what did it mean to be a writer? 'I used to be able to convince myself that I was what I was doing,' he wrote in 1981. 'Now it is not easy. I'm not sure what I am. I can define myself by negatives. Once I was by choice a writer, now I am a writer because it is the only occupation where I seem to be me.' But he wondered whether his facility with words was truly the noblest of artistic powers:

> *Sometimes I wonder why I have been forced to spend my creative life grappling with words & the logic & rationality they demand. And words are the coins of the realm of the thought. They are instruments of common barter; they belong to rich & poor, stupid & bright. I would rather, I wish I could paint; I wish I could dance; I wish I could go beyond language. I wish I could find a way of reaching directly into another's heart. Words are my only tool. Sometimes I think perhaps I have not worked hard enough. I am still alive. There is time.*

The apartment at 250 West 85th Street, New York, during the 1980s. Robert would keep the apartment until the end of his time in New York. Reminders of New Zealand in this room include a model wharenui, Michael Tubberty's famous 1975 photograph of Whina Cooper and child, and a poster from the Christchurch production of *Unfamiliar Steps*.

Words can be limiting and powerful, demanding discipline while promising freedom. Lord's process of writing required fastidiousness and gave rise to existential uncertainty, and like many authors and dramatists he often suffered a 'creative block'. He wrote and rewrote scripts, boiling them down to the basics – 'I go through a process of removing things, I write very spare scripts normally,' he told Amey.[41] He did not want for inspiration. He read voraciously and went to a great many plays. Katherine Mansfield, Janet Frame, Somerset Maugham, Patrick White, Thornton Wilder, Edward Albee, Tennessee Williams, Eugene O'Neill, Harold Pinter and Joe Orton all informed his work. He had a particular interest in 'the human condition', especially its stresses and small-scale crises, and he talked of feelings and observations of life that 'strike a chord – an emotional response, and you want to try and explore that area of human relationships'.[42] Theatre need not be 'revolutionary', he said, but plays could help audiences come to new understandings of the world.[43]

Many of Lord's own radio and stage plays give the impression of 'a rollercoaster between surrealism and social satire'.[44] *Well Hung*, for instance, is both dark and funny. Roger Hall compared the play to the work of English playwright Joe Orton, concluding Lord had Orton's wit 'without Orton's cruelty'.[45] Lord couched his social criticism in humour. When Wally, a new recruit, asks, 'Can I spend all day telling people off, and can I whack them with a truncheon when I don't like them?' Detective Jasper Sharp responds, 'Wally, you're a natural. Already you've embraced the ethos of the New Zealand police service.'[46]

Much of Lord's work explores 'the shifting and treacherous sands of personal relations'.[47] Longstanding married couples are the basis of several plays, including *Bert and Maisy*, *China Wars* and *Joyful and Triumphant*.[48] Lord wrote *Bert and Maisy* in 1979, and the play, set in a small, unnamed town, made its first stage appearance in Christchurch in 1983 under the title *Unfamiliar Steps*. It was performed around New Zealand, in Sydney and at the Old Globe Theatre in San Diego, and later became a television series. In *Bert and Maisy*, which Lord described as 'a low-keyed comedy of New Zealand manners', Bert meets a young man, Tom, at the local railway station. Tom brings a hint of cosmopolitanism to Bert and Maisy's routine life.[49] He has travelled overseas,

drinks wine and coffee rather than beer and tea, gets the couple dancing around the living room, and upends gendered divisions of labour by sending Bert into the kitchen and Maisy out into the vegetable garden. Maisy's niece Shona and her upwardly mobile insurance broker husband Grant are both committed to respectability and they resent Tom's influence: 'What will the neighbours think?'[50]

In the late 1980s, Circa Theatre commissioned Lord's final play, *Joyful and Triumphant*. It follows the small-town Bishop family over eight successive Christmas Days between 1949 and 1989. Lord mulls over themes of family, propriety, conformity, social mobility, changing political sensitivities, and intimate relationships between Māori and Pākehā. One of the Pākehā characters is Raewyn, who gave up for adoption the baby boy she had with a young Māori man many years before. She is reunited with her adult son and meets his children at the end of the play. Her father, known for his prejudiced views of Māori, declares that his newly discovered grandson 'had a good head on his shoulders and it was obvious where that came from'.[51]

Family life was a recurring focus in Lord's creative work. He wrote about the tensions festering in suburban living rooms at a time when the nuclear family's lustre had begun to tarnish. Some of Lord's characters, including Bert, Maisy and Raewyn, visibly chafe at expectations of male breadwinning and female domestic confinement. In her discussion of Lord's plays, Susan Williams refers to the 'brutalized society' of middle-class suburbia and the failure of the conventional family to 'provide either health or happiness to those who are trapped within it'.[52] Lord had no wish to live a suburban life. He regarded 'the homogeneous nature of New Zealand society as somewhat claustrophobic', and in 1983 bridled at a suggestion he might return from New York and live in his parents' basement.[53] Such a plan 'would put an end to any possibility of a career as a dramatist,' he wrote in his diary. 'I would move out of touch in more ways than one & heighten the cultural confusion that I am finally coming to terms with.' Nevertheless, Robert's family became increasingly important as he entered his forties. He wrote regularly to his parents while he was in New York and kept up with family news, and his mother Bebe became immensely proud of her writer son.

Lord's critique of suburban existence sat alongside a persistent focus on erotic ambiguities, and not just in the pub at Lake Ōhau. Almost all the characters in the American play *China Wars* have a bisexual component, and queerness appears in the New Zealand plays too.[54] In *Joyful and Triumphant*, Raewyn has a brief relationship with Liz. This bothers Raewyn's traditionalist father, who exclaims, 'I can just see her driving through the front door on her Harley-Davidson.'[55] In *Bert and Maisy*, Grant suggests Bert picked up his urbane friend Tom in the railway station toilets: 'men's rooms, mirrors, sideways glances'.[56] Most reviewers ignored the innuendo, seeing Tom as a substitute for Bert and Maisy's wayward and absent son.[57] But Lord often

Robert stands on the porch of his parents' house in suburban Meadowbank during the early 1980s. MS-1907/004, Hocken Collections

twisted the conventions of sexual conformity into unusual forms. The middle-aged parents in *Balance of Payments*, a 1972 play that Lord later described as 'a bit naughty', live off the earnings of their well-endowed rent-boy son.[58] His ability to attract men at swimming pools and saunas interests them so much they demand to know the finer details while insisting he make more money. One day, when he brings home only eight dollars, his furious mother stabs and kills him with a knitting needle before shooting two subsequent visitors to the house – the vicar and a client of her son – as she tries to cover her tracks.

Ostensibly about heterosexual relationships, the enigmatic *Meeting Place*, also first staged in 1972, is just as gay – and even more grim. There are ongoing homoerotic tensions between its two female and two male characters, a considerable amount of same-sex touching, a vivid description of a casual pickup that turns into a gay-bashing, and an altercation between the two men staged to look like a sexual assault.[59] Even in the darkest of moments, however, Lord insisted on the presence of comedy and irony. Actors rehearsed what they found a heavy scene in *Meeting Place*, only to discover how funny the playwright thought it was.

Lord introduced queer themes onto the stage just as the gay liberation movement was making its mark in New Zealand.[60] Few local playwrights had anything to say about homosexuality during the 1970s when sex between men was still illegal.[61] Gordon Dryland's *If I Bought Her the Wool*, from 1971, was a kind of 'queer romcom' that rehearsed old and new ideas about homoeroticism.[62] It, along with *Balance of Payments* and *Meeting Place*, appeared only a few years after Mart Crowley's landmark American production *Boys in the Band*, a 1968 play about a gay man's birthday party and the testy relationships between his friends.

After many years based in America, Robert returned to New Zealand in 1987 to take up the Robert Burns Fellowship in Dunedin. He wrote charmingly about the southern city, describing the clouds hanging over the hills and the tendency of the sun to come out when the day is nearly over. 'Dunedin really is peculiar and makes me feel melancholic,' he wrote. 'It seems to be not of this world and it isn't. It's like visiting your grandmother. But I like it.'

The Affair, from 1987, is set in the city. This play tells of events that occur in a series of familiar places: the Robbie Burns and Captain Cook pubs, Governor's Café and Centre City New World supermarket. An incomplete manuscript in several rough drafts, *Academic Circles*, pokes fun at a fictionalised English Department in an 'unattractive modern building' at the University of Otago. Illicit liaisons and intellectual snobberies come to the surface during a power struggle that ensues when the much-loved head of department can no longer continue in his job. The pretender to the throne is 'a sexy man whom we don't want to believe is as evil as he seems but who, in the end, turns out to be even worse'.[63] Another character gives the whole of New Zealand a drubbing: 'Culture? In this country? You'd be better off burying a bottle of Steinlager in a time capsule.'[64]

Opposite: The poster for *Meeting Place*, 1972. Terence Taylor photographed the cast members on Mt Victoria. From left to right: Craig Ashley, Nonnita Rees, Susan Wilson and Tony Ditchburn. MS-1907/090, Hocken Collections

MEETING PLACE

by Robert Lord
directed by
Anthony Taylor
opening Oct. 24
Downstage ↻

As Burns Fellow, Robert took part in academic life, socialising on campus and elsewhere. Young people gravitated towards him at the Gardens Tavern in North Dunedin, finding him to be a warm, humorous conversationalist.[65] He mentored gay students, including those with an interest in the theatre, and a memorable diary entry describes a lesbian and gay dance at the Māori Hill Community Centre. In October 1987, he picked up the keys to the small cottage he bought at 3 Titan Street, in the student area: 'Absolutely tiny. One bedroom. Tiny courtyard out the back. Brick. Old (turn of century).' Faced one day with the prospect of having two guests at once, Robert described it as 'the smallest house in the southern hemisphere if not the world'. He had it modified to suit his height by relocating the kitchen light switches high up on the walls, having the kitchen benches raised, and setting up two showers – one of them outdoors – suitable for his tall frame. Boswell, a Jack Russell terrier, kept him company for a time.[66]

In 1989, Robert went to see doctors in New York and was prescribed medication, including AZT, for AIDS-related symptoms. Back in New Zealand he had treatment for skin lesions and a large and painful brain tumour. Still, he carried on writing and arranging for his work to be performed. In November 1991, extremely sick, he was admitted to Dunedin Hospital where many of his friends and family came to see him for the last time. He died on 7 January 1992. *Joyful and Triumphant* was first performed six weeks after his death. This, his most popular and well-received play, earned him a posthumous award for Playwright of the Year. His home in Titan Street is now Robert Lord Writers' Cottage, a retreat for visiting writers.

• • •

The diaries in this volume span a 17-year period of Robert Lord's life, from the first trip to the United States in 1974 to the final entry in March 1991, less than a year before his death. There are many gaps, including the six years that disappear in the late 1970s. Towards the end of his 1974 diary, Robert wrote, 'New York I just love love but doubt if I could work there'; by the start of the next diary, in 1980, he had been there for several years and was well embedded in Manhattan life.

The front room of Lord's Titan Street cottage in 2022. Chris Brickell collection

Lord's brown 1981–83 diary and blue 1984–85 diary. The diaries are not fancy: two of the eight volumes are wire-bound notebooks with card covers, and the rest consist of unbound A4 pages. Some are typewritten, others are computer printouts.

MS-2438/110, MS-2438/109, Hocken Collections

In 1987, when packages of Robert's papers arrived in Dunedin from New York, he decided to donate them to the Hocken Library. 'Called Stuart Strachan of the Hocken who came over and we discussed the gift of the papers to the Library – on loan during my lifetime, gift thereafter. I retain copyright. He is sending over boxes and over the next few weeks I will go through everything and sort it out. What a relief it will be to have them off my hands. He seemed pleased I had retained personal correspondence.'[67] Sorting through his papers was not always easy, though. 'Came across pieces of a diary which made me cringe. Don't know if I can force myself to read it all.'

Robert was a self-conscious diary writer. He chastised himself for his irregular recording habits – 'I have no ability when it comes to keeping an ongoing diary' – and he worried about coming across badly: 'Have a feeling that I am a neurotic bitch & that these pages will bear testament to that. Oh dear. I'm not really, just confused, insecure & broke.' At one point he even asked, 'Are diaries an act of narcissism or self torture?' Robert also wondered who their audience might be. He found it difficult to find a 'natural voice' in which to write because he imagined any one of his diaries being read by others, 'a stab for posterity or something', and this gave rise to technical problems.[68] 'If it was just for me I wouldn't have to explain certain things, etc.' The idea of unknown readers delving into his thoughts also made him uneasy. He saw diaries, in general, as 'a device for gaining perspective on one's own behaviour, not a window for strangers'.

Despite Robert's discomfort with the idea of an audience, the donation of his papers to the Hocken Library suggests an awareness of a potential readership. Some of the diaries appear to have been written with an eye on future publication. He began his handwritten journal for 1981–83, including a long account of a trip home to New Zealand, with 'the concept of a book' in mind, but quickly found it 'unworkable'. In 1987, when he recorded his year in Dunedin, he mentioned a 'Burns Fellow Diary' he might write for the magazine *North & South*: 'I must strive to make it upbeat as when I analyze the year most of the news is bad but I don't want to appear grumpy.'[69] The 1989–90 diary largely consists of letters, both 'real' and unsent, that would be the basis of a 'non-fiction epistolary novel' to be called *The Goodbye Book*.

Playwriting for the live theatre is the diaries' major creative focus, and Lord tells of the vagaries and frustrations of his attempts to establish a career in the industry. In a practical sense, his diaries are extended to-do lists that record the development of well-known works as well as ideas that never made it past the concept stage. He traces the ups and downs of the development of *Well Hung, Bert and Maisy, China Wars, The Travelling Squirrel* and *Joyful and Triumphant*. There are detailed and lively accounts of what is or isn't working in a play as a whole or a specific scene. We include about half of the diaries' total text in this book, but the unabridged diaries provide ample opportunity for a theatre historian to explore the writing of Lord's works in sometimes forensic detail. In this abridged volume we have restricted our selections to material that covers key elements of his life and work without demanding readers' familiarity with the plays. We include a list of Lord's works at the back of this book.

For consistency's sake, we have corrected typographical errors and standardised spellings throughout (though we have retained Robert's mix of US and English spelling). The 1989–90 diary's 'epistolary novel' format lends itself to repetition and self-editorialising, with multiple letters on the same topics and explanatory comments describing the recipients. We have cut back this framing device, instead keeping the diaristic sections of the letters in chronological order and, in some cases, combining letters, especially where several were written on the same date. Where possible, we have provided brief notes on the many friends and colleagues who people the diaries, but there are gaps: in some cases the context is clear for passing acquaintances, and in others we have been unable to track down information. As noted in the text, we have changed some names where details in the text may affect the privacy of living people.

Robert Lord's diaries invite their readers to compare their writer's inner life and the cultural worlds of his time.[70] They tell of a wryly funny, perceptive man who occupied a curious position as both an insider and outsider, active participant and looker-on, New Zealander and New Yorker. His ambiguous status provided him with unique insights and fodder for his writing, and the evocative and passionately emotional diaries present a warts-and-all picture of a pioneering playwright's relationships, personal struggles and creative spirit.

NOTES

1. Phillip Mann, 'Introduction', in *Three Plays: Robert Lord*, ed. Phillip Mann (Wellington: Playmarket, 2013), p. 21.
2. Ibid., p. 29.
3. Susan Williams, 'Metamorphosis at "The Margin": Bruce Mason, James K Baxter, Mervyn Thompson, Renée and Robert Lord, Five Playwrights Who Have Helped to Change the Face of New Zealand Drama', PhD thesis, Massey University, Palmerston North, 2006, p. 262.
4. Robert Lord, 'Hamilton: Scenes from a Life', *Landfall 180*, December 1991, p. 403.
5. Ibid., p. 405.

6. Ibid. This story, or at least Lord's remembered version of it, appears in the script of the play *The Travelling Squirrel*: see Robert Lord, *The Travelling Squirrel*, in *Three Plays*, ed. Mann, pp. 135–37.

7. Robert Lord, 'Two Years in the Wilderness', unpublished typescript, MS-1907/052, Hocken Collections (HC). Lord also refers to this story in the script of *Travelling Squirrel*, p. 155.

8. Lord, 'Hamilton', p. 406.

9. Steve Dakin, 'Hitching a Ride with Bob', 2016, unpublished notes in editors' possession.

10. Robert Lord, 'Autobiographical notes', unpublished manuscript in editors' possession.

11. Robert Lord, 'Mrs Weeve', MS-2440/049, HC; Mann, 'Introduction', p. 17.

12. John Reid, *Whatever It Takes: Pacific Films and John O'Shea 1948–2000* (Wellington: Victoria University Press, 2018), p. 204.

13. John O'Shea, *Don't Let It Get You – Memories, Documents* (Wellington: Victoria University Press, 1999), p. 107.

14. Mann, 'Introduction', p. 19.

15. Nonnita Rees, 'Introduction', in *Number 8 Wire*, ed. David O'Donnell (Wellington: Playmarket, 2011), p. 79; John Smythe, *Downstage Upfront: The First 40 Years of New Zealand's Longest-running Professional Theatre* (Wellington: Victoria University Press, 2004), p. 132; 'Robert's Scrapbook', MS-1907/049, HC.

16. Smythe, *Downstage Upfront*, p. 58.

17. Rosemary Vincent, 'The Lord Touch on TV', *New Zealand Woman's Weekly*, 18 July 1988, p. 34.

18. Phillip Mann, 'Introduction', in *Three Plays*, ed. Mann, pp. 33–41.

19. On the history of Unity, see Smythe, *Downstage Upfront*, p. 67; Sarah Gaitanos, *Nola Millar: A Theatrical Life* (Wellington: Victoria University Press, 2006), ch. 7.

20. Rees, 'Introduction', p. 80.

21. Smythe, *Downstage Upfront*, p. 139.

22. Nonnita Rees, 'Getting New Zealand Writing into Theatres: The Story of Playmarket', in *Playmarket 40: 40 Years of Playwriting in New Zealand*, ed. Laurie Atkinson (Wellington: Playmarket, 2013), p. 15.

23. For a discussion, see Smyth, *Downstage Upfront*, p. 149; Mann, 'Introduction', in *Three Plays*, ed. Mann, pp. 217–22.

24. Susan Williams, 'Advocating Interaction with "The Other": Robert Lord's Use of the Food Metaphor', in *Performing Aotearoa: New Zealand Drama and Theatre in an Age of Transition*, eds David O'Donnell and Marc Maufort (Brussels: P.I.E. Peter Lang, 2007), p. 88.

25. Sunny Amey, 'Robert Lord: Interviewed by Sunny Amey', *Act 24*, 1974, p. 10.

26. Williams, 'Advocating Interaction', p. 88.

27. James Wenley, *Aotearoa New Zealand in the Global Theatre Marketplace: Travelling Theatre* (London and New York: Routledge, 2020), pp. 206–07.

28. Miles Fairburn, *Nearly Out of Heart and Hope: The Puzzle of a Colonial Labourer's Diary* (Auckland: Auckland University Press, 1995), pp. 2–5.

29. Genevieve De Pont, 'Hiding and Revealing: The Emotional History of a Travel Diary', in *The Lives of Colonial Objects*, eds Annabel Cooper, Lachy Paterson and Angela Wanhalla (Dunedin: Otago University Press, 2015), pp. 268–74, esp. p. 272.

30. Hilary Halba, 'Robert Lord's New York: Big and Small, Notes on Life and Art', *Australasian Drama Studies 60*, 2012, p. 33.

31. On the typesetting job, see 'US-based NZer Home for Own Play', unattributed clipping, Scrapbook, MS-1907/002, HC.

32. Roger Hall, 'Robert Lord – Last Lines', *North and South*, April 1992, p. 15.

33. Robert Lord, 'Symposium of NZ Playwrights Abroad', *Landfall 116*, 1975, p. 298.

34. Paula Treichler, *How to Have Theory in an Epidemic: Cultural Chronicles of AIDS* (Durham: Duke University Press, 1999).

35. Robert Lord, 'Burns Fellow 1987', Recorded interview with Rowena Cullen, Dunedin, 1988.

36. 'Small Town Enzed', *Press*, 13 July 1983, Scrapbook, MS-1907/002, HC.

37. Sunny Amey, conversation with Nonnita Rees, 6 November 2022.

38. George Webby, *Just Who Does He Think He Is? A Theatrical Life* (Wellington: Steele Roberts, 2006), p. 252.

39. Michael Metzger, email to Chris Brickell, 14 November 2022.

40. Sunny Amey, conversation with Nonnita Rees, 6 November 2022.

41. Amey, 'Robert Lord', p. 7.

42. Ibid.

43. Ibid.

44. David O'Donnell, 'Foreword', in *Three Plays*, ed. Mann, p. 12.

45. Hall, 'Robert Lord', p. 15.

46. Robert Lord, *Well Hung*, in *Three Plays*, ed. Mann, p. 287.

47. David Carnegie, 'High as a Kite', *Act 4*, November 1979, p. 72.

48. Williams, 'Metamorphosis', p. 268.

49. Robert Lord, 'Introduction', in *Bert and Maisy: A Play by Robert Lord* (Dunedin: Otago University Press, 1988), p. 5.

50. Lord, *Bert and Maisy*, p. 67.

51. Robert Lord, *Joyful and Triumphant* (Wellington: Victoria University Press, 1993), p. 96.

52. Williams, 'Advocating Interaction', p. 90; Williams, 'Metamorphosis', p. 284.

53. Lord, 'Symposium', p. 298.

54. On homoerotic themes in *China Wars*, see Halba, 'Robert Lord's New York', p. 36.

55. Lord, *Joyful and Triumphant*, p. 90.

56. Lord, *Bert and Maisy*, p. 74.

57. An exception that hints at Bert's challenge to social respectability is 'Unfamiliar Steps', *Press*, 6 July 1983. For this review and others, see Scrapbook, MS-1907/002, HC.

58. Robert Lord, 'Burns Fellow 1987'.

59. Smythe, *Downstage Upfront*, p. 132.

60. For a discussion of the gay liberation movement in New Zealand, see Chris Brickell, *Mates and Lovers: A History of Gay New Zealand* (Auckland: Godwit, 2008), ch. 5.

61.   James Courage, who was born in Canterbury in 1903 and moved to England in 1922, wrote two plays with homoerotic themes: *New Country*, in 1926, and *Private History*, in 1938. It appears neither was ever staged in New Zealand. See Chris Brickell (ed.), *James Courage Diaries* (Dunedin: Otago University Press, 2021), pp. 31–32; James Courage, *New Country: Plays and Stories* (Dunedin: Genre Books, 2015). After Lord's and Dryland's 1970s work, it seems the next queer-themed play was Bruce Mason's *Blood of the Lamb*, about a lesbian couple: John Smythe, *The Plays of Bruce Mason: A Survey* (Wellington: Victoria University Press and Playmarket, 2015), ch. 16.

62.   Shane Bosher, 'Firing the Canon', *Playmarket Annual 55*, 2020, pp. 52–59; Gordon Dryland, 'If I Bought Her the Wool', *Act 28*, August 1975, pp. 1–20.

63.   Robert Lord, Notes related to 'Academic Circles', MS-2241/026, HC, p. 1.

64.   Robert Lord, 'Academic Circles', incomplete typescript, MS-2241/050, HC, p. 12.

65.   Mike Arthur, email to Nonnita Rees, 4 February 2023.

66.   Hall, 'Robert Lord', p. 14.

67.   Robert Lord, diary entry, 29 April 1987, MS-2438/111, HC, p. 13.

68.   Robert Lord, diary entry, 2 April 1985, MS-2438/110, HC, p. 27.

69.   Robert Lord, diary entry, 10 December 1987, MS-2438/111, HC, p. 102.

70.   Irina Paperno, 'What Can be Done with Diaries?', *Russian Review 63*, 4, 2004, pp. 561–73, esp. p. 572.

Overleaf: Robert Lord during the 1970s. MS-2438/223/004, Hocken Collections

DIARIES

1974

Robert at the Golden Gate Bridge, San Francisco. MS-1907/007/001, Hocken Collections

14 August 1974

Last week spent time in the company of Arthur Ballet, Edith Oliver & Lloyd Richards.* I went to East Haddam, Conn, about 20 miles from Waterford – thru most delicious countryside – many trees, houses set among them & no sign of farming & East Haddam itself a delight, quite unreal, on the Conn River, an old stopover for river transport & since the late 18thC the home of an opera house, recently restored – seating 300 & now operates as a theatre for the region (The Goodspeed), quite marvellous with an elegant appearance – beautiful bars & so forth & the theatre on the top floor. Loved it. Saw dress rehearsal of a new musical destined for B'way: *Shenandoah*, based on a 65 James Stewart movie & somewhat old hat, though with good dance numbers – most of the party despised it & offended by cutie Black boy part & so at lunch afterwards a great debate & Edith sounding off, Arthur getting uptight about everyone being negative & so forth – but a great lunch overlooking the river. And the O'Neill is over – strange feelings about it but good to watch, though I was often bored as had nothing to do.

The O'Neill is a beautiful place & could be duplicated in Aust or NZ – should pursue that. Saw great people & actors there (John Hawkins, Bobby Christian, Ben Masters). Also saw in that last week *Anything Goes* at a summer theatre with Ann Miller, which was dull except for some tap numbers – & realize some odd things – like originally it was to be about a shipboard fire, while in rehearsal a tragedy at sea meant it all had to be changed, also it has the Aimee McPherson-type character that appears in *Vile Bodies* & her angels,† which leads to the thought that novel might make a great musical. Also in the week that Nixon resigned, an act which caused great tension & left everyone flat at the end – got v. drunk watching tele &

---

*   **Arthur Ballet** (1928–2012), academic, dramaturg and director known as a champion of new plays, and regular dramaturg at the National Playwrights Conference. With Martin Esslin, dramaturg for workshop of RL's *Dead and Never Called Me Mother* at the 1975 conference. **Edith Oliver** (1913–1998), theatre and film critic, and *New Yorker* writer. Worked with new playwrights as a dramaturg at the National Playwrights Conference 1975–95. **Lloyd Richards** (1919–2006), Canadian-American theatre director, actor and academic. Dean of the Yale School of Drama 1979–91, and artistic director of the National Playwrights Conference for 32 years.

†   **Aimee Semple McPherson** (1890–1944), Canadian celebrity evangelist and faith healer.

Above: The Eugene O'Neill Center. Robert sent this postcard to his Aunt Rose, and on the back he wrote: 'I am certainly having a marvellous time in America. It is only five weeks since I left New Zealand but it seems so much longer than that – I've seen so much and met so many good people.' MS-1907/007/004, Hocken Collections

Left: Robert in the USA, 1974. MS-1907/011/095, Hocken Collections

rang Craig & Donna in Sydney (& it was 8/8, Craig's birthday).* One of the joys of the USA is the vocal experience – the extraordinary array of accents – each rich, expressive – Italian etc. Then with farewells at the O'Neill on Sunday we went to a vast ocean beach in Rhode Island where the water was that tourist ad blue & then back to Waterford. Then the train to Bridgeport in the unexpected company of Brian Syron, who confuses me but think he is good.† And we talked about greater NZ involvement in Aust Conf the Bondi Project – must write to him this week. Then in Bridgeport (ugh) a bus to Stratford & to find I have been put in a motel miles away from the theatre & expensive – colour TV but shabby, anyway stayed there one night but am now staying in an amazing home but more of that later. Saw *12th Night*, which after a slow start was very good – a strange painted set that looks as if it has risen from the sea & why does the play start in the court? But an observation on the American way of life – it is hot & people prance with such flair, & the area in front of the theatre (where I am now writing) has tables etc and people have lunches, dinner here & minstrels wander round singing. Great. At Bridgeport bus station saw a lady talking silently to herself & gesticulating wildly. Haunted? Why can't a summer theatre start in Auckland? The American Shakespeare Theatre – Stratford, Conn – is a vast wooden building, big auditorium but not forbidding. Outside the theatre today stalls selling goodies & curios. It really is an idyllic place. A river floats nearby with many pleasure craft. Loved *R&J* – elegant production & beautiful sets & costumes, extraordinary girl Roberta Maxwell playing Juliet. Now here again for *Cat on a Hot Tin Roof*, which I refuse to call *Cat*. Another marvellous evening & many many people picnicking, a rather elegant feeling with cloths spread on the grass, with marvellous salads being served and wine bottles opened. And free tickets for me, which is very good.

---

* **Craig Ashley**, New Zealand actor based in Australia since 1975. He was in the Downstage company from 1971 to 1974, and appeared in several of RL's early plays. **Donna Akersten**, New Zealand actor who played many roles at both Downstage and Circa theatres, Wellington.

† **Brian Syron** (1934–1993), Australian actor, teacher, activist and the country's first Indigenous film director. Trained in New York and London in the 1960s, and co-founded the Australian National Playwrights Conference with Katharine Brisbane in 1973.

Really an extraordinary way of life. Now for the good news – went and saw Robert Gordon after *R&J* (have an idea about that play),* we meet at about 5 & talk and walk to the restaurant getting there about 5.30 & then he casually says he has a message for me to ring Trinity Square Theatre in Providence, Rhode Island about *Well Hung* – so cool he was and I of course all excited – Arthur B had sent them the script, how they knew I was in this country I do not know – and by then too late to ring so will ring them tomorrow morning. Began to think that neither Downstage nor [Sydney's] Nimrod had anything to do with this production, or my agent for that matter and all those percentages I have to shell out. So maybe all will happen.

I must find a country where I can rest up and work. I'm sure it will be Australia. I am confused but must keep on I think. By the way, how much Shakespeare will I see on my travels – so far very good productions of *King Lear* and *Love's Labour's Lost* (Guthrie) & *Twelfth Night* & *Romeo & Juliet*.† The place is idyllic & people have obviously showered & changed after a hot day & this for them is an occasion. *Cat on a Hot Tin Roof* was great – quite intriguing, if that is the word, to see it now – 19 years later & not at all dated – in fact with its discussion of mediocrity & personal truth it is very pertinent.

Well rang Trinity Square Rep Co & yes they do want to do *Well Hung* & that is the best news to come my way for ages, will go & see them on my way to Britain I think, they have to deal with Howard but must get myself some sort of agent here.‡ Am very excited re the play & of course am dreaming as usual.

Westport is the most beautiful small town I've seen so far – far ahead of New London or Stratford, really pleasant streets, trees & shops & a remarkable bookshop called, surprise, surprise, The Remarkable Bookshop. Left Stratford about midday & managed to get a bus right to Westport,

---

* **Robert Gordon**, American author and playwright, later Professor of Creative Writing at San Francisco State University.
† Both *King Lear* and *Love's Labour's Lost* were directed by Michael Langham for the 1974–75 season at Minneapolis's Guthrie Theater.
‡ **Howard Nicholson**, RL's Australian agent.

Well Hung at Downstage in Wellington, 1974, with Michael Haigh (left) and Craig Ashley (right). Photograph by Terence Taylor. MS-2438/063/002, Hocken Collections

which is good, & am now waiting round for Ed Hastings,* who is in rehearsal till about 5.30, so having done the shops I am now sitting in a cocktail bar, which is somewhat decadent at 3.15 but at least it is cool here.

So many ideas at present and simply must get to work on them. Let one enumerate: 1) *Dead & Never Called Me Mother* – a social, financial, sexual comedy for six characters. 2) Sarah Bernhardt's *Hamlet* – my play for Reg.†
3) a play in an old people's home during a performance of *Romeo & Juliet* – 2 old people in love etc with scenes from the play. 4) *Vile Bodies* – a musical, witty but I cannot find a copy of the book. 5) Also want to work on *Kite* and

---

* **Edward Hastings** (1931–2011), a founding member of San Francisco's American Conservatory Theater and its artistic director 1986–92.
† **Reg Livermore**, Australian actor, singer, performer, presenter and painter; known for roles in musicals such as *Hair* and *The Rocky Horror Show*, and the one-man show *Betty Blokk-buster Follies*.

Dead and Never Called Me Mother, a tragicomedy set in a large suburban home, tells of mistaken intentions, seduction and strained family loyalties. Meryl Streep (top left) plays Alice, a friend of the family who longs in vain for a relationship with pianist John (played by Joel Brooks, top right). John is utterly devoted to his mother, Sarah (Jill Andre, bottom left), who is having an affair with the gardener, Sean (Ben Masters, bottom right).

MS 2438/148/002, Hocken Collections

Workshopping *Dead and Never Called Me Mother* at the National Playwrights Conference, 1975. From left: Arthur Ballet, Martin Esslin, Meryl Streep, Joel Brooks, Robert Lord, Jill Andre. Ben Masters sits on the far right. MS-2438/148/001, Hocken Collections

6) want to rewrite *Heroes & Butterflies* getting it into two acts making it funnier and 7) rework *Body In The Park* for BBC & 8) write a new radio piece for the NZBC, so there is much to be done in the next short while.

The flight from Auckland to Sydney had me all atwitter – but it was good to be in Sydney again. Delighted to hear the Nimrod want to do *Well Hung* – hope it goes well & also that it makes some cash. Then the flight to San Francisco – so long that I couldn't be frightened all that distance & I ended up enjoying it. San Francisco was good. I was tired & strange but enjoyed all. Then on to Minneapolis – an amazing flight – where I saw great productions of *King Lear* & *Love's Labour's Lost*. Loved Minneapolis – very green. And on to New York, which is so dirty I cannot describe it but vital & alive &

A friend poses in front of the Transamerica Pyramid in San Francisco. MS-1907/007/002, Hocken Collections

saw Russell, Steve, Sue Kedgley & so forth – stayed in Brooklyn – loud, hot, scary.* Indeed a relief to escape to Waterford & the Playwrights Conference. Westport really is very beautiful – have just walked thru part of it & am somewhat delighted by the trees & the old houses. Very tranquil. Have arrived at the rehearsal rooms, which are very close to the theatre.

17/8 Last night went to an extraordinary restaurant, The Red Barn, & had shrimps, crabs, lobster & chestnuts glacés – the latter being awful – & then went later to a bar & drank a great deal. Must stop drinking beer, am getting too fat. Not a pretty sight.

---

* **Stephen Whitehouse** (1945–2017), New Zealand journalist and broadcaster, son of Davina Whitehouse. He worked in the Department of Information at the United Nations in New York, later becoming head of Public Affairs. **Sue Kedgley**, New Zealand journalist, author and politician. She lived in New York from 1973 to 1981, where she worked on women's issues at the United Nations.

This evening dined out at yet another ritzy restaurant – The 3 Bears & then on to White Barn Theatre to see *Ti-Jean & His Brothers* by Derek Walcott (*Dream on Monkey Mountain*) – fascinating, amateur, messy but charming. Audience quiet – very wealthy – count the Gucci shoes! Then I have moved into the home of an elderly lady (76) – Mrs Nader, & at $5 a night it is great. Sunday rested a lot – dreamt of Craig, which was strange.

6/9 and I wonder what I was going to say there, lying in the sun in Westport an age ago – left there on 20th & was driven to New York by a composer and his wife, who is a designer – they were both staying at Mrs Nader's. A hair-raising hour-long drive to the city because of the giant trucks that kept trying to force us off the road. By the way I'm now in Montreal, but must fill in the various details of the past few weeks. They have certainly been very busy & theatre-packed. On return to NY spent the first night with Sue & Steve after an afternoon shopping* – overcame my fear of New York & found I could use the subways with such finesse – bought a new pair of trou, a hideous Midwest sports coat, 2 shirts, & a beret. And spent many days just walking round 'the city' and getting the feel of it. So very hot & humid most of the time & so dirty all the time but fascinating & 6th Ave a joy – quite inspiring. Bob you must get this up to date.

17/10 at last a little time – in the Empress Hotel at Victoria – charming, English, quaint – having High Tea at 4.30 having spent the day here. To recap very briefly. After Westport I returned to NY 20/8 & embarked on a theatre spree – saw *Over Here*, *Moonchildren*, *Bad Habits*, *Candide*, *El Grande de Coca Cola* (ugh), *Scapino*, *Pippin*, *My Fat Friend*. Stayed at either Steve's or at Sue Kedgley's flat. One night went to an all-NZ party (Sue K, Steve & Sue, Mary V, Ray Thorburn, Miles X who was going back to NZ to marry).†

Did a great deal of sightseeing & aimless wandering about & enjoyed all. Met Hamish Tristram while crossing 5th Ave – he in the company of some gorgeous French men & staying in the Hotel Pierre & popping back &

---

*   **Sue Watt** (d.2018), New Zealand community activist who formed the Women's Group at the United Nations with Sue Kedgley and others. Steve Whitehouse's then wife.

†   **Mary Varnham**, New Zealand writer, publisher and former local body politician. Lived in New York from 1972 to 1978, where she worked in PR and publishing. **Ray Thorburn**, New Zealand artist and educator.

Robert in May 1974. MS-1907/11/007, Hocken Collections

forth to Fire Island – all very strange indeed.* Normally he lives in London
and was on holiday. Life is fucking weird & I really am a manic depressive
or something & in fact do get worried about the state of mind & also the
preoccupation with suicide. But I've got to make myself work & write down
in here all the time, else I'll forget all.

Moonchildren a delicious play, haunting, truthful & honest about
some people sharing a home while at university – in addition a very good
production.† New York I just love love but doubt if I could work there.
And it was so hot! And went sailing with Sue & Steve & a Jamaican doctor
friend who has a 35′ yacht & he can't sail & the 5-hour trip to Fire Island
turned into a 42-hour nightmare. Labour Day went to Boston – sat next to
an Indian recently arrived in the US who was in a state of culture shock &
thought it all too much. In Boston stayed at the Y where met a man who had
lived there 3 years – liked sucking people off & it was a good pickup place –

---

*   **Hamish Tristram**, London-based New Zealand lawyer and academic. RL also uses 'FIP'
     and 'the Pines' to refer to the Fire Island Pines vacation destination on Long Island.

†   *Moonchildren* (originally titled *Cancer*), 1970 play by New York playwright Michael Weller.

Robert (centre), Brian Syron (right) and an American friend, 1974. Robert wears a Eugene O'Neill Playwrights Conference sweatshirt. MS-2438/226, Hocken Collections

he didn't work. Saw Angela Lansbury in *Gypsy* in Boston – she was great but the show dullsville – ineptly written & directed & too long. Then travelled up thru Mass & Vermont to Montreal – sat next to Irene, a ghastly woman with a loud voice whose spouse died of cancer at the age of 51, whose son was an engineer, who hated Blacks & Nixon.

Montreal was a dream, clean, French, old & charming. Took a tour & saw among other things the Oratory of St Joseph, founded in recent times by the late Brother André – a school custodian who was illiterate but had a gift of healing – very impressive building from the outside but so kitsch inside & lots of canes & crutches from the cured. Awful. Then on to Toronto & another Y & sat next to a young American returning to Chicago after 12 weeks in Europe. Born in Egypt, he came to the States when 2 & had stayed in Europe with wealthy Egyptian relatives. Toronto & dinner with Maarten

VD & Margaret & their daughter Beatrice & also with Russell Poole & family.* Then on to Calgary (50 hours) & some odd ones in the bus.

6 December 1974

Far too much later a return to the diary – & that was very shortlived for it is now Dec 6th & I wonder if I'll ever be able to get into this habit with any degree of regularity at all. Well I am as usual flipping in & out of moods with a great deal of ease. What a bore & a bugger it is. It is not easy being a writer, believe me, and the depressing, constant belief that one isn't, the hope one is, the tedious moods. Oh shit, what's it all about, Alfie? The depressing realization that quite soon, one has to be serious. What are you up to Robert L? *Vile Bodies* a daunting project, potentially very commercial & also potentially a great work of <u>art</u>!!! (bullshit). And I am not going to lose an opportunity of staying here. No. This is where I should be now. London, if it still exists, after.

27 December 1974

Getting letters is a delight & a shock. I find them painful to read. Quickly one is back with you, sharing. But the truth dawns that we are far apart & our battles with life/spirit/all go on – as they must – alone. They allow me to enter a world of memories & also show me how brittle that world & this world are.

Have decided that one problem with this book & with my failure to relate to it is that I do not like its messiness. Therefore, I will now start a new format.

• • •

---

*   **Maarten Van Dijk**, who RL had met through the Drama Club at Victoria University, was studying towards a PhD in Drama at the University of Toronto. He later became Professor of Theatre at the University of Waterloo, Ontario. **Margaret Van Dijk**, who had been friends with RL since their schooldays in Hamilton, was a professor of Communications and Publishing at Centennial College in Toronto. **Russell Poole**, who had been at Southland Boys' High School with RL, was studying towards a PhD in Medieval Studies at the University of Toronto; his then wife Fiona Farrell was completing an MPhil in Drama.

There is a large gap in Robert Lord's early diaries; there are none between the end of 1974 and August 1980. In 1975, after Auckland's Mercury Theatre had staged Richard Campion's production of *Heroes and Butterflies*, a play about the costs of political ambition in a time of war, Robert made the call to live in New York. Sunny Amey visited him there. He soon had three agents: Gilbert Parker in New York (from 1979, at William Morris), Howard Nicholson in Sydney, and Playmarket in New Zealand. In 1975, at the National Playwrights Conference in Waterford, Connecticut, he workshopped his new play *Dead and Never Called Me Mother*. At Robert's suggestion, playwright Roger Hall spent time at the Eugene O'Neill Theater Center during the late 1970s.

I'll Scream If I Want To tells of disgruntled twenty-somethings and their shifting allegiances. It was broadcast on New Zealand radio as *Blood On My Sprigs* in 1975 and staged at Provincetown Playhouse in Provincetown, Massachusetts, in 1976. *Well Hung* had been performed in 1974 by the Trinity Square Repertory Company in Providence, Rhode Island, on the recommendation of dramaturg Arthur Ballet, a champion of new American playwriting. *Well Hung* had several Australian productions before reemerging for North American audiences as *Cop Shop*. One of these was a 1979 Toronto production marked by a wariness of New Zealand accents and idioms. In 1977 Anthony Taylor became artistic director at Downstage, and he programmed two of Lord's plays: a lush production of *Heroes and Butterflies* in 1978 (the play also appeared at the Christchurch Festival), and *High as a Kite*, a major rewrite of *I'll Scream If I Want To*, in 1979.

Filmmaker John O'Shea ran into scriptwriting and directing challenges with his ambitious film about nineteenth-century photographers Alfred and Walter Burton, and in 1979 he commissioned a new treatment from Robert. *Pictures* was shot on the Whanganui River over seven weeks early in 1980, and the film screened at Cannes and in London a year later.

Robert Lord looked back on these years as a 'necessary purgatory' of writing for wider audiences. He felt alienated from the immediacy and fluency he had experienced at the start of the decade, and he struggled to capture authentic American subtexts in his writing. When he returned to playwriting in 1979, and began what would become *Bert and Maisy*, he found he could write fluently again and finished the first script in a week. He was very pleased with the play, but it failed to spark any interest in New Zealand or the USA at the time.

1980–1981

Gary Lisz on Fire Island, 1982. Photograph by Bobby Miller. Bobby Miller collection

22 August 1980

I no longer love her, that's certain, but maybe I love her
Love is so short, forgetting is so long

Because through nights like this one I held her in my arms
My soul is not satisfied that it has lost her

Pablo Neruda
'Tonight I Can Write (The Saddest Lines)'

Yesterday I had breakfast with Granny Lisz and we were both feeling like
shit and somewhat suicidal – after leaving the American we went up to
her house and had coffee and there was very sepulchral music on the radio
and she showed me some Pablo Neruda poetry including the above which
I copied down and that put me in a very weird frame of mind or confirmed
the one I was already in.* Leaving Granny and feeling very weak I wandered
through the park to pay off the phone service with money Gary Bond had
donated to the cause.† Refuse to get a job which is hideous and have to dodge
the phone as the doctor is always calling wanting payment I don't have.
There is no solution. Went and saw Jay as I was feeling weak and wanted
him and I guess I do love him still, which is annoying.‡ There is something
wrong with me – I think when I love I depend too much. Anyway Jay came
home with me and we cried for ages, which was good and bad and he is good
but we are very different and I expect that is the problem. Had a long phone
conversation with Sally Hartman, who is crazed, and the latest in the saga
is that she went up to Boston after no sleep for several days – one night
dancing, the next talking with Donald – anyway up to Boston and a long day
at work followed by a party and then in her hotel room a torrid phone call

---

*   **Gary ('Granny') Lisz** (1953–1988), American fashion, costume and set designer for
theatre, film and ballet.

†   **Gary Bond** (1940–1995), English stage and film actor and singer, partner of EJ Taylor
from 1979.

‡   **Jay Kevin Funk** (1958–1994), RL's friend and former lover. Then a bartender; later an
AIDS activist, involved in ACT UP New York alongside his former lover Mark Harrington.

to Walter, her latest beau, during which Sally masturbated to a climax and passed out.* The poor young Walter, not knowing what had provoked the silence on the other end of the phone, panicked and called the hotel. The security men could not rouse Sally by knocking on the door and when she came to an hour later they were removing the door from its hinges. What madness. I felt obliged to suggest that she get her life together but she told me that it was very much together.

Am reminded of another Sally story related by Jackie O'Hofsiss at Dobson's earlier this week.† Early one Sunday out on the deck Sally was making out with all and sundry including Granny Lisz and decided to fuck Granny, which delighted that queen. So Sally is off to the bedroom to strap on the dildo and Jack gets out of bed to watch. Meantime the phone goes and Martine van Hamel is asking Granny to design a cossie for some new ballet.‡ So when Sally emerges from the bedroom with the dildo strapped into place Granny is planning to drape this here and that there and on another plane altogether. Sally looks at dear Granny, who has obviously forgotten she was going to get fucked, says 'fuck', pulls at a toggle and the dildo crashes to the floor.

Today I slept very late and avoided the phone like the plague but did lunch with Granny again and brought her up to date with the latest Sally Hartman stories and we giggled and we're both off to dinner with EJ and Gary [Bond] at Bobby's tonight.§ Granny went to the Peking Opera and then to Danceteria last night and of course, troll that she is, picked up some number on the way home – a young man of German descent and somewhat into violence from what I can gather.

---

* Names have been changed.
† **Jack Hofsiss** (1950–2016), American theatre, film and television director, who won a Tony award for the 1979 Broadway production of *The Elephant Man*.
‡ **Martine van Hamel**, Dutch ballerina, choreographer, teacher and director, at the time principal dancer at the American Ballet Theatre.
§ **EJ Taylor** (d.2022), American artist and partner of Gary Bond. He lived in RL's building and often used his phone. **Bobby Miller**, American photographer, poet, actor and makeup artist.

Gary Lisz (left) and Bobby Miller. Bobby Miller collection

24 August 1980

Sunday and a beautiful day, I actually went up onto the roof and lay in the
sun for an hour or three and was surprised by a man from the 15th floor
who made a brief appearance but was startled off by my nakedness. So
where did we leave off? Friday lunch as usual with Granny Lisz and a brief
run over all the gossip and now I've decided to write a book called *September*
about everything that happens to me that month. And tie in all the
members of the family and their fucked-up lives. Slept late Friday, Saturday

and Sunday – am I sick or just being lazy? Who can tell? Friday evening out to Bobby's for dinner – Granny, EJ, Gary and moi and EJ's godchild Paige and her father Dan. Clams and Jackie O'Hofsiss turned up after dinner.* Very amusing but I felt strangely removed from it all. I didn't feel up to exposing my soul in front of all and sundry – never do. Find it hard to explain to anyone about Jay at all. Is it jealousy on my part? I can't believe that he doesn't love me but I know he loves me but he doesn't want to be my lover. And there is nothing I can do about that – or is there? I cannot be angry because he is honest. Am I hurt or is it just my pride? Did I love him too much? Do I always love too much – is that my flaw – is it the wanting of someone to lift the burden of being alone that makes it impossible for someone to love me? There are several things that have to be done. There has to be a refining of goals. There has to be a working each day. Things must be achieved.

Saturday slept late and then Granny came over and we worked on a fashion column he has to write and that quite wore my mind out and God knows what it was about. I don't. Then off to Melvin B's and Silent Steve's for dinner.† Steve was silent, the dinner excellent, and Melvin took second place to George Baxt,‡ who recounted cast lists of countless old plays and movies and told me to write write write. And I borrowed several books from Melvin. One of George's – *A Queer Kind of Death*, *The Philadelphia Story*, a Beryl Bainbridge and a Susan Hill. So have my reading cut out for me – and am now over halfway through *The Story of Harold*, which is good but not great. And today – what of today? The sun as mentioned above and then a brief encounter on 80th Street, which was jolly and got my rocks off, and now off with Granny to see slides of Singapore.

---

* **Keith ('Clams') Edmondson** (1953–1995), friend who worked for TWA before becoming an assistant to Jack Hofsiss, including on *The Elephant Man* and the New York City Opera production of *The Student Prince*.
† **Melvin Bernhardt** (1931–2015), American stage and television director, and his partner **Steve Durham** (d.1987).
‡ **George Baxt** (1923–2003), writer of screenplays and crime fiction, best known for gay Black detective character Pharoah Love.

26 August 1980

Feel very disgruntled and disenchanted with everything at the moment.
Am being very negative about myself and EJ has just given me a talking
to – what he says is correct – negative energy is negative time. One cannot
afford that. Jay came round and I suppose that started it off. Well it did. I
do love him so much and when he holds me and kisses me it feels – it is so
wonderful – and I suppose that when he does that I hope that he will return.
He seems to be offering out the hope but he is not. He loves me and wants
my approval. At the same time he is going out on a fuck date tonight with
someone he picked up at the baths. I must tell him, and this I have known
and EJ said also, that I cannot have this. It does upset me, which would
in some lights seem to be a sign of immaturity on my part. Do seem to be
a strange and lonely person right now. This life I lead is not good – but is
going to Connecticut to share an apartment with Gary the right answer? I
do not know. Should I get a job in a production office or with an agent? Or
should I go back to New Zealand for a while and maybe work in the theatre
there? Oh, the choices do not inspire me. I want oblivion and I want life at
the same time and that does seem to be the most ultimate of contradictions.
There is such a gap in experience and attitude between Jay and myself and
I know that he feels he is acting decently and indeed he is. But from my
perspective ...

Love. It is so hard to believe how much I love Jay. But I do. And I
remember the intensity and the strangeness and the places we visited
together in other worlds. He doesn't. Maybe he was never with me. There is
a sadness.

27 August 1980

There is something slightly wrong with the typewriter and I hope it
doesn't get serious as I haven't the money to get it repaired. Went out and
got fucked last night, which seemed to be the best thing to do under the
circumstances. Wanted to get stoned and phoned David Lawson for some
dope but evidently he has given it up.* So then worked my way through
the phone book and got in touch with Al Godfrey and went down and

---

*   **David Lawson**, American filmmaker.

visited him in his rather hideous apartment on 25th St between 9th and 10th.* Turns out it is the anniversary of his affair with Rob – and Rob was expected – and we had sex but I couldn't come, which was odd. I thought it was healthy to go as it was a trouble getting over him and at that time I had the same violated feeling that obsessed me yesterday. Violation is the word. To have shared a world, to have known a world, to have believed a state existed and then to be told it doesn't. Something is ripped in two. A curtain. A dress. And behind it – that nothing state, that emptiness. Strange. But to see Al again and to be intimate I suppose is the word. And to feel nothing. To be slightly bored throughout. Sadness in that too. And I toddled off to Man's Country, where I got plunged a couple of times and quite enjoyed it but basically a tacky group there. And home to bed. Now at 3.15 in the afternoon it is well over 90 and I'm sweating and listening to Marianne Faithfull and think I will turn my attention to writing for a while. Must. Have to. Must.

28 August 1980

Did a lot of C with RB[†] and then to dinner at The Bakery, where Lyn Williamson – a NZer – was playing, and then back to RB's and on the Barbaras and getting higher and higher and in the early hours sodomy in bookstall and then home and not being able to sleep and watching Mary Tyler Moore then the Marx Brothers. Slept very late. Woke in a foul and depressed mood and scared that I was having a relapse of hepatitis.

31 August 1980

Last day of August and poverty still persists. No sign of anything. No cavalry of dimes appearing on the horizon. Not so much as even an indication from NZ that anyone is interested in *Family Portrait*. The fuckers. What has happened? Friday was the opening of *Student Prince* and went toddling along dutifully. Of what was once called the family the following were in attendance: Sally, Eddy B (with the famous Abe), Moi, Granny, Julie, Bobby,

---

*   Name has been changed.

†   **Robert Boykin** (1949–1988), owner of iconic late-1970s New York nightclub Hurrah; partner of **Marc Jacobs** from 1979.

EJ Taylor and his partner Gary Bond, 1986. MS-1907/005, Hocken Collections

Louis, Peter Fonseca, Peter B, Ellen Greene.* Boykin was absent. There
was a party in the G&W building in the Paramount suite catered by Doug
Watts – very good.† Most of the people showed, including Eddy Columbia.
Not drinking and feeling a little ill, I was bored but stayed till quite late
but avoided the after-party party at Jack's. Donald Cass was present. He is
thin and strange. Is now living in a hotel on Lexington with bloodstains on
the walls. What is he trying to do to himself? Sally got drunk and did some
rather flamboyant dancing.

---

*   **Edward Betz**, actor and production assistant to Jack Hofsiss on the 1982 film *I'm
    Dancing as Fast as I Can*. **Julie Weiss**, costume designer and actress. Worked with Hofsiss,
    including on *The Elephant Man*. **Peter Fonseca** (1958–1986), lead dancer with the
    American Ballet Theatre. **Peter ('Mother') Buckley** (1938–1991), photographer, editor,
    and arts and travel writer for *Vogue*, the *New York Times* and *Vanity Fair*. **Ellen Greene**,
    American stage and film singer and actor, best known for her role as Audrey in stage and
    film versions of *Little Shop of Horrors*.
†   **Doug Watts** (d.1987), friend of RL's whose firm Douglas Watts Caterers worked many
    high-end New York events.

Saturday slept late and refused to go to the island. Jay came round in the afternoon and we played Scrabble and for once I won. I then played with his body, which was okay I guess but he does rather lie there like a dead fish. Evening I wandered around and ended up at St Mark's Baths, where for once I felt quite good about my body and got laid. Gary and EJ turned up Saturday morning and then off to DC till tomorrow night. Arthur Ballet turned up this morning and we had a couple of hours together. He is to be dramaturg of the Guthrie and do a TV news show there. Also teaching of course. He seemed in good spirits and happy in love. Then he left and I have decided to take the 4.30 train to Isle de Flambe [Fire Island], stay over and come back tomorrow. Must talk to Cappy while I am there and try to get some money coming in from real estate.* Have been thinking about the new play – Jean/Grant – he comes to visit about the house and knowing of the stamp collection. It is his intention to get the valuable stamp. The love affair happens. She turns against him, not because of his deception, but because of the various family pressures. I think that should work. Must away.

3 September 1980

At the beach it was Jack Hofsiss Adoration Weekend. Very funny. When I arrived the house was empty but it soon filled up. They had had a frantic night on Saturday and quite worn themselves out. Present were: Jack Hofsiss. Julie Weiss. Clams Edmondson. Gary Lisz. Bobbi Pearlman. Lola Herman. Rosie Halston. Annette Ascosi. Eddy Betz. Self. Bill Pitt for a time. John Dolf.† And in and out: Peter Buckley. Doug Watts. Jeffrey Sanker. David Lawson.‡ Well there was your basic tension between Clams and Eddy Betz. Both reading each other all weekend. Clams was a bitch the entire time. My dear, you'd think she singlehandedly ran the City Opera. And as for her fawning over Jack. It is too sick to take.

---

* 'Cappy' (unidentified), Long Island realtor who employed RL and lent him money.

† **Barbara ('Bobbi') Pearlman**, American fashion illustrator, painter and sculptor. **Rosie Halston**: name has been changed. **John Dolf** (1960–1990), American actor and producer, and RL's sometime flatmate. RL refers to him as both 'John Boy' and 'Debby from Dallas'.

‡ **Jeffrey Sanker** (1955–2021), promoter and special-event producer who worked at New York clubs in the 1980s, including Studio 54.

Some members of Robert's New York family during the 1980s, clockwise from top left: Jack Hofsiss, Keith ('Clams') Edmondson, Robert La Fosse and Peter Buckley, photographed by Bobby Miller. Bobby Miller collection

John Dolf slept with several people, including Lawson and Sanker, who now try and sleep with each other's tricks – such being the ways of ex-lovers. Sunday night Gary set fire to the stove by broiling taco shells. Rosie Halston said she slept with Doug Watts but didn't. Larry and Dwight had, on Saturday, slept with Eddy Betz's trick (Rosie watched) and Eddy kicked him out. Lola is going to run for Mayor of NY and says she will be in office by 1986. Oh dear.

On the dance floor Sunday night was quite fun but I didn't really get off. Everyone delighted that Julie is doing poppers – one would think a child had learned to walk. Julie also confessed to me that her idea of pleasure on earth was riding in a limo with Jack Hofsiss and David Bowie – evidently her Berkeley friends feel she has sold out. Am I surprised? Jay rang today and wants me to take him to Hurrah's tonight as he wants to get in free. Little shit. He is also off to *Evita* tonight. Collected Becky today and she is home and quiet now.

4 September 1980

Last night had dinner with John Dolf, who is pleasant but overly cheerful and truly boring when he tries to dish people – our over-tired rhetoric, which sounds passably amusing from the mouth of a jaded queen, sounds as hollow as it truly is from the mouth of a 20-year-old innocent. He is going to move in here and that will help with the rent. Yesterday received a letter from John O'Shea, which was very complimentary about *A Family Portrait* but no mention of money.* Jay came round in the evening.

This morning at some ungodly hour Alan Seymour phoned from NZ.† He approached me in 1973 to direct *Balance of Payments* for his school – I declined and Craig directed. Anyway he now sounds like an apprentice Paul Minifie‡ but is probably very nice and certainly has good taste for he wants to mount a season of all my plays at some new theatre company in Wellington and to fly me out for the event. Strange. Anyway have written off

---

* **John O'Shea** (1920–2001), New Zealand independent filmmaker and producer.

† **Alan Seymour**, New Zealand actor who taught at the Workers' Educational Association in Upper Hutt.

‡ **Paul Minifie**, New Zealand actor, director and arts manager.

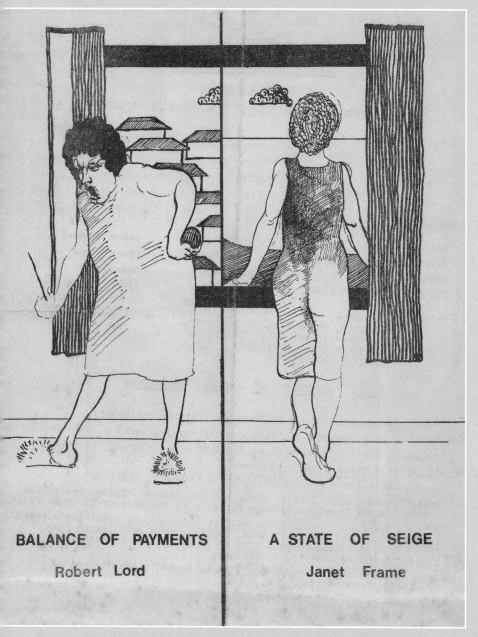

BALANCE OF PAYMENTS

Robert Lord

A STATE OF SEIGE

Janet Frame

Wellington's Unity Theatre performed Robert Lord's *Balance of Payments* and Janet Frame's *A State of Siege* in a double bill in 1972. MS-1907/049/001, Hocken Collections

to Judy Russell to find out what the company is like as it would be tedious to fly out for such an event if it were terrible.*

Have come to the conclusion that I was brought up to believe I was stupid. That if I could understand something then it wasn't worth understanding. Of course I always thought I was brought up as a retard – and that is borne out by the old story of one of Richard's [brother's] friends being surprised that I was normal – as everyone spoke of me in whispers. But it is more than that. I really do think that I was downgraded to the point where I could not believe I had brains and that as a consequence I didn't. I presumed I could not understand things when actually I've a rather good brain. Remember in Standard 3 or 4 at Remuera Primary having to learn a poem and memorizing some very obscure piece and being asked, by a teacher, why I had chosen it – I had no answer at the time but feel that I must have chosen it because I did not understand it. Oh dear. And this would reflect my whole academic career. How strange it was when I became a teacher that I could then suddenly understand math. This realization is not, I think, minor. Because it has without a doubt affected my whole psyche and development. It has dictated choices in subject matter of my writing and now that I am concentrating on NZ I can see through those choices. I trust that that is a major breakthrough. It has also affected my own self-perception. I have always known that I felt that once I'd achieved something it was not worth it – that if I could do it then it could not be difficult. It could be that these achievements are very difficult. This has wormed its way into my private life. But it is also a part of the Groucho syndrome, 'I don't want to join any club that will have me for a member'. So maybe this will all go to help fashion the new aggressive and successful Robert Lord. Hope so.

7 September 1980

Went to *Charlie and Algernon* on Thursday night – it was truly hateful. Could only take about an hour of it and then fled the theatre. Those hideous sets which rumble in and out. Also frightful acting and PJ Benjamin, the lead, far too cute. Left before the hit number where the man sings to the mouse

---

* **Judy Russell**, New Zealand arts administrator. Co-founder and first administrator of Playmarket 1974–81, and distribution manager at NZ Film Commission 1981–86.

but my most hated song was 'Chocolate Cake and Jelly Donuts'. Terrifyingly bad. Went with Jay and Peter Buckley and we had dinner at Joe Allen's after, which was jolly, and Jay went down to [Greenwich Village] to hang out and I went home. Friday had a typically lazy day and achieved nil.

Am regretting my decision to let John Dolf move into the apartment as he is très young and noisy. Don't think I can manage with all that going on. What did I do Friday? Refused to have breakfast with Gary, Annette, EJ et al. Why? Gary arrived back from the beach Thursday claiming, proclaiming to be madly in love and the breakfast was to meet the new amour. Did not feel strong enough. Gary B hated the breakfast as Lisz and love kept kissing and caressing in the diner and Annette was in one of her outrageous moods, which he did not care for. In the afternoon Jay came by wanting me to get some acid for him from Terri. Well, I did the phoning and Jay, Alex and I walked down to Terri's and I picked up 15 half-moons.*

Then went out to dinner at Melvin Bernhardt's, which was quite interesting. Explained the plot of my murder/mystery to Melvin and he was not impressed and thought it lacked surprise etc. So back to the drawing board with that one. Melvin then asked how my finances were and I thought he was going to offer to loan me some money. But no. Instead he offered me a job cleaning an apartment! Life. Then home and over to Gary Lisz's, where I met up with him and Annette and we were off to Cahoots to meet Jeffrey Schlong [Sanker], Gregory Osborne and Stuart and Robby La Fosse and then on to Hurrah's.† Robert was not there and Hurrah's was dull. We ended up hanging out on the streets smoking hash and so forth till about 4, when we went to Osborne's and picked up Ellen Greene and went up to the roof. Gregory walked round the edge of the building and pretended to jump off, which made me leave. Then Annette, Gary, Stephen (Gary's amour) and I went to Ruskay's and had coffee. Then home. Slept all Saturday morning then had breakfast at Clarence's. Annette leaving for London, as was Gary

---

* **Alex Ely**, friend and roommate of Jay Funk. Studied photography at the ICP; later worked as a photographer, agent and a production and creative director in advertising.

† **Gregory Osborne** (1954–1994), American ballet dancer, lead dancer with the American Ballet Theatre. **Robert La Fosse**, American dancer and choreographer. A lead dancer with the American Ballet Theatre and New York City Ballet, he also appeared in Broadway shows.

John Dolf, 1986.
MS-1907/005, Hocken Collections

Bond. Went out in a limo with Annette and Granny and spent all evening
there. Bond and EJ also present. Then subway home and the *Sunday Times*
and sleep most of Sunday – wasted time wasted time.

Don't know if I can afford to go to the beach this week. Feel I really
should try and get a job. John O'Shea please send me some money. Shit.

8 September 1980

New York really stinks – early morning and I've just got in from Hurrah's
et al and the streets smell something fierce. Gary and I watched *Jezebel* and
then had dinner and wandered to Boykin's and the Club, where the video
dance party was great. Got into myself and started thinking about right and
wrong – there is no. Only sanity and insanity. And sanity is only rational
behaviour, but all behaviour is irrational. Or is it rational? The message of
this is to stay out of rock clubs. Anyway, met Iggy Pop and then, once home,
rang Russell Craig and spoke to him for a long time and felt very good about

Russell Craig at the 1973 Rolling Stones concert he attended with Robert.

Russell Craig collection

that.* It was nice to speak to him and I didn't feel on edge or threatened or any of those things – actually felt I wanted to be with him. Will write him a letter soon.

12 September 1980

It has all been going on. Since Sunday morning (I mean Monday) when the above was written things have continued on their downward path and it has all been too much. Monday I felt a mess all day and accomplished zero but finally got a good night's sleep and John Dolf moved his stuff into the apartment and I'm not too sure how I'm going to cope with that. Tuesday I went to the Pines against my better judgement. Left in the late afternoon and who is sitting at the Cultured Elephant but [Jay] Funk et al so saw them.

Richard (Louis's friend) came for dinner and was as tedious as ever. Funk

---

* **Russell Craig**, New Zealand-born, London-based stage designer. In 1989 RL described him as 'probably the great love of my life. A love I managed to mishandle disastrously' (MS-2441/054, p. 38, Hocken Collections).

and Ely picked me up and we watched *Foul Play* at the Pavilion and then went down to [Cherry] Grove and hung out there for a while – for too long – there was some 'Wet Jockey Shorts' contest and a drag queen by the name of Tiffany who with a sprained foot mimed to Eartha Kitt and others and then MC'd the event but was drunk, 'luded out and tedious and we stayed only for the first three contestants, who were pretty dull I thought. Jay was affectionate and charming to be with but didn't really want to spend time with me, which was one of the reasons why I didn't want to go out in the first place.

Received a long letter from John O'Shea which contained a brief report on *Pictures*, which apparently is better than anyone thought – but that doesn't convince me. He also wants Gilbert to try and find money.* Then John went on and on about *A Family Portrait*, which he feels is: dated, not sufficiently illuminating about the human condition, making little sense outside of New Zealand and more. So that puts me in a down. He also wants that I should write with more passion and suggested that the current illness, poverty and so forth might lead to a release of said passion. Who knows. Also had a letter from George Webby, who sounded well and excited about his trip this way and gave much news of Downstage, which sounds to be in very bad shape.†

Jay doesn't want to see me, he wants to get into Hurrah's for nothing. He rang later to see what I could do – I hadn't spoken to Robert – and Jay was calling from the baths. This all puts me in a ridiculous bind. I want to be with Jay but he does not want to be with me. He loves me, by which he means he wants to be my friend. I guess I want more. But what more do I want? The touch of him and the closeness makes me feel content. His absence and rejection make me feel old and unattractive. He isn't really doing anything to hurt me but he is being unsubtle and strange and hurtful even if it is without intention. Does he just want me to be fucked up? Does

---

* **Gilbert Parker** (1927–2019), RL's US agent, initially at Curtis Brown and from 1979 at William Morris. Noted theatrical literary agent, sometimes called the last of the gentleman agents.

† **George Webby** (1925–2012), teacher, training college lecturer, actor and theatre director, closely associated with Unity and Downstage theatres in Wellington, and director of Toi Whakaari New Zealand Drama School 1974–88.

he understand how I feel? I thought I explained it to him last week. Does he just want a free ticket to Hurrah's? Really. And did he ever love me? Did he ever really care? Will he love me again? Why can't I get over it?

14 September 1980

At this point I phoned Peter Buckley and talked for ages moaning about everything and he told me to get over it. During the conversation Robert Boykin phoned and suggested I meet him and EJ at the Club and I told him of Jay's request and RB said Jay could look after himself. I then felt guilty and RB phoned again to ask me to his house post haste and I went, forgetting (or trying to) about Jay. RB and EJ both convinced I should take the job with Charles.* Had champagne and cocaine with them and then we went to the Club, which depressed EJ and which I quite enjoyed but it was très hot as the air conditioning wasn't working. But the group 'The Feelies' were good. I hoped, of course, to see Jay but he was not there. Later I went off and was trashy at a bookstore. Boring. Arrived home and could not sleep for hours and then wasted the day doing not a thing but did talk to Charles Hunt and have to see him on Monday. Friday night Gary and Stephen and I went to *My Bodyguard*, which was quite sweet but not extraordinary, and then came home to be joined by EJ and Clams and Kenny to watch a Gary Bond movie on Channel 9, which never came on due to the ball game. Boring. Then to bed and up early and on the train to Mystic. Slept all the way – as did Gary. Picked up by Elaine and her daughter Ivy. Very pleasant even if I did think E too ebullient at first but that was my mood. Then with her husband Fox we went to a wedding at the Bocci Club in Westerly. A lot of Italians and a very depressing crowd they were. Felt the move would not be a good idea – nothing in common with anyone. Pizza at the wedding and Heineken. Then to Stonington and it is adorable and the apartment wonderful. In awful shape but the top floor of an old house with two nice rooms for me and a widow's watch up a flight of stairs. Right in the heart of the town – which has a tiny narrow main street and some small shops.

---

*   **Charles Hunt**, vice-president at the Fifi Oscard theatrical and literary agency. He had offered RL a job as his assistant but it turned out to be a 'gopher position' (MS-2438/108, p. 15, Hocken Collections).

Friend and sometime roommate Ethan Silverman in Robert's kitchen. Robert's apartment, 14J, was the only one on its floor with a kitchen; the other apartments had a kitchen recess in the living room. MS-1907/002/001/001, Hocken Collections

Really rather fancy living there but need something to cook on, a wood stove, and somehow to do washing – no laundromat in town. And how does one support oneself? We also looked at the outside of a converted barn, which was beautiful but out of reach. Then finished reading *True Confessions* by John Gregory Dunne, which is well written but a little pointless I thought. Fell asleep and then went out for dinner and slept again. Then started reading *Dodsworth*, which I am enjoying. Elaine found out that the apartment is $220 a month. Returned on train this morning and had a quiet day with *Dodsworth*. The terrible ache is still travelling round my body and is lodged in the right wrist today. It makes typing très hard.

17 September 1980

Saturday night they – Doug, Sally, John et al – had been to the Elton John party organized by Rosie at the *Peking*, which is a boat at South Port [South Street Seaport]. According to Sally – phone conversation late Sunday night – it was yet another party of the century and they all got shit-faced and did lots of poppers (she now calls them snappers) and X and Y were wonderful, whoever X and Y might be – actually one of them is Elton's manager, the man banned from NZ for hitting Sue Keith's friend.* Life. John said the party was a bore with lots of faggot models and disco and Doug at first hating it all and then, once his quaalude hit in, not wanting to leave the family. Fuck the family.

Evidently after my phone call from Sally – and she hadn't rung to call me, she wanted to speak to John – she heard from Donald Cass, who was drunk in Cahoots and wanted to come by. Sally was with Walter and had just seen *The Women's Room* and was in no shape for the argument – do you love me or do you love Walter? – or for the tears and suicide threat, but did relent and let DC sleep in her bed and then went to Walter's apartment and slept with him and his ex-lover and the ex-lover's current boyfriend. How quaint life is. Picked up details of this conversation Monday night with Peter.

Tuesday I went on a massive walk and to the new doctor, who was a great relief. The pain and swelling is related to the hepatitis and he has put me

---

* **John Reid**, Elton John's manager and former partner, had been arrested and sentenced to a month in jail in New Zealand in 1974 for assaulting a journalist.

on a massive dosage of aspirin, which has been quite miraculous and makes me more than a little annoyed with Dr Jacobs, who never gave me anything for the pain. Anyway, he took more blood tests and I will get those results on Friday. From the urine sample it transpired that there was bilirubin in the blood and I hope that does not mean I'm still sick. However, there is no temperature and my blood is clotting so I think I am okay. No more drinking for 6 to 9 months.

I did go to the baths Sunday night and got plunged quite pleasantly and plunged a very nubile young man. Most enjoyable I expect but I don't think my heart was in it. Life. Gary called me with news that Clams is sick and has to go to hospital and it might be cancer. Something to do with lymph nodes. Anyway he does not have to go to hospital – or is not going – until next week and is going to Washington for that. Quite clearly Jay is not weighing so heavily on my mind at present. Well, I am worried. I'm worried because I feel that I'm going to end up not liking him at all. He really does only call when he wants something and that is depressing. Selfish. Right now I could care less. Right now I'm happy with the way things are.

Am also thinking a lot about 'The Short Happy Life of Frankie Jones', which is my dullard in the disco set story. Poor boy – 30 – from the country comes to NY when his wife kicks him out – gets a job and falls in love with elegant socialite – a cross between Sally Hartman and Rosie – he follows her round and eventually gets swept up in her group and into Studio [54]. Finally, one 'luded night he ends up in bed with her and she can't remember and rejects his offers of marriage. No way. He then decides to kill himself and goes to throw himself under a subway but is deflected by a mugging and saves an old lady. He then goes to throw himself off the Brooklyn Bridge and meets another man there and talks the other man out of doing it. Finally he finds a derelict house and is going to take pills and burn himself to death. But as the fire starts he realizes there are children in danger and is forced to save them. He becomes a hero. He is awarded a medal for all his fine deeds. The girl comes to greet him, he rushes to her and is struck down by a car. Nasty ending. How do we avoid it? We do two endings. The first – she rushes to him and leads him off to a triumphant party at Studio where all praise him and she confesses she is over it all and wants him and so we cut to a small log cabin where he fishes and she cleans house and has babies. That is the fantasy story. The real ending is that he gets killed by an out-of-control car. We tell the endings in that order. I like it. Could be a screenplay but people would be confused. I'm over people. Must do what I want. Feel the *September* book can hold all these things. I wonder if it can? There might even be room for the story about the man who bumps off derelicts. All these stories part of the narrator's perceptions as he goes through the month and looks at the city and at his circle of friends. Put them all in. Write. That is the most important thing. Must take control of destiny. Must connect the dots oneself. Must go to the country and write. That is the only answer.

19 September 1980
Jay and Alex came round yesterday evening finally returning EJ's record player and they did their ironing. Funny. And maybe a touch depressing. Then went and had dinner with EJ and later we watched TV, which was très boring and I went to sleep. Today molto tedioso. Laundry and housework. Yesterday walked to Gilbert's with Ray Edkins and dropped off Becky.* Becky found a dead squirrel in the park and rubbed herself on top of it so I took her to Bloomies and sprayed her with cologne. Evidently the cologne wore off and Gilbert is going to wash her. Latest gossip: Gary and others went to Zandra Rhodes' showing at the Plaza and it was Divine! And then to 123 and Bonds and Fabulous! Tonight I have to go to dinner with Mark Wilde and Nick so that will be fairly dull I guess. Do hope I survive. No money at all. Boring.

23 September 1980
What has happened since I last wrote? Managed to get myself into a dreadful mood on Friday, which was tedious. The day dragged on and I felt worse and worse. Met Nick Edwards and Mark Wilde in the Wildwood at 7pm and once there didn't know what to say to them and felt stupid. Went to Nick's for a vast dinner which Mark had cooked. Mark très attractive and

---

* **Ray Edkins**, now known as Steven Ray, New Zealand stage and screen actor and director; member of Auckland's Central and Mercury theatres, and original presenter of *Play School*.

spent the weekend debauching himself. They both told me to get a job and be sensible, which is not the advice I wanted. Boring. Came home early and fell asleep and slept forever. Saturday was a mess of a day. In the evening EJ and I dressed up and went over to Gary's for tea, which was moderately amusing. Gary was rushing off to Jack Hofsiss's and we were home by about 9. Gary in a somewhat strange mood and I feel estranged from him. Also am getting paranoid and think everyone is plotting against me. Boring. Sunday was the day of EJ's dinner for Robert Boykin. Panic stations when he discovered that Gary, Clams et al had not purchased any vino and he was

Gilbert Parker on Fire Island with Becky and Robert. MS-1907/004, Hocken Collections

unable to get anyone to help him up to Riverdale with the goodies. I went up with him in the subway and then we discovered that he had left stuff behind and I came back again. Before returning with the food had a blowjob at the bookstore. Naughty. The dinner was most elegant. It being the last night of summer and very warm, we ate on the porch and then lay under the trees. All rather idyllic. Jack, Gary, Clams, Julie, Bobby, EJ, Boykin, and Moi. Lots of conversation but I had nothing to say. Everyone talking about ART and the agony of it. Oh dear. Then home again and John was here and we talked for a while before I went back to the bookshop.

Peter went to the opening of 'The Saint' Saturday – when they arrived at 2am a line round the block and a wait of 90 minutes. They went to Flamingo and returned at 5. Evidently it is most spectacular and exciting but very acid trip and hard to work out where you are and where everything is. Went to the baths last night and was plunged and I guess I enjoyed that. Today received a call from Alex with the news that Jay was most ill and so sent Jay off to Dr Marmer and trust he is better soon. No news on any front of anything that sounds exciting or fun. John Dolf has just come in – he inadvertently told Sally Hartman and Ed Betz that there had been a birthday party for Jack and Robert and Ed was distraught and could hardly finish his fish. Life. Also, John is pissed because Doug has announced that he passed inspection by Doug's friends. Oh dear. But that is life. Have had a reasonably productive day and feel quite up but no doubt will be down again soon. Have tickets for *Passione* tomorrow matinee and will go with JT, Buckley and John Dolf. Work is the answer.

My dear, this is a day for gossip. What fun. Peter cannot come to *Passione* tomorrow as he is too busy – which is a first. Jay was fired from Boodles. That is also a first. He claims he arranged for someone to double for him tonight as he is sick and the double did not appear and as a result Jay was fired. I have nothing to say about that, but I do think that Jay probably never worked too hard. But what is he to do? And the naughty child has not enrolled for classes this semester, which annoys me as he tends to indolence. I think I shocked EJ the other night when, in the depths of my depression, I claimed that the world totally depressed me because everyone deluded themselves and that was how they survived and that I saw through the delusions and was disgusted. There is indeed some truth in that but delusions are essential and my problem is that I cannot delude myself. I am too willing to believe the worst about me. Poor fool.

I am in too good a mood today and that is scary. Will I be a mess tomorrow? Then, a long conversation ('telephonic') with Buckley while another person was masturbating on Peter's couch. And Peter was telling me he was working! Oh! So, Peter took Doug a 'lude and the doctors gave Doug demerol. So Doug phoned Peter and went on and on about Dolf. What did he say? Let me tell you. He said: he loved John but thought John was using him, he thought he loved John but John bored him. Why did John bore him? Because John was a user. Is this true? What is the truth of the situation? Is Doug just saying this because he wants Peter to feel sorry for him? Peter said his two hours this afternoon with Doug were most gratifying. No doubt Doug told Peter how much he loved him. This is all too much. What is it all about? Does anyone love anyone? I am beginning to doubt it. Is John really a user? Is he any more a user than Douglas is and was? Or is he an innocent? Is anyone innocent? All this must be explored.

25 September 1980

After the tremendous spurt of activity two days ago I feel quite exhausted, which is usual. Yesterday was full of incident but none too exciting. Have been thinking a lot about theatre and feel that probably it is not for me. Can I mean this? But it seems that what interests me may not really belong in the theatre and maybe I should attempt short stories and the novel. I wonder. Have been taking notes etc but in this strange state of flux have too many small projects and nothing which is grabbing me and dragging me on. Went to *Passione* yesterday with John Boy, JT and Jay. Hated it with much passione. It is terrible. At least the first act is. I couldn't stay for the second. Some of the audience attempted to get their money back at half time. Insulting and boring. A couple of interesting speeches but nothing which shows insight, intelligence or a love for the theatre.

Jay, it transpires, has amoebas in his stomach. The result of some naughty sexual activity which I will not try and imagine. As a result he is in great pain and taking many pills, which are expensive. He is here at the moment and in bed. I have made soup and it is something like the past but I do not feel emotionally vulnerable so that is good as long as it lasts. Am getting into very serious financial difficulties with bills piling up and up and now letters from agencies. Tut Tut. What will happen? Will I be sent to jail? Will I have to go to court? Yesterday walked from *Passione* over to a pharmacy on the East Side to get pills for Jay and then home. In the evening 2 one-act plays by Don Wollner at New Dramatists and they did not elevate my affection for the theatre. Slight. Slight. Slight. Nicely written. Nice characters. But really TV with a bit more oomph. This is doing nothing. This is taking us nowhere. Why can't theatre have more imagination? I am getting very worried about this lack of imagination. This regressive dependence on realism which stems from the literal quality of television. Everything is being reduced to what we know. Nothing seems to fly. It is the familiar being rehashed. Again and again the same. What is worst about *Passione* is that Innaurato becomes embroiled in realism and stereotypes and his true genius, his bizarre strokes, are absent or if they are present they are flattened by the rest. Hate going to events at New Dramatists. They strike me as having a somewhat revivalist quality.

Walked home from the plays last night and John Boy was here when I arrived. EJ also came down. John Boy in pain because of his ankle and, as it transpired, because of a slight fever. Is the whole world falling apart? And of course lest it be thought at a later date that I am apolitical, I am fully aware that there is a nasty conflagration going on in Iran and Iraq and it does seem strange that at this late date there should still be trouble over a stretch of water.

Today I slept late as usual and let the phone ring a few times, which is naughty. Then went and found Jay and brought him home here. Clams phoned yesterday and evidently I'm invited to the exclusive party after the play on Sunday, which should be quite jolly.

26 September 1980

My typewriter turned epileptic last night much to my chagrin and even now, having had a surgeon tamper with it for a good 90 minutes, it is still randomly inserting marks. Most irritating. What is happening? Jay lies in

bed still ailing. More pills were ordered today as tests have shown he has yet
another bacteria lying in his stomach. The child is extremely ill, I only hope
the half hour of ecstasy was worth it. Bitter queen that I am. Flip-flopped
yesterday and did some work here and there and went to the panel at ND
[New Dramatists] on Don Wollner's plays. Still am having this problem
regarding the theatre. Regarding the fact that everything I see I have already
seen. Lay awake a long time last night trying to think what theatre is for
me. It is not in staging. It is not in daring language etc. Those things have
been done and do not come to grips with the fundamental problem. Maybe
I should return to the idea of a play about Katherine Mansfield. Well, she
would not be Katherine Mansfield but me and the play would be about
departing from NZ and trying to come to grips with the world. Is there a
play there or not? Do not know. Think so. Have some ideas. Will try and
sort them out. There are too many projects. Also heard of a job at the NZ
Consulate and have an interview on Tuesday – it is a 9 to 5.15 job which I
would hate but it is tax free and who knows – might be good for me. Oh shit.
Don't really want to do that. This typewriter is going to drive me mad unless
it starts behaving itself.

The thing about writing a play is that you don't want to make it seem
as if you're writing a play. What I mean is that if you have a statement to
make you don't want to make the statement out cold. You can do that in an
article. You want to embody the statement to make the statement implicit.
To make the statement appear in the mind of the audience as they watch
the play – because they have perceived the statement implicitly. It's not like
a whodunnit and the audience working it out. A good play should create a
response in the audience which cannot be wrapped up in words. They should
be left with an emotional response. With a thought. Now you can't say that
thought. You don't even plant it. You let it rise of its own accord. That is not
easy. The real drama happens between the words as spoken and the minds
that receive – however many yards between the seat and the stage. In that
space the idea that is the play, the statement of the play, must come alive.
Or does the real drama take place in the head of the audience? What this is
all leading up to saying is that to say this is what I am writing about, here it
is, is not necessarily the best approach. It might seem logical but it is wrong.

The question you have to ask is how do I make the audience feel this thought that I feel and in doing that you might have to write things which have no relationship to what you are actually saying. Is this bullshit? I wonder. The problem with all the shit I see is that the author is not trying to make the audience feel anything. The author wants the audience to laugh, to be scared, to want to spend $25. He does not want the audience to share his own perceptions.

30 October 1980

Typewriter still not a well woman and so frustrated by that. There is much to report. First of all the man was meant to come and fix this machine yesterday and now will arrive tomorrow. He had better. Financial problems worsen and am now getting phone calls as well as threatening letters. Went and saw Kathleen Norris today and am borrowing $500 from New Dramatists, which might help me through the next month – especially if John Boy stays on and helps with the rent.* Must stay here and try and get my finances together and write a new play. It is all a matter of discipline. Have had several good ideas for work of late and want to follow them all up. Jay has just come in – he has an infection of the cornea which is very serious and can lead to scars on the cornea if not properly treated, it is a form of herpes. Poor thing.

Granny has been a touch evasive about everything of late. Oh dear. Well it turned out neither EJ nor I was actually invited to what turned out to be a dinner at Mr Chow's followed by a party at Linda Stein's† at which everyone drank too much cheap wine causing Granny to be very ill on Sunday afternoon – Clams had to put a Bible on her stomach. Of course they are all doing an inordinate amount of drugs right now for no good reason as none of them has any money. So I stayed at home.

Anyway, Sunday. I wore a black shirt of EJ's and a bright blue tie and a brown jacket and cowboy boots. A most elegant party at Robert Boykin's

---

*   **Kathleen Norris**, executive director of the New Dramatists, later executive director of the Australian Film Institute.

†   **Linda Stein** (1945–2007), American manager of rock bands including the Ramones, later a celebrity real estate broker.

Jay Funk in Robert's apartment, 1986. MS-1907/005, Hocken Collections

at 5 – great food and a lot of record/music people. Then the play itself with several celebs, Vreeland, Warhol, Princess Lee, Aaron Copland, Helen Hayes and so forth,* then the party at the loft just off 5th on 11th street – great place and about 500 there and so exclusive I could have brought a football team. I asked Buckley to point out the celebs but he thought I was joking and knew them, so I remained in the dark about most of them, but did talk to Sylvia Miles† and Don Boyd, who is the exec producer for many Brit and US films, he seemed a very nice man indeed. Monice Van Varoon was there and a great many rock people and a wonderful band 'The Coasters', who played until the police arrived to stop them. Lots of food and liquor and a generally

---

*   **Diana Vreeland** (1903–1989), French-American fashion columnist and editor. **Andy Warhol** (1928–1987), American visual artist, film director and producer, and a leading figure in the Pop Art movement. **Princess Lee Radziwill** (Caroline Bouvier, 1933–2019), American socialite, PR executive and interior decorator, and the sister of Jackie Kennedy. **Aaron Copland** (1900–1990), American composer, teacher, writer and conductor. **Helen Hayes** (1900–1993), American actress nicknamed the First Lady of American theatre.

†   **Sylvia Miles** (1924–2019), American actress and socialite.

polite event until the band, when there was much dancing. Bowie took forever to get his makeup off and arrived with a phalanx of photographers – a great sweep around the room and much kissing and flashlighting and so forth. The great moment for 'our crowd' was when Sally Hartman saw David and threw herself at him, great kisses and tears and grabbing of the buns as if they were the best of friends and the most sympatico of artists. Jack H most pissed by this and hailed Ellen Greene, who swept Sally off to a bedroom. Sally was out of sorts for most of the evening. It transpires that Eddy Betz has been telling her for years that there is only one woman who is her equal – Christine Jones – well Sally finally met Christine at Robert's and was most upset for Christine's ex (Skip Stein) is Sally's current! How do you like that. But Skip is dull and only his supply of cocaine seems to favour him. However, Sally does tell me that she is becoming very fond of him! My arse. Chris Stein also there.* After Sally's moment with Bowie she soon departed and evidently Jack highly pissed off, which is interesting as I think a year ago her behaviour was probably the same but he was different.

Thinking in bed last night came up with an idea for a play about King Hongi which might be interesting – must go to library tomorrow and do research. But the play would be about the colonial experience but from the Maori point of view. The noble savage. But instead of showing the Maori as the innocent try and show it the other way round – just as the English thought him quaint, try to show how he sees them. For he used the English. Also try and show the death of a culture and its replacement by an unsatisfactory void. I think this could be quite a powerful and interesting piece for non-Kiwis.

Tomorrow I have a gallery showing with EJ and Barbara Lackey and then *Division Street* with Judy Popkin.† Next week I have to have my new tooth done. Life.

---

*   **Chris Stein**, American photographer and musician, best known as guitarist and co-founder of Blondie.

†   **Barbara Lackey**, co-owner of nightclub Hurrah with Robert Boykin. **Judy Popkin** (née Lessing), RNZ foreign correspondent, chief of radio for three UN peacekeeping missions, and international tennis umpire/commentator. New Zealand friend of RL's in New York, married to American theatre critic, academic and dramaturg Henry Popkin.

14 November 1980

Two weeks have passed and nothing has been accomplished at all. Have maintained reasonable health but these last couple of days have had pains in the arms but am now fired up with aspirin and they have abated. What is there to report? Firstly EJ went back to London last week – a last-minute panic and then off with nothing quite finished but at least he is out of that apartment and that worry is off his shoulders. Had a small party for him here – decorated the house with leaves and called it the R Beagle Galleries and had lots of mock-EJ art around and a programme and terrible food – spam on wonderbread toast, marshmallows, cheese whiz and the most revolting cocktail sausages – and after the guests had left went with EJ, Peter Buckley and Charles Hunt to Teacher's for dinner. Molto tedioso. Jay's eye eventually cleared up and he is better now, he spent much time here and professed to John Boy that he loves me but will not indulge in any sort of intimacy and then disappeared for two days and returned with hickeys on his neck. I don't think he realizes what he is doing to me, but I am feeling better about it now and my nostalgia for the intense intimacy that characterized the early days of our relationship is not quite so painful. Really I am silly about it all but there was a time when the lovemaking seemed sacramental, which is, I expect, what lovemaking is meant to be. How strange. No money has come in and of course that worries me and also nothing has happened on the career front.

Do want to write something about the group of people I know and maybe the novel is the best form for that. Also have an idea for a play done from two points of view. First the man, and how he has come to end up in bed with the woman, and then the woman and how she has come to end up in bed with the man – the same story and characters both times but from the other point of view and one could use different scenes. This should give a cumulative comic effect. The pivotal point is the bed scene, which should probably be played three times at the beginning of Act One, beginning of Act Two and end of Act Two – or maybe just twice. And it would be called *His and Hers* which seems to be a nice way of putting it. This might be the right framework for the play about these people I know. And then there is the idea for the play about the party to which no one gets invited and everyone

wants to go – the giver decides not to have the party and so everyone has
to crash the non-existent event, I think I like the idea. And then have some
thoughts about a play about the likes of Muldoon – some sort of angry
farce about New Zealand and about the corruption of the people and their
stupidity and the contempt in which they are held by the leaders. To be set
in the PM's office. Think about it.

Received two letters from Reg Livermore last week and it was a joy to
hear from him again even if to learn that his London season was a disaster
but Hal Prince wants to produce his show in NYC.* Then yesterday Reg is on
the phone and he is staying at the Algonquin and here to see *Barnum*, which
Edgley wants him to do in Australia, and to meet with Prince.† He wanted
me to go to Hollywood/Ukraine with him last night but he could not go –
dinner with the Princes – and so I took JT and really had a good time, which
I was not expecting. Anyway did see Reg for an hour at the hotel and enjoyed
that and tonight we are seeing *Barnum* and tomorrow *42nd Street* so look
forward to all that. Strange meeting old friends again. But I admire him so.

9 January 1981

It is shortly after 3am and I've just got in from work – work being IGI and
typesetting. But the good news is here I am in front of the typewriter and
actually using it for the first time in months. But it is clear that I need a
new seat, having become used to sitting for hours before a typing machine
I now find my personal desk and chair to be at odds with each other. Have
been building up to this moment – the moment of actually sitting down and
using my typewriter again – for weeks. 1980 ended with terrible terrible
depression – it was so bad that it was beyond depression. Somehow my
illness, the lack of interest in my career, the chipper presence of John Dolf
and the concurrent presence of George Webby – and the process of adjusting
to the new working situation – conspired to create a frame of mind so full of
gloom and doom. When George and John left I had hoped for a parting of

---

* **Harold ('Hal') Prince** (1928–2019), American theatre producer and director, known for
   his work in musical theatre.
† **Michael Edgley** then ran Edgley International, Australian theatre and concert
   promotions company.

the clouds and had rushed out to spend some of my few pennies on a pile of books from Barnes and Noble. When John departed for Thanksgiving there was an enormous sense of peace and calm – which made his ever living here again with me impossible – I was hoping for the same at Christmas but it wasn't to be. No, alone I sank even lower. I saw no one except the people at work and briefly Sally/Donald and that crowd but felt uncomfortable with them and no doubt rudely rushed away, or I should say, rushed away, no doubt rudely. However. And then my mind would travel back over all the terrible incidents in my life and this while without the comfort of liquor – but no, liquor is not a comfort, it is a blind. However, since the start of this year I have begun to improve. I have felt a certain strength returning and have thought kindly about writing again. The *Travelling Squirrel* play I read and hated over Christmas but have been thinking about lately and see the problems and want to work on it. Have also been thinking about my life in New Zealand as a source for more plays and perhaps even a film script. And the story of the man coming to NY and falling in love and getting involved in the disco set and then trying to kill himself I now want to work on as a film script and tie it all in with a Capote-type narrator who introduces and interrupts the story as well as appearing in the background. And to have the hero leave the city at the end. It seems as if it would/should be an easy task and I am going to start taking notes. This is good.

The apartment is too expensive, that is for sure, but right now I feel I will not give it up. If I get a raise and if I can make some money writing and out of real estate then I will get by. I hope so. But also now I do not feel the need for great clumps of money – I would like to go home this year but that is all. I want enough to get the apartment looking decent and to keep me in books – which if I could just get used to the idea of the library I wouldn't have to worry about. And I think it important that I do continue with the daily notetaking or whatever this is. The most extraordinary thing is the difference one feels without the liquor. The perspective changed. But it is also quite clear that I am a manic depressive and I must watch these moods very carefully though I don't know how much I can do about them. I certainly don't want to take drugs (lithium or whatever). The lows are tedious and the highs frustrating because one wants, when high, to take

Robert, Becky and George Webby in Robert's apartment. Photograph by Martin Webby.

on the world and is apt to start 3 trillion projects and be unable to advance sufficiently with any, which is likely to cause another low which is suffused with the knowledge that the world has defeated one. The answer has probably been obvious to everyone else for years – channel, control. I feel if I can use this to contain the thousand thoughts and then concentrate on one project at a time – not hoping for cosmic breakthroughs, but for some gentle progress – then we might get somewhere. So this is the beginning. And I will, I have, begun.

11 January 1981

Not quite. Have felt strangely exhausted these past few days which is, I think, the result of the weather, which is bitterly cold. Have done very little other than watch TV (*The Philadelphia Story* and *Hospital* – both excellent) and sleep – also saw the Preston Sturges movie *The Lady Eve*. Had a wonderful Saturday afternoon with Jim Mag and we talked much and walked up to his house and I met Hester, his wife.* Apart from that have seen no one. Did have a long chat with Gilbert and a short chat with Gary Lisz, who phoned me pretending to want to talk to me but really after John Dolf's phone number. Talked to Mag about the novel/screenplay idea and he suggested I do it as a screenplay and if it doesn't work out then redo it as a novel, which would seem to be sensible. Also spoke to him about *The Travelling Squirrel* and he seemed to like the idea very much and was greatly encouraging. It would be good if I could get the projects done this year that I want to get done – *The Travelling Squirrel*, the screenplay (*A Short and Happy Life*, or *How the Good Die*), the play about the unmarried NZ woman and the *September* book. Is that too much? Probably. Will I just drift on? Possibly.

• • •

* **James Magnuson**, American author and playwright, later director of the Michener Center for Writers at the University of Texas, Austin, 1994–2017.

There is a gap in the diary between January and October 1981. Robert mentions he had been ill with bouts of hepatitis in 1980–81. When he resumed the diary in October, he had been living for six months on Fire Island, selling real estate and continuing work on *The Travelling Squirrel*. He was also revising the play that would become *Bert and Maisy*, though was still in search of an opportunity to produce it in either New Zealand or the USA.

1981–1983

Robert at 'The Quest', Fire Island, 1981. MS-2438/223/021, Hocken Collections

27 October 1981

Sitting in the restaurant of the Northwestern terminal of JFK & feeling somewhat queasy about flying. Had a lousy night's sleep after exhausting myself packing & writing notes & paying bills. So I'm leaving NY with $15 and $20 in the bank. Here I am, 36 & penniless, which is not exactly how I thought I would be in younger & more ambitious days. I'm wondering if I can actually do what I'm planning. If I can write the book I want to write. Passages of it have formed in my mind over the last several months and then been lost in the shuffle of my rather pointless daily life. But I do want to write the book. I do want to write about New Zealand & my life, I want to find out if I ever could live there again & how that country has shaped this 36-year-old penniless writer, typesetter, realtor.

Left Fire Island about three weeks ago and reentered the village of Manhattan. Left that strip of sand for the city. Went back again to say goodbye on a glorious autumn day. Pastel shades. Pale reds & yellows & the sun casting pink over the beach. Enormous clarity. Clear. Wandered along the beach. A few clusters of people casting long shadows. Looking posed. Posed by who? And a larger group surrounding a prone young man. His girl stroking his forehead. What happened? He dove into a wave & hit his head on the sand. Unable to move now & lying with clothes piled over him. A Lilco van parked on the sand next to him. And then a police car. And then a helicopter to take him to the mainland. Later that night I said a prayer for him – whoever he was.

And the next day grey & damp as I tidy the 3-bedroom shack that had been home for 6 months. The shack with an ill-shaped swordfish cut out of plywood & tacked over the front door in tribute to Hemingway we were told. Hemingway who called the shack 'The Quest' when he stayed there once 30 years ago. So rumour, legend, has it. The shack where six, seven, eight, more often, had gathered on weekends & partied, got high, been frivolous, pointless. Dressed & redressed for late-night dancing. Made love. Bitched each other. Laughed. The shack where during the weeks I'd made some futile attempts at writing, where I recovered from a second bout of hepatitis, bringing to 18 months a time of illness. The shack where during one wet weekend trapped with 3 other New Zealanders I came to realize I have many unresolved problems with my attitude to my homeland & perhaps I had better return to examine them.

Being with Kiwis in New York irritates me beyond belief. Of course it could be that they, the ones I meet, are irritating people but no, it is more. It's a memory of the frustrations & regrets, it's an unwelcome mirror revealing blemishes one had ignored & had hoped were forgotten. And so is this journey. The 18 hours of flight. And so is being in this banal restaurant. Eating the eggs & bacon & feeling queasy. Popping the Valium & wishing it were a 'lude. Wishing I was in bed with Rebecca – the beagle – wishing for another day of wandering the city. Of shooting the breeze with Robert Boykin & others equally underemployed. Of dreaming dreams, of scheming schemes. Yesterday I ran round the city like a crazy woman. Trying to scrape together money to pay those essential bills. Screaming through Bloomingdales to buy gifts for Hilary & Nathan* – and I had to do it at Bloomies. I have a card. Payment can wait. And all this in the company of Jay, whom I still love & who loves me but who has found more in his Christianity, which I do not understand but he has given me a book to read.

For some reason there are no clocks in this terminal. And I carry no watch. I keep asking strangers the time. I haven't told many people I am returning to New Zealand but for some reason these last few weeks have brought me in contact with many from the past. Alan and Valerie dashing into NYC on the way to the Prêt in Paris.† That quaint shop in Tinakori Road now a string of shops with one in Sydney, where they will probably settle. NZ they say is a mess. A cripple. Morally & physically in decline, & people leaving in droves. And Reg Livermore here to learn to tightrope walk for his role as Barnum in the Australian production of that show. Reminding of 10 years ago when he came into my life & overwhelmed me with his talent & insight & warmth. And letters from Sunny & Donna touring in London & from George Webby in New Zealand sending clippings of strife surrounding the rugby tour by the South Africans which has seemingly polarized the NZ

---

*   RL's niece and nephew.

†   **Alan Svendsen** (1928?–2012) was a buyer, manager and shop designer for the Vance Vivian menswear chain. **Valerie Svendsen** (1930?–2017) had worked in costume design at Downstage from the late 1960s before opening her boutique Memsahib in 1971.

populace.* My parents writing & worried about the poor police – ignoring on moral issues. And Nick Enright phoning about Amendment 78 to the 1961 Crimes Act, which will impose jail terms of 14 years on those who write, record, disseminate information deemed prejudicial to the image of NZ abroad.† If it comes law it will be the only such law in any non-totalitarian country. New Zealand has been in my mind. But not to forget my American friends in the last 3 weeks. Peter Buckley at 43 and penniless. Gary Lisz at 28 and penniless. Jack Hofsiss in Hollywood putting the final touches to his first major motion picture. Gary Lisz having become enthused with a Canadian mystic who predicts the millennium in 1983. It would appear, this is what I gleaned from a 30-minute crash course, that God was/is a gas similar to ether who, while wandering through the universe, left some of himself on Earth, which, interacting with gases etc here, formed man, who indeed lived in the Garden of Eden, which at that time shared a diet of oxygen & xenon.

Gary announced he would from now on be aloof & eschew frivolity & drugs. Indeed the previous Saturday night at The Saint he had made an earnest attempt to do this but was bored rigid & finally decided, when offered, to sniff up some cocaine – but he accepts responsibility for this and will pay the consequences. A young man, David, arrived & was dazzled by all this sophisticated spiritual nonsense & urged that Taylor take up the ouija board & thus we communicated with Sobrax, who told us to pray for France (this new/old religion seems right-wing) which is in danger of going Communist. An evil spirit interfered & spelled out Fuck, we had to pray to get him out. After an hour I was exhausted & fled. I wonder what Gary will be into when I return.

I am now on the plane, a rather ancient DC8, & we are taxiing to the runway. There is so much to write & I know I'm going into a time-warp where my Fire Island/New York life with its discos, drugs, spiritualism,

---

* **Sunny Amey**, New Zealand director and educator. Worked in UK theatre, including five years at the newly formed National Theatre. Artistic director at Downstage Theatre 1970–74; curriculum officer for drama at Department of Education 1975–88; and director of Toi Whakaari New Zealand Drama School 1988–91.

† **Nick Enright** (1950–2003), Australian actor, playwright and director. RL met him in Melbourne in 1973 and the two shared an apartment in New York in the mid-70s.

enthusiasms & speeches will seem unreal, a dream, just as New Zealand this moment seems an absurdity. I want to continue to talk about New York for a moment. To sketch in a few characters. But this book will freewheel. Names will appear & explanations eventually will follow. Events both past & present will be discussed. I always feel exhausted on planes. Does it have to do with oxygen? (Bring on the xenon.) Or is it a nervous reaction? There is very thick fog about but we seem to be leaving on schedule. Does Andy Warhol really enjoy flying, is it true that he loves planes? There is something about the interior of this Capitol plane that reeks of mediocre design, which is inherently plastic. Is that the attraction?

Someone has approached Robert [Boykin] to co-produce a children's show at the Felt Forum in Madison Square Garden & Robert came to me & I almost handed him my best idea to date (*Roger, The Travelling Squirrel*) but managed to get out of that. Anyway I was taken to meet the producer & as one might expect in his apartment high above Lincoln Center one discovered he was an asshole. I suggest a revamped *Owl & Pussycat*, which he thinks is a show about a hooker & why would Streisand do it in the Felt Forum? Horrors.

In the city this week I did have a great NY Sunday – wandered past the marathoners & on to the theatre. A good feeling in the air, & the play *Einstein & the Polar Bear* by Tom Griffin was deliciously literate, warm & compassionate.* I delight for Tom, who acted in my first play done in the States – *Well Hung* – & wish I'd written this piece. But it has helped to redefine my goals. After years of bad experiences I was on the verge of putting down the pen but now I want to write those plays. But there is the cultural problem, I am not now & never will be an American but I have ceased to be a New Zealander. I exist in a limbo. It is very hard to write plays of weight that do not come out of a real world. I still can write with ease about New Zealand. I find it very hard to write about America. A gut understanding is missing. But there is my impression of America & that is probably where I should work.

---

* **Tom Griffin** (1946–2018), actor and playwright. Member of the Trinity Square company 1974–83. *Einstein and the Polar Bear*, his fourth play, about a reclusive writer, was adapted for the screen in 1984.

A New York street scene from Robert's archive. MS-1907/007/005, Hocken Collections

Reg & I talked about this last week. He wondered if perhaps I hadn't got caught up in that city syndrome that can keep one busy for months only to show you that you weren't busy at all. New York is the easiest city in the world to do nothing in – and not notice it. And being gay accentuates this. One is trapped in a ghetto of parties & hunts. Sometimes I wish I was a eunuch. The vanities. I hate my body but not enough to sweat daily at a Nautilus machine forming those curves & bulges so desired. Am I the last of the wimps? I am also possessive on an emotional level but rationally a very liberated man. A guru tells me I am working out sex karma from a life in Egypt. Sometimes this worries & depresses me but for the most part I am staggered as to why the masses don't respond to my sparkling wit & occasionally dazzling repartee. Today my gay angst is elsewhere. With luck we won't have to deal with it again.

Reg, I have already mentioned Reg. Reg I admire more than anyone else. I admire his talent & his center. He is Australian, he is of Australia, he is part of Australia. There is no doubt. His talent as a performer, writer & painter is considerable, is overwhelming. His show was hated in London. I know not why. He speaks from the heart but is outrageous, is funny & always real. Reg saw this large book. 200 blank sheets. Look, I said, I will fill this up. 'Will you?' he replied, 'I wonder.' He wonders if I am in the world of nonsense. I do too. What happened to the eager beaver grossly overconfident young writer? Were there really too many disappointments? Or am I lazy? Reg daunts me. I find him attractive. Always have. I don't know if I want to sleep with him anymore. Why do my palms sweat when I write on planes?

We are over Pennsylvania. There is nothing but cloud. There is 'occasional turbulence'. My Valium is kicking in. Reg has spent time, he would say 'done time', in New Zealand. First in *The Legend of King O'Malley*,* one of those discover our past docu-plays so popular in the antipodes in the late 60s & early 70s when theatre was said to be emerging. He returned in *Hair* playing Berger & stayed in my apartment. A tumble-down affair – the top floor of an old house. Downstairs Graham Kerr once lived & had a mock-up of his TV kitchen.† Rumour had it that Igor Stravinsky once drank tea on the front

---

* Australian 1970 musical by Bob Ellis and Michael Boddy about politician King O'Malley.
† **Graham Kerr**, British-born chef known as the Galloping Gourmet. He moved to New Zealand in 1958 and hosted his first television show, *Entertaining with Kerr*, from 1959.

lawn. I'm inclined to doubt it. It certainly was not a lawn of elegance. Once this apartment looked down over a valley of old wooden cottages & then to the city of Wellington with its harbour so beautiful, trapped by mountains & similar in design to San Francisco. Before I left for New York the valley of houses had become a motorway going nowhere but no doubt of fine design if one cares about the design of such things. Hating cars I also hate motorways. And the harbour was still here but smaller as vast reclamation schemes which have marked the history of that earthquake-ridden city continued to push into the always blue sky. The view was being destroyed. I have no reason to think this progress may have been arrested.

My apartment had crooked floors, an old gas stove, a gas copper in lieu of a washing machine. We bought a fridge at an auction. My friend Tim kept it full of lobsters, which he dove for off the rocky coast.* Many people lived there from time to time. For several weeks a group of hippies camped in the living room. We called them the Afghanistanians, presumably because they'd been there. They moved in with their brown rice & sewing machine, with strips of leather & some old car tires. They made shirts out of flour sacks & sandals from the tires and leather. I was less tolerant in those days & hated them.

Reg came into this madness & adapted. I wanted to show him how beautiful New Zealand was & with my friend Willy we set off to drive him to Lake Taupo.† We got lost, which is quite hard to do, & ended up in Wanganui, a city(?) of the most depressing demeanour. The day was grey. We drove across a mountain range surrounded by thunderclouds. We seemed to be in some Norwegian folk tale & waited for trolls. We then arrived in Raetihi, the carrot capital of NZ, a town with 2 collapsing shops & an abandoned opera house surrounded by dirty fields of carrots.‡ What was an opera house doing here? Was *Tristan* ever performed? A terrible anomaly lost in a world of carrots. It was all too much. We drove home. Every village looked more bleak than the one before. My country looked like a third-world backwater. I was

---

*   **Tim Brosnahan**, friend, fisherman, and flatmate at 26 Clifton Terrace.
†   **Jan Williams**, RL's friend whom he'd known 'since 1970 when she lived over the street from me in Wellington' (MS-2438/109, p.42, Hocken Collections). He visited her in Hastings on his 1981 trip and she travelled to Auckland with him and his parents.
‡   Theatre Royal (1915), Seddon Street, Raetihi.

Robert on the verandah of his flat in Clifton Terrace, Wellington, in 1972. Photograph by
Terence Taylor. MS-2438/223/001, Hocken Collections

embarrassed. Reg & I laughed about it last week. I had wanted to show him what was important to me. I'm not sure what we found.

Later I visited Reg in Australia & was stunned by the vibrancy and richness of Sydney. Bars were open past 10 at night. I was drunk on Australian beer & Australian life. I wanted to leave New Zealand. In those days I was innocent. Not that I knew it. As a matter of fact I considered myself to be sophisticated. A cut above the rest. I could discuss sex openly, but not with my family. I could discuss theatre & believed it to be important. To be vital, necessary, a contribution. That a few hundred others were the only ones who shared my views confirmed their correctness. Of course being gay & effeminate in a country which above all prizes rude masculinity doesn't make life simple & maybe explains my need for arrogance. America today seems covered by clouds but I'm sure it's down there some 31,000 feet. The clouds have cleared. I see Chicago below.

Flying always amazes me. Right now we are over Colorado, I think. There is snow about but not much. Last time I took this NY–LA flight was on my way to New Zealand to work on *Pictures*, my one and only movie. The in-flight movie was an epic about photographers arriving in the US last century from France & moving east overland & as I watched them trudge & agonize their way I was zooming over that same territory. This provoked a number of no doubt banal thoughts but the essence still fascinates. The changing appreciation of time as one grows older. This is very apropos in my thinking about NZ. But 100 years ago those photographers spent the better parts of several years doing what I now do in six hours, & I complain that my palms sweat! Happy Rockefeller said at the time of the bicentenary that it amazed her that the country was only four times older than she.*

New Zealand was hardly colonized at all when claimed by the British 140 years ago, & the major immigration to there did not start until 1860. In the space of 3 lifetimes a virgin land populated sparsely by Polynesians, with a unique & exquisite natural life, has become – what? The home for 60 million sheep & a population constantly shrinking from 3 million. What is it? A pattern of English behaviour transplanted & allowed to flourish/diminish/

* **Margaretta Large ('Happy') Rockefeller** (1926–2015), philanthropist and widow of Governor of New York and US Vice-President Nelson Rockefeller (1908–1979).

revert/pervert. As a country it has produced an extraordinary catalogue
of eccentrics & has developed an insularity appropriate to its location and
a rigid manner of behaviour – stronger I think than I ever realized when
I lived there. And this country, God's Own we called it when I was young.
Later I mocked that but it still seemed something like paradise; this country
seems on the verge of shrouding itself in totalitarian oppression. The
private codes of repressed emotion, understatement, of never accepting
achievement in others, of distaste for success & excess (except in sports), is
it finally finding a codified expression in law? Can this really be true?

How can a country which professes to enjoy racial equality between
Pakehas & Maoris act in such a way as to internationally demonstrate it does
not care a damn about oppressed people? You cannot say sports & politics
are not related when every other country in the world relates them. It is
absurd. And when my parents write to me of the protests & riots, it is the
'poor police' they worry for. Has the insularity, the physical isolation, really
engendered a belief that the rest of the world does not exist – or should
not be taken seriously? Watching our Prime Minister strut and fret on the
international stage only confirms this. Or am I a dangerous radical? There
was a time when I found it hard to believe the rest of the world existed.
When the news from abroad – the wars, the international tensions – seemed
absurd enough to be the figment of some zealous fractioneer.

Indeed I invented a theory (if one invents a theory) that all there was
was New Zealand, that those who left were placed on a large aircraft carrier
just over the horizon where they were fed drugs & otherwise told they
were experiencing 'the world'. And the dissidents, the ones who spat out
the drugs, they were trapped on the carrier & charged with inventing news
designed to make those at home safe & secure. It's a whimsical fantasy but
it did help explain why one was living in this strange & rigid paradise. Of
course now, living in New York, when I think about New Zealand and my life
there it seems strange and unreal. What is it? What is this country? Above
the Rockies I wonder why I am going. I have to. I have something to work
out. I must confront it.

Yes, I am a writer and I work in real estate & schemes. The writing has
been going on for longer than I can remember, as have the schemes. The real

estate is more recent, begun on Fire Island, where, during one summer when penniless as usual & rewriting a play that bogged me down for three years & which ultimately wasn't worth it, I started cleaning summer rental houses & then segued into renting the same working for Cappy, an extraordinary woman whose fascination with business, whose total preoccupation with it, is not a matter of greed for money, it is a passion. But I'm not that dedicated. If I roleplay I can do it but it isn't me. I used to be able to convince myself that I was what I was doing. Now it is not easy. I'm not sure what I am. I can define myself by negatives. Once I was by choice a writer, now I am a writer because it is the only occupation where I seem to be me. And even I have to be careful. I have to remember what writer I am. What truth, what attitude, what manner of thinking is really mine. It is too easy to mimic & easy to accept the mimicry as oneself. I read Paul Theroux's travel books & wanted to use them as models for my book about New Zealand. They are excellent and absorbing books & his prose is a delight. But I am not he and cannot force myself into his mould or ape his manner. I must be me.

It's hard to say anything about LA that hasn't been said. But I always want to work out where its bits & pieces begin. But it looks the same. All the same & the cars & rental car depots & the fast food places & the names of streets which have no relationship, as far as I can see, to their spelling. I wandered to the beach & saw the men and their muscles, a man roller skating with an amp & electric guitar twanging. Bought a hot dog which the blond blue-eyed California boy cook told me he had soaked in beer. I was hungry. The paddle tennis courts are full but the promenade is quiet. Leaving the airport was trying. Aware of the $10 alone in my pocket (I bought 2 screwdrivers on the flight) I sought a bank but was trapped with my case & had to reenter the terminal & have it x-rayed then opened and the gifts I charged at Bloomingdales opened for inspection. And getting a cab! Having to deal with a rabbit-toothed despatcher. LA. I want a drink but don't know where to buy one. Shortly the hour should be up. I feel I should say something definitive about this city. How can I possibly? Something pithy, witty & Vidalese. But I have nothing to say, I do not know this city of freeways & low-slung houses.

28 October 1981

I've already arrived & I'm still in LA; after an horrendous taxi ride to the airport on a freeway which belied such description, four lanes each way loaded with the vehicles this city was created for & which seem to be choking it to death. And here I am, a late arrival to the departure lounge which is chock-a-block with Kiwis, many of whom belong to the 'Temuka Rugby Club 1981 American Tour'. They sport their labelled travel bags & a plethora of gifts for the kids at home. In the bar 4 of them are gathered round one who is a 'character', he wears a giant purple sombrero with silver trim, they call him Hombre. They drink beer & pronounce Michelob to be 'not bad', which is high praise. The bartender & I both notice the stinginess of their tipping – but I know it is a habit for which the Kiwi has an ingrained disgust. They enjoyed the Grand Canyon; 'yes it was alright wasn't it?' They joke rather loudly & they look like NZers – with stocky bodies & weathered faces & none of them can wear a shirt, the shirt buckles & bulges & defies fitting neatly into the trousers. It is odd to be back among NZers so soon. I hadn't expected it. There is also a collection of senior citizens whom I imagine to be returning from their 'trip' for which years of saving & anticipation paved the way. I wonder how they found the world – or did they notice it? Most conversations seem to be about home. But it is the accent that does most for me. I could be blind & know I was in NZ. Those strange vowels! It is a voice that sounds to me homely & naïve. It gives me a warm feeling & it puts me on edge all at once. Do I sound like this? I think I do & don't wonder that NYers listen to me curiously. Tommy Tune did tell me that next to Tommy Grimes I had the strangest speech patterns he had ever heard.[*] And the men seem to dress consciously to deny any sexuality; there are no tight jeans & no carefully composed looks such as bombard the eye in the Big Apple. But no one dresses for travel anymore. There must have been an age not too distant where travel demanded a certain sense of style.

Anyway I have entered culture shock in this vulgar & plastic airport where I grabbed a screwdriver to wash down a Valium. Actually it is culture shock two. LA was one. NYers hate LA. Everyone knows that. It sprawls.

[*]   **Tommy Tune**, American actor, dancer, singer, theatre director, producer and choreographer.

You drive everywhere. You go to bed early. The smog. I could go on. Being a New Yorker I feel duty bound to hate LA as well. But Liz, my friend, abounds with enthusiasm for it & that is infectious.* Down at Venice I find a sense of community. Sitting on the stoop in the morning one is greeted by the neighbours; they stop by to chat, they talk to the mailman. Other people arrive, open their mail, talk about what they are doing, reading, seeing. It is a neighbourhood, not like a NY neigh., not an enclave. But warm, there is a caring. I like it.

And now I'm on the plane. I did find the paper, the *Observer*, about Mr Muldoon's schemes. I've shown it to my travel companions. The female (a nurse from Wellington about to relocate to Napier & returning from a vacation with friends in Ontario) says after reading: 'Muldoon is a wanker.' The male, about 30, who works for the government but who wants to go out on his own & leave NZ, doesn't like Muldoon & doesn't like people who oppose NZ/SA sporting contacts. He thinks there is no leadership in any political party but suggests Muldoon is mad. 'Hitler was mad,' he adds as an afterthought, 'how did he get to power?' There is a silence which mirrors the silent consent he has referred to. We all agree Air New Zealand is a very good airline – but I'm not sure I want to see the scheduled film about Elvis.

Thursday 29 and/or 30 October 1981
A day has been mislaid somewhere in the middle of the Pacific. I'm drinking New Zealand beer, real beer, not lager & not too chilled, a warmed & warming taste I had forgotten. Sitting in the sunroom at home looking out over the Orakei Basin to the harbour, clumpy grey cloud & rather cold. A strange contrast to the glorious morning that greeted me – we flew down the coast from Whangarei, over the Hen & Chickens, over the Great Barrier, seeing Kawau & then the Waitemata & the city & an easy landing at Mangere. And that strange ritual where the cabin is sprayed for bugs. Keeping our virgin land free from medfly & other nasties. And I'm confused as we come flying over the city, the land is lush, the hills, those small extinct

---

* **Elizabeth Coulter**, New Zealand actor who RL met at Victoria University. Performed in RL's *Pictures* (Pacific Films) and at Auckland's Mercury Theatre in the 1970s, before moving to Los Angeles. Came to New York to take part in RL's productions and readings.

volcanoes green green among the houses. It looks beautiful. And Mum &
Dad there as I arrive. They ask me if they look older but in truth they don't.
Dad has a little arthritis, he tells me, but he manages to play several games
of bowls & at least one of golf each w/e. So it stands to reason it can't be
too bad. They have brought the Mini, which looks ludicrously small but we
manage to pile in. Driving home I'm a little dazed, relief at having arrived,
tiredness, the familiarity & the strangeness of it all. What do we talk about?
They want to know about my career, anxious for success.

Auckland is Auckland, the land fertile, the growth lush, the colours
bright, the houses on their small sections neat and clean. We drive past the
Mangere Bridge, which was half finished when I left in 1974 & was then left
alone because of union troubles & is finally being finished. Dad has a pithy
comment about unions & unionists. Home & it's more chatter – lightly we
touch on the Springbok tour, my parents stand firmly on the right. They too
distrust Muldoon but see no alternative. I mention Amendment 78 but it
is not seen as a threat. We rifle through the list of relatives, who is married,
who is divorced, who is well. Many are coming for drinks on Sunday so
I can be inspected. Hideous! They will all ask what I do. How things are
going. What sort of life I have. I will lie. Am I going to tell them I dance
my life away, that I'm a disco maven? That I'm a faggot slut who behaved
like a whore during her last weeks in NY & now wonders if she has an anal
infection?

Since starting these notes I've moved from sundeck to fireside to dinner
table (corned beef, broad beans, potato, pumpkin, spinach) to fireside &
now to bed. I am exhausted. Went into town to clear up some tedious money
matters. Went to the Mercury Theatre & was swamped with feelings of love
hate regret. Russell was there in my heart & nowhere to be seen. An era
returned & a sadness. I saw Jonathan Hardy & arranged to contact him on
the weekend.* I am too tired to do this now. Will continue in the a.m.

---

*   **Jonathan Hardy** (1940–2012), New Zealand stage, television and film actor, writer and
director. Artistic director of the Mercury Theatre 1980–85, and also worked extensively
in Australia and the UK.

31 October 1981

This is all too much. I am saturated, smothered, barraged. Too many images, visual & otherwise. Too many remembrances of things past. I'm not at all sure if this idea is going to work – for a book – so much is going on in my mind & I want to relate it all. We visited Pam* yesterday after going into town & she & Mum immediately leapt into a conversation about Pam's toe, which is giving her trouble. Pam asks me what I think of Reagan. I don't know what to say. Reagan? I don't think about him at all. And there is more discussing of rugby & the racing situation. The world, it can be agreed, is no longer a pleasant place, but sitting at Pam's looking out over the twin harbours this city is built on, all the neat houses, the trees that dapple the city, one cannot imagine that this is still not God's Own, the country founded by lesser English & thought for so long to be a haven. And Pam is full of stories of her children & grandchildren, all of whom are nearby, and I know my mother wishes I too was settled here with my quarter acre and correct percentage of little ones. Father had worried that I do not have a NZ driver's license & this has provoked a visit to the traffic department – my NY State license is acceptable.

In the Mercury I saw a programme for *Heroes & Butterflies* & that caused a moment of – what is it? Not regret. An intense sense of my youth, of when all was possible, of when I loved Russell & he loved me and all was about to happen for us. It is one thing that can be said in my favour I think, that I do not stop loving even if it becomes perverted for a time. The love is always there & I do still love Russell. Now, as I write this, I wish he was here and I could turn to him. But he is in London & our lives seem to have parted quite beyond any form of reunification.

I met Russell in 1972 when I lived in Wellington. It was at Tony Taylor's house.† I remember thinking he was the most beautiful person I had ever seen. I wanted to be with him from the moment I first laid eyes on him, which is something of a clichéd situation. I was rather doughy & intense, garrulous too & occasionally amusing in those days. I was intense about the

---

*   **Pam Smith**, RL's aunt, Bebe Lord's sister.

†   **Anthony (Tony) Taylor** (1937–2009), Radio New Zealand producer in the 1970s, and artistic director at Downstage Theatre 1977–81 and Fortune Theatre 1984–85.

Mercury Theatre

Heroes and Butterflies

Robert Lord

theatre & believed I would write great plays. It seemed simple in theory. I was dedicated to Downstage & worked my butt off for it – a blind loyalty to George, then Sunny, then Tony Taylor. The thought of living in, of even visiting America, was remote, it did not exist. This was the Vietnam period, America was an enemy, America was not understood. Certainly not by me. It was a monolith telling the world how to behave. Iron fisting & being flashy. The world was simpler, I was simpler.

I met Russell again & tried to make his acquaintance without success. Then one night when he was working on his set for *Narrow Road to the Deep North* I stayed up for hours & helped him & took him home & we had sex & my heart sang with the chance, with the opportunity, the possibility of love. I lived in Wellington, he lived in Auckland. We traded visits. I remember & I know he remembers my tears one day when I had to leave him. I was too possessive, not in matters sexual, but I wanted him all. And later I was the one who let everything collapse. Who actually destroyed the relationship. We were both travelling abroad & I wanted freedom again. I should have made a commitment. I think towards the end of our NZ time I was very cruel to him. No excuse. Naïveté. Wanting the world. And I think now if I had been easier in my relationship with my parents, been honest about my sexuality & if they had accepted it, then my turning away from Russell would not have happened & I would not have hurt him so badly.

Once in New York & going through the rapid changes that city demanded, I wanted him again & would write long declarations of love, would call & drunkenly implore his affection. But I had lost him, I had lost part of myself I think. I never realized how much I loved him & had hurt him until I visited him in London in early 1979 & stayed in his flat there. One night we drank Guinness at the local pub & then Jamieson's at the flat & he catalogued my crimes. There was nothing to say. I couldn't explain myself. Yes I tried, I told how the sex had ceased to work for me. But what does that mean? It could have worked again.

Left: Russell Craig designed both the stage set and the programme's cover artwork for the 1974 Mercury Theatre production of *Heroes and Butterflies*. MS-1907/029, Hocken Collections

I think now that when I left NZ I wanted freedom to enjoy the success that I knew would be mine. What arrogance & whatever happened to the success? At that time (79) I'd finished the first draft of *Family Portrait*, Russell read it & concluded I'd sold out. Given up. Failed. This did have an effect. I didn't write anything more for 2 years. It is only recently that I have tried again. And yesterday, wandering through the Mercury, all the best times were with me. Russell! I spoke to him a few months ago. He has a lover. He sounded happy & he said he would write. He hasn't. I don't expect him to. But now I miss him. And the irony is the story of Jay, which placed me in Russell's shoes. Not that Jay wants me back. He is happy & good & has God. But with Jay at least if the sex has gone the love is still there. He loves me very much, of that I have no doubt. The day before I left NY & was in such a state he spent with me & helped me shop for my nephew & niece. He is a good man.

I visited Flo, 93 years old & now going blind, my last surviving great-aunt, who lives with her daughter Pat, who has never married. They are pleased to see me, they are worried about my health, they tumble out a thousand stories of what they've seen on television & how beautiful NY looked when they saw the marathon on television. How proud I must've been when a NZ girl came in first. I love them. They are eccentric & they potter through their rather pleasant bungalow. We have sherry. They ask me what I think of Reagan. Flo thinks he's a bit of a warmonger. Flo thinks it's terrible what happened over the football tour. That there should be barbed wire in a country like this! And elections coming up! Muldoon will have to get in, if he doesn't who will all the cartoonists satirize? It is a healthy attitude.

I wonder if I have become too glib. It is too easy in NY to skate across the surface of experience & to imagine the thin slice on the ice as a deep and revealing slash. This is not so. I am here now in New Zealand. I cannot avoid the fact that these are my roots. I sense I am home. It cannot be otherwise. I must find a way of dealing with it. I could bury myself here. Build a house in the bottom of my parents' garden as we often discuss. But that would be an escape. But I feel I want to write. Just being here & the flood of feelings makes me want to write a new play. I will never be an American. These are my roots. But something tells me I cannot stay in this city of neat, clean streets & well-tended gardens, of all English cars preserved lovingly not out of affection but because a new one costs too damn much.

Today I drove through Remuera, where I was a 9-year-old. It was perhaps 10 shops, I remember the grocery, the bookstore & the library. The library where I first started writing. Later this day: I am surrounded by ghosts and I know no one. I know everything, my past is here, I am here now – but I am invisible. It occurred to me as we drove this afternoon to look at some cottages such as might be suitable to build at the bottom of the garden for a writer like myself to live in; it occurred to me as we drove that I have no friends here. I know no one here. When I left seven years ago, which is not a long time, I knew many many people. They have all gone. All. I've been

Russell Craig in Newcastle, England, 1986. MS-1907/005, Hocken Collections

through my address book. No names. No people to call. So I drive through these familiar streets. I expect to see the familiar faces. Ghost town. And every corner another memory. It is an experience of far more intensity than I imagined. On other visits I was busy, I was being a writer, role-playing. Now I am wandering through the city with no real purpose & am being assaulted by my own mind at every turn. Had I left, been gone, 30 years – I could expect this. But 7? I knew people were leaving, I knew they were going to Australia, to England, seeking to escape, seeking a chance at something more. This is a small & beautiful pond. Maybe there is a limit as to how many fish can survive in it at any one time. If the pond fills up do they turn on each other & kill; perhaps if they have no taste for blood they leave. The people I saw today at the many displays of mobile homes were young, the women pregnant, the men standing back with somewhat worried brows. I felt no kinship.

Jean-Pierre Gauthier appeared as a ghost.* Out of nowhere & not having thought of him for years he was there. A very handsome French Canadian, he came and settled in NZ for a time as part of a mime troupe. I worked with him. It was strange because he accepted his gayness in a manner that I did not. I knew I was gay & I knew there was no great sin in this but I knew I had to be apart from the rest, from family, in this aspect of my life. Jean-Pierre's adjustment was different, family accepted, there was no problem. It seemed to me at the time that it gave him a strength I lacked. I don't know what happened to him. I remember he was an excellent cook & could make an excellent chocolate mousse & good bread. I am writing this in the den my father built under the house. It is a small & cosy room but cold right now as I have all the windows open – I'm smoking, a habit for which my parents have the utmost contempt. For 20 years I've been smoking behind their backs. Jean-Pierre, sandy hair, blue eyes, & exotic by virtue of being French. But what was he really like? Did I invent him, this dashing mousse-making Frenchman?

---

*   **Jean-Pierre Gauthier**, French-Canadian member of Francis Batten's Theatre Action mime/physical theatre company. The company began with performers trained at the Paris-based École Jacques Lecoq, and was resident with Downstage in Wellington in 1972 and 1973.

After our tour of model houses Mother and I visited Sir Denis & Lady Blundell; Lady B is my mother's cousin.* She first dated her husband from my parents' house where she was a visitor in the late 40s. I was just a nipper. Sir Denis, a lawyer, a soldier who distinguished himself in WW2, later became the NZ High Commissioner in London & then Governor General. At the time he was Governor I was a young man dedicated to theatre and art, something of a hippie I guess but confused in my role-playing. My background is of extreme conservatism, by inclination I am bohemian. As a result I have been frequently an embarrassment. But also I have an aptitude for organization & management. There is no need for me to be modest about this. It is not a skill I prize; though had I done so, and perhaps if I was familiar with the world then as I am now, I might have chosen to champion these skills. My homosexuality & the fact that I could not let it find expression within my family lead me into strange avenues. If I had been born in America I think I would not have found it necessary to enter the theatre.

One last cigarette & I will go upstairs and join the folks for a drink. I have travelled 9 or 10,000 miles this week, already New York is like a dream. The Saturday night ritual, the coke & Quaaludes, The Saint, the high-powered nonsense of that world seems just that. As Davina[†] once told me, & this is a peculiar metaphor, when you return home it is always as if you have never left, you fit in perfectly but you don't quite belong; like a child who has lost a tooth & tries to fit the tooth back in the socket; it fits there but does not belong there. Sometimes I wonder why I have been forced to spend my creative life grappling with words & the logic & rationality they demand. And words are the coins of the realm of the thought. They are instruments of common barter; they belong to rich & poor, stupid & bright. I would rather, I wish I could paint; I wish I could dance; I wish I could go beyond language. I wish I could find a way of reaching directly into another's heart.

---

[*] **Sir Edward Denis Blundell** (1907–1984), lawyer, cricketer and diplomat, and 12th Governor-General of New Zealand 1972–77. **June Blundell** (1922–2012) was known for her community service and welfare work.

[†] **Davina Whitehouse** (1912–2002), English-born actress who emigrated to New Zealand in 1952 and worked in stage, radio, television and film.

Words are my only tool. Sometimes I think perhaps I have not worked hard enough. I am still alive. There is time.

1 November 1981

This is the first day on which no one has asked me what I think of President Reagan. On the other hand many have commented on my lack of an American accent. This morning a drove of relatives appeared. Bobby & Henry of my parents' vintage arrived with their somewhat regal air, Mother & Bobby are cousins. They are retired & spend two months of each year in Honolulu. Sir Denis and Lady B arrived & Sir D read the article from the *Observer* with interest but little comment. Two of Pam's daughters arrived. Sandy with her 14-year-old son Stuart who is something of a tennis player & has a wry sense of humour. Kim, the 11-year-old daughter who seems distinguished by her height, was also present. Jenny, Pam's other and youngest daughter, came with Garth, her husband, & I liked them both. They are young, decent, hard-working & unsophisticated. Of the Cookes (Mother's brother) Jack, the patriarch, arrives first, followed by John the eldest & his wife Kate, who I'd not met before. John is definitely a decent chap but something of a fool & we all laugh about him, which is probably unfair as he seems to have the best of intentions. Nigel & his wife Liz appear with Amelia, their daughter, over whom they dote. Nigel always looks as if the world is a little too much for him. Liz is full of opinions & politics & gossip. Juliet arrives without her husband, who is studying. The other of Jack's children, Rosamund, is about to arrive here from London, where she has left an unsatisfactory husband & a brain-damaged child. Everyone wants to know when Rosamund is coming but no one asks. Pat also arrives. I surprise myself with the ease with which I manage to deal with the influx. I'm not exactly floating through it, I'm not exactly part. Actually my visits seem to provide an excuse for the various factions of Mother's family to come together and size each other up. We are in strong National territory. There is a confidence, and ease, and assumed superiority. But these are not vindictive or arrogant people. They are all off to work and their gardens when the party is over, they are off to improve their houses if not their minds.

2 November 1981

Total exhaustion has set in but I trust it is only temporary. Where does one begin to describe this day? For the first time since arriving I didn't take a Valium so woke early but lay in bed. A gafuddle of packing & loading the car coupled with getting a warrant of fitness led to us leaving about 11.30. The drive confirmed the extraordinary impression of lushness & pleasant comfortability. Though the wind has been blowing like crazy & it is somewhat unseasonal, the countryside still looks extraordinaire. We leave the main highway after the Bombay Hills & head across the Hauraki Plains, a former outlet for the Waikato River & once site of a vast kauri forest. Now huge stumps of kauri roots dot the landscape, strange & twisted haunted shapes. The land, once given over to cattle, is now being turned to maize. The stretch from Auckland to the bottom of the Hills has seemed to be an unbroken string of suburbs, across the plain one is entering real rural life. The first of two gorges brings us to Waihi, an old gold mining town now thought to harbour another $100M worth of gold. The land is magnificently rugged through the gorge, the hills jagged. Waikino, a small town in the gorge, is now reduced to one hotel, the rest of the shops were washed away in the floods of last year which were apparently epic & one can still see the damage to the undergrowth & bush.

At Waihi we visit Delma Brake, Mother's cousin, who is now 66 & who for the past few years has owned a small house on the outskirts of the town. It is a tumbledown affair, one of the original gold miners' cottages, but it is here she has chosen to live & paint. Del has been married three times. The first marriage, to a gentleman who later became a successful industrialist, ended as Del pursued a theatrical career & toured the country with Dick Campion's NZ Players. Most of the family thinks she is mad. She wonders if I would like the house & says she will leave it to me. She has a book she wants to show me, written by a local whom she describes with a sashay as gay. She encouraged him to write the book but had trouble getting him to tone down the homosexual theme. All this is told to me as if I were some acclaimed heterosexual. It is too bizarre.

We leave Waihi & through another gorge enter the Bay of Plenty, which is phenomenal. Beautiful, that word again, & lush, that word again. Another former dairy region, it is now given over to produce – kiwifruit plantations & citrus orchards. No one is hungry here. And finally we arrive at Te Puke, where Renais and the children greet us. Nathan (8) & Hilary (3½) are beautiful & delight in their grandparents but are somewhat wary of me. I must be tired. Beautiful has appeared umpteen times in this. Will finish tomorrow. Bert & Doris (Renais' parents) are here. It is a large family for once.

2 November 1981

The intimacies of family life, the private jokes, the shared sensibility. It is interesting how Dirt & Boris (as Rich calls them) have formed a connection with my parents. Bert, the Sheik of Shaggy Creek, has sold his orchard in Pahiatua (resting place of the Gods) & now lives in retirement there. The orchard with its grapes, tea bushes & rambling old house was a favourite haunt of mine. A private little world in which Bert could rummage to his eccentric heart's content. And he's eccentric, last night going on at length about some mathematical problem no one else could decipher, he has decided to vote National for the first time because 'Muldoon stuck to his guns over the Springboks', whatever that means. The election campaign opened last night with Muldoon speaking in Hamilton. Hilary Rose, who I'd only seen as a very small baby while here in 79, is now vivacious, active & noisy. She is also 'on the go', as Mother says, while Nathan is something of a dreamer. Last night the kids & I bunked down in a caravan behind the house. In the morning, early, Hilary fell out of bed or, as she put it with all her confidence, 'the bed dumped me'.

It is the first decent day since I arrived here, warm, not very cloudy & thank God, no wind. Have begun to read *Man Alone* by John Mulgan, a book I managed to avoid reading at school, which was a mistake. It's very good. Mother announced that she went out with Mulgan once. I want to call the States & check on plays & schemes but feel that probably I am being pushy. Will wait till I get to Wellington before calling. I'm also reading [Maurice] Shadbolt's *Shell Guide to NZ*, which is quite tautly written. Keeping this journal is, I believe, good for me, because it is pointing out the vast weaknesses in my descriptive powers; Nick Enright used to say I had a novelist's eye for detail. I'm not so sure. But soon perhaps I will be able to write something good. Early in *Man Alone*, there is a choice piece of dialogue behind the hero & a soldier as they sail into Auckland harbour: 'That's Auckland, mate – the Queen of the North.' / 'The what?' / 'The Queen of the North. That's what they call it – in Auckland. This is God's own, this country.' / 'It looks all right.' / 'It's not a bad little town – nor a bad little country neither. It looks small after London though, don't it, mate? It looks different now to me to what it did.'// 'It looks different now to me to what it did' – a wonderfully New Zealand locution which means exactly what it says but hints at more – at a former dream of a Queen City shattered – but attempting to maintain the illusion – of never admitting this may not be the best but believing that probably it isn't.

Oh, but these blossoms, these hills, these rolling hills, the vines, the trees – this must be some type of paradise. But we are in the Bay of Plenty. An apter name is hard to imagine. Nathan & Hilary have rabbits – Thumper & Lerm. Nathan is supposed to feed them. He does not. He seems to have become a more affectionate child as he's grown older. I like him. Again it is the quietness of this country that amazes me. Still. Of course it is deceptive. Beneath the surface … Renais has already mentioned the number of separated & divorced couples she and Rich know here. 'It's shocking,' she tells me. Renais is too busy to contemplate such naughtiness for long – treasurer for the Red Cross, a member of an antique society, a student of woodwork (she has made a towel rack which Richard compares to a church pew), she also distributes library books to the elderly & runs the house & garden. She told me they are thinking of selling the pram but thought maybe they should keep it in case that I … can you believe it?

I've never been to Te Puke before but lived on the ocean about 18 miles away in the winter of 73 – wrote *Well Hung* there & directed *It Isn't Cricket* for a theatre in Tauranga. I felt it was very romantic to closet myself by the sea to write. It was. This morning's paper has an article about the article I read in the *Observer*, it will be interesting to see if it provokes any response. Later: Muldoon on news tonight claiming *Observer* article misrepresents situation, that the bill is being considered by parliament but was drafted by some committee of which he had no part. It does sound as if it has been

misrepresented; but it does still carry vague & ominous passages which one would rather were eliminated. Strange that the *Observer* article October 25 only had any impact today – November 3. Slow. And in this lackadaisical society it doesn't seem important, it won't happen; they won't let it go through & so on, seem to be the general responses. Strange how typical a response, how cliched a Kiwi response.

Today Renais drove the folks & me & Hilary throughout the region – through miles of kiwifruit orchards, acres of citrus fruit – much rotting on the ground – too extraordinary. More signs of wealth & ease & complacency. Went to the Mount & swam in crystal clear water, warm & beautiful. The only people on the beach. Major picnic. Fun & very NZ. As one drives, the views out over the Bay of Plenty constantly surprise. Went to a small beach community – Maketu – where the mighty canoe 'Arawa' landed, a few derelict huts here but most houses modern & comfortable. Then to an agricultural fair with miles of horticultural equipment on display – most of it Japanese. Drank wine made from kiwifruit, which is rather pleasant.

Left: The extended family at Pahiatua during the mid-1970s. From left to right: Dick Lord (Robert's father), his aunt Lorelle, Robert, his nephew Nathan, Jack (Robert's uncle), his mother Bebe, his brother Richard and sister-in-law Renais.
MS-1907/004, Hocken Collections

Right: Renais, Robert and Nathan. MS-1907/004, Hocken Collections

Below: Robert and Nathan. MS-1907/004, Hocken Collections

A river running through the town has been diverted in the plain before the sea – evidently to open up more land for cultivation. We follow it down to the sea, through stumpy, swampy land. New York seems very far away.

Was strange driving through the Mount, where we spent so many summers as children. Remember summering there with Godfrey Nicholson & jerking off for the first time. Remember also when Richard broke his leg at the beach – a log rolled over it as we played in the surf. I ran home to get my mother & told her to bring her purse. Then felt quite put out when Richard was given a bright green ice cream in the shop to which he had been carried & I was not. What a good place this was to discover sex.

Tonight we watch Rowling of the Labour Party open his election campaign. He is quite forceful but says nothing. Mum thinks he rants & raves. Bert thinks he talks bullshit. Dad can't see the economic basis & thinks they have no policy. Nothing has changed. National wants to 'think big' & has huge industrial projects scheduled for fruition over the next ten years. Labour wants jobs now. 'If we could send troops to Europe to fight a war, we can turn this country round.' It all seems vague & naïve & one wonders what difference anyone could make. Tomorrow we are off to Rotorua & Taupo.

4 November 1981

The day began at the crack of dawn with Nathan & Hilary getting in my bed. After breakfast (whitebait) Renais & I went to Papamoa for a swim; it was bloody freezing but clean, clear & good & the day hot & perfect. We then left the land of kiwifruit & headed inland to Rotorua. The scenery continues to dazzle. The first stop at the Okere Falls took us through bush for several minutes, then down steps cut through rock to a pool at the bottom of the waterfall. It is almost beyond words. Then we drive round very blue & clean lakes, we see the wisps of geothermal steam & enter Rotorua, yet another prosperous town, where we have lunch with [family friends] Barbie & John Todd.

We drive up a mountain & see the city & the lake spread below, we visit the first house I ever lived in. A small house in a row of similar houses built by the town & rented, then, for 30s 6p a week. My mother informs me I was born at 6am – I have been asking her what time for years. There was an earthquake that night & all the Maori patients left the hospital. We head for Taupo next, through what my father remembers as very rugged & poor country – it is a road he used to travel weekly from Rotorua to collect Taupo banking. It is now good farmland. The horizon is of jagged hills & humped mountains. In the distance we see the flat top of Mt Tarawera. I have an urgent desire to see mud pools & such & we visit Waiotapu & my needs are met – wander for about an hour through steaming pools, strange craters, multi-coloured lakes, & misty bush, and then an extraordinary view out over a valley to a small lake, & behind it another small & steaming pale green lake. And so on to the Dickies [family friends] at Taupo, whose house has the most amazing view yet – out over this huge lake to Ruapehu, Tongariro & Ngauruhoe. The evening is clear, the mountains extraordinary. Tomorrow we drive to Wellington. Conversations lament the past. Jack Todd announces: 'There was a time when a woman could walk down any street in New Zealand & be safe. That time has gone.' Affluence continues to be in evidence. Todd takes us to the pool part of Rotorua. It looked good to me.

Father continues to try & identify every tree, bird & person – to link family names, to tie people up with the past. And bowls & golf & banking are constant topics. But we can all laugh at each other. It does strike me however that this me is only part of me, that the real me is in hiding for the duration. I swam in the lake this evening. Very warm & clean. I also jogged & did push-ups & used the wheel. Most impressed, I was. Vanity.

5 November 1981

Guy Fawkes Day! The morning is overcast but I am told it will clear. The mountains cannot be seen. Around 8 I went for a short jog & a semi-swim then push-ups on the grass. Can I sustain all this physical activity, it is most unlike me. Late at night – by which I mean 10.30 which seems late these days. There have been too many images this day & one does not know quite how to assimilate them. Have gone through a variety of moods, at one stage got quite out of temper with Dad & his continual chatter about obscure points of banking. Then later, in Waikanae, got quite pissed with Mother, who wanted to see an old friend but had no idea where she lived.

Death, gardens, illness are the constant themes. Last night had extremely erotic dreams no doubt inspired by Kiwi deprivation. The highlight was a scene with a man who seemed to think I had been unfaithful to him & then grabbed & kissed me & kept saying: 'this is right, this is so right' with such assurance & conviction that one knew one had met one's twin at last. The dream was so powerful I had a comfortable feeling all day that before the year is out I will meet someone & that it will be right. Such idle romantic fantasies give us strength I suppose.

We left the Dickies early with father proclaiming it would take us hours to reach Wellington. It is another day of bewilderingly dynamic scenery. The early part of the Desert Road with its quick steep canyons leading on to the desert plateau with the mountains standing over us. It is here that countless rivers are being diverted into Lake Taupo as part of a massive power project. It is here that American troops winter in order to acclimatise themselves to tough terrain. And wandering through these volcanic plateaus one wonders when the next big bang will occur as it must & decimate how much of New Zealand. We passed the army museum at Waiouru with its guns & tanks – this wasteland is a perfect place for a monument to inhumanity. And then the land changes again, green & lush once more as we pass through a series of dying villages.

A stop at Waikanae to visit a bedridden friend of Father's. On to Jack & Lorelle's house & family chatter.* Ruminations. Remembrances. Dad & his brother debate who was married to whom & when. Mother knits. Lorelle cooks. I laugh a lot & phone some old friends, Mary Varnham, John O'Shea, Tony Taylor & set up some meetings. There are more ghosts here. I very much want to see Alan & Val [Svendsen] & to unwind. To work on these notes & sketch in details. Alan & Val do not respond to the phone, maybe they have yet to return from the States. I feel peculiar & know I am entering another waste land, another ghost town. Passed Onslow College, where I used to pick up Matthew Abram & head for clandestine encounters.† Hope to hold onto my sense of reality for the next few days. We do not move on to Picton until Sunday. Feel very far away from NYC & quite torn. I could

---

*   **Jack** and **Lorelle Lord**, RL's uncle and aunt.
†   Name has been changed.

live anywhere. I am adaptable. But where do I belong? This is all too strange. Need a good day alone to get myself together. Maybe if the Svendsens do not turn up I will go & visit George Webby. Oh, this town. There is much to tell.

6 November 1981

Am beginning to have decided misgivings about this entire undertaking. It is all vastly unsettling emotionally & I doubt if I can work anything into a book. But will continue to try. It is a lousy overcast day with Wellington shrouded in mist. The Svendsens do not seem to have returned & no one knows where they are. Have spoken to a variety of old friends: Tony Taylor, Raymond Boyce,[*] George Webby & others. It is all too queer. Have a doctor's appointment this afternoon. Am very horny & my strange dreams continue. Last night dreamt my father was arrested for embezzling $350 & that I was heavily involved with Studio 54. Can make no sense of any of it. One of the images from yesterday is of seductively blossomed trees, ripe with flowers & foliage. Today the world is bleaker. Have moved from the solidly National territory of family into the hotbed of Labour fermentation at Downstage & am writing this in Tony's office. He is off rehearsing a new musical. I'm drinking ouzo & have a buzz on.

Need to decompress somewhere. Saw George Webby this morning at the Drama School – a strange building which in its previous incarnation was a massage parlour & is full of cubicles and knee-high light switches. The world is too much with me today. I have a strange feeling of sour anticipation in my stomach, I'm not sure how or why it is there. Images are coming too fast. It all got too much for a white woman, as George Webby would say, & I ran off & had a tender encounter which alleviated some stress & was rewarding into itself. I can see that this Wellington section is either going to make or break me. Who can tell? I'm having another ouzo to help ease the tension. Fool that I am. Spoke to Nonnita, whom I haven't seen for 8 years, will see her Saturday afternoon.[†]

---

[*] **Raymond Boyce** (1928–9), British-New Zealand stage designer, costume designer, puppeteer and puppet designer.

[†] **Nonnita Rees**, co-founder of Playmarket with RL, Judy Russell and Ian Fraser. Actor, director and administrator at Downstage 1970–77, director of Playmarket 1981–86, and from the 1980s worked in cultural administration and as a policy analyst. Married to Phillip Mann and RL refers to her by both surnames.

7 November 1981

Rain. Depression. Too many conversations.

8 November 1981

Rain. Spoke to Robert Boykin in New York where it is snowing. Homesick. Want to be sitting in my apartment watching the snow drift down. However, I am not. Have just returned to Jack & Lorelle's after a brunch with Mike Nicolaidi & ruminations with him.*

Yesterday visited John O'Shea in the morning, Tony Taylor for lunch, Nonnita Mann in afternoon & then dinner with Phil & Non & Harry Seresin & Marilyn Duckworth.† All in all a full day discussing film, theatre, art & so forth. Very wearying. Also visited Mary Varnham. A lot of 'why don't you return.' But I really don't know many people & the feeling of emptiness persists. The lack of energy is palpable. I feel that the energy one once knew here which became introverted, twisted & neurotic & finally exorcised has not been replaced. A state of vacuum. If that makes sense. Have had terrible yearnings to get the hell out of here & go back but must serve out my time. Wellington looks a great deal less opulent than the rest of the country, though that might be the miserable weather. The funny shacks of Thorndon, Mt Victoria etc look cold & not very inviting as the mist shrouds the hills & the harbour. Have a strange series of impressions.

Nonnita is full of energy & ideas. She has 2 children now. She lives in a wondrous clutter with burly Phil who has written a sci-fi novel shortly to be published by Gollancz. They talk of their bizarre Chinese adventure of 2 years. Their 5-year-old son who grew up speaking Chinese now speaks English with Chinese syntax. Strange. And genders get confused. Later. Am

---

* **Mike Nicolaidi**, journalist, critic, arts administrator and author. Founding president of Playmarket 1975–81, and director of Queen Elizabeth II Arts Council 1971–74. RL often refers to him as 'Mike Nic'.

† **Phillip Mann** (1942–2022), British-born New Zealand writer, teacher and theatre director. **Harry Seresin** (1919–1994), New Zealand entrepreneur who was involved in setting up the Coffee Gallery in Parson's Bookstore, Downstage Theatre and the Settlement restaurant and café. Born in Hamburg to Russian Jewish parents, he emigrated to New Zealand in 1939. **Marilyn Duckworth**, New Zealand novelist, poet and short-story writer.

on the MV Aratika in the Marlborough Sounds. Very beautiful and desolate. Hills rolling down into the sea. The weather is a little better than when we left Wellington but still a lot of cloud & mist round the hills.

Mike Nicolaidi was interesting. He is absolute enthusiasm as ever. His affair with Michael Houstoun seems to be in full flower.* Michael is returning to conduct his career from NZ which has brought a lot of nonsense about his head – 'NZ Pianist Gives Up' etc. How lacking in generosity these people are. I believe now that *Family Portrait* is better than I'd ever thought. Spoke to Ross Jolly about it.† Mike Nic was in Japan last year, an experience he enjoyed because he found the Japanese – being non-Christian – lack guilt, which enables them to be efficient. Moral issues do not exist. Now I am on the move again I feel happier.

9 November 1981

Stayed in a pleasant motel in Picton last night with a view of the town & harbour. We had a 'spa pool' before bedding down. I wrote a couple of letters while Mum & Dad watched some interminable debate on the economy & the election. Then this morning got on the road & stopped first at Blenheim to visit some colleagues of the family. I remained in a reasonably obnoxious mood all day, which I must attempt to correct but my reaction to this country is not a simple or an easy one. As we headed toward Kaikoura, the weather worsened. The coast road with its jagged rocks & turquoise sea – made milky with mud from recent heavy rain – was, as always, spectacular. And beyond Kaikoura, more spectacular coastline with the road veering into tunnels through rocky outcrops & we passed the spot where Mother stood on a seal thinking it was a rock! And then we are at the top of the Canterbury Plains & the scenery unfolds in a different & more gentle fashion. We passed forms of deer which I have never seen & more crops. And then a pitstop at other retired friends at Amberley & we drive on into Christchurch, which is crowded with tourists as it is show week & the races.

---

* **Michael Houstoun**, New Zealand pianist. From 1974 to 1981 he lived away from New Zealand, studying in Philadelphia and London. He continued to perform internationally after returning to New Zealand.

† **Ross Jolly**, New Zealand theatre, television, radio and film actor and director.

We have accommodation in a 'bed & breakfast' house (breakfast: 7.30–8.30!). I have a 'sleep in' in the garden which suits me. We eat at the Carlton pub. The old main bar is now a self-service dining room smelling a little too much of fat & smoke & hideously decorated in pinks & reds. The steaks are thin, wafer thin & overcooked. But the price is right.

Then I call Steve Dakin, whom I haven't spoken to for years, & more memories come flooding back, he is married and has a family.* I will try & see him tomorrow. Then I wander round the edges of Hagley Park, which looks, as everyone says, so English; past the old houses with their lush gardens, past a very fecund honeysuckle & to the old university which is now an arts centre. I almost get lost on my return. Strange that in this town of 500,000 I see about 6 people in my hour's walk & few cars. It is only 9pm now & just dark. Twilight lingers on later as we head south. I had forgotten that. The feeling of emptiness, of not particularly joyful nostalgia, persists. Tomorrow I must get in a better frame of mind. In the midst of all this family I feel lonely & not very successful – a sort of eccentric black sheep & that is what I suppose I am.

10 November 1981

Dropped the folks & [family friend] Mabel de la Perelle, with whom we are now staying, off at their pensioners' function & shortly I'm going to visit Steve Dakin – whom I've already seen twice today. Round midday I visited Elric Hooper & was very taken with the Court Theatre – its excellent auditoriums & rehearsal spaces.† Quite the best equipped plant in NZ & this year it has done 27 productions, which puts Downstage to shame.

Noticed in this beautiful blossoming city the absence of pornography, dirt & graffiti one has become so familiar with in New York. Did see graffiti in Wellington: Dead Men Don't Rape; Lesbians Unite; Punks Support Black Power. Wellington is a neurotic city & I feel it is the hemmed-in nature of

---

*   **Steve Dakin**, university lecturer in industrial psychology and friend of RL's from Southland Boys' High School days. After leaving school, the two hitched around New Zealand together.

†   **Elric Hooper**, New Zealand actor and director, and artistic director at Christchurch's Court Theatre 1979– 2000. Began his career in productions directed by Ngaio Marsh, and also worked in the UK, including with Joan Littlewood.

the place, the way it is turned in on itself with no natural way out. Here vast planes stretch to distant mountains, the world is open. The absence of people continues to amaze one; on a night like this Central Park would be alive with people & music. But the bird songs are pleasant & the quietness blissful. Just wish there was more life.

Tomorrow we travel through the Mackenzie Country past a vast new power plant which is cutting up the countryside. Mabel chatters on, she thinks it terrible that jokes can't be made about the Maoris, she loves Rob Muldoon & his National Party. I take the bait but in a pleasant way.

Horse chestnut trees are an extraordinary pink, trout are in the Avon, ducklings abound. Two ducks are sitting just by me now. It feels good here. Life in New York seems far away today. I'm thinking of a new play, want to write something immediate & funny about NZ but maybe I am out of touch. Don't think so. Am reading *Foreskin's Lament*, which is very good & crude & alive.* We need more of that. Am watching a young father & his daughter. Am I a little jealous? No. A magpie is sitting on a bench next to me bathing in the sun. He looks quite regal. A little girl is chasing ducks. I always used to feel, & perhaps still do, that a great deal goes on behind drawn curtains in Christchurch. All the people must be doing something. I remember a strange party at Norrie Rogers'.† But I never spent much time here. Remember a New Year's Eve encounter & walking home at 3am in incredible dry heat. Remember also selling Tabac Men's Cosmetics at the DIC & a brief encounter at the Christmas party. My brother was also at the party. A confused night. Also remember coming here after my famous broken engagement to Gloria.‡

11 November 1981

Am feeling quite drunk, which is rather pleasant – but also have severe back pains due to exercise with the wheel. Now do 3 sets of 10 with the wheel, 3

---

*   *Foreskin's Lament*, Greg McGee's 1981 play set in a rugby changing room after a practice, and at an after-match party, a landmark in New Zealand theatre.
†   **William Norrie Rogers** (1914–1985), New Zealand doctor.
‡   Gloria, RL's girlfriend in Clifton Terrace days; RL had proposed to her in the shower but the engagement was shortlived.

sets of push-ups (10), & have started sit-ups (5) tonight. All this activity is fine but seems to be having no effect on my stomach, which is the area of maximum concern. Have a feeling that I could get into serious exercise on my return to the States & hope this is true. It would be pleasant to enter my 37th summer with a firm stomach even if I do not have fame or fortune.

Today has been without doubt the most spectacular since I started this diary. An extraordinary series of visuals such as to stun me into silence, beginning with the drive from Christchurch to the Rakaia Gorge with magnificent mountains appearing from behind & through clouds at heights quite unnatural. And the gorge itself with its ambling milk-blue snow river & hillsides of yellow broom. Then on through the plains of Canterbury – miles of flat with stony pastures & dirty merino sheep with mountains climbing up on the west. And after Geraldine the flat giving way to rolling green hills & tree-lined roofs, old cobb houses, still delightful & suddenly no green but brown tawny tussock as we enter the mountain regions of the upper Waitaki – a major & total contrast – then we turn a corner & before us the most extraordinary assemblage of blue snow-capped mountains – a line so high and so long the breath is literally taken away. I have seen nothing like this barren landscape which is empty yet complete. Satisfying unto itself. Like the scenery from some vast epic but unpopulated.

Then we are at Lake Tekapo – an expanse of milk blue and a bowl of mountains dominated by Cook – which we then see from every possible angle. We visit the small church with its spectacular view over the lake, we visit the monument to collie dogs. The lake, the mountains hovering. Perfection. And we drive to Pukaki, now part of a giant complex of hydro-electric stations & acting as a holding tank. Mt Cook is seen again. We drive on to Twizel, which is where we plan to stay – a small town of workers involved in the power scheme. Hideous & no room at the inn. So we drive on & detour to Lake Ohau – a small gem & we stay at a lodge overlooking the lake – & Mt Cook – & eat a homecooked meal – we are 3 of about 6 guests at what is a large lodge.

It has indeed been the best day of the trek & we have all agreed what a damper Wellington put on our proceedings – but we are over it now & I have spoken to Michael Arthur, with whom I will stay in Invercargill &

whom I love & cannot imagine what it will be like to see again.* I love it here – so clean & empty & powerful, this is where I identify with NZ most yet it is not really where I come from. But it speaks to me & I feel at peace. Thank God we, Mum, Dad & I, are having fun again. I was getting worried. This is what I came to see. It is pure here – but has such potential.

12 November 1981

Hungover all day. Boring.

13 November 1981

A glorious morning in Dunedin & my body is feeling stronger. Thank God. Managed to get very drunk in Lake Ohau with two shearers who were on a pub crawl, two bus drivers from Timaru & the bartender. Most amusing & silly. Naturally the following day was a wash-out but we drove from Ohau to Dunedin along the Waitaki River with its huge power projects. An easy drive. In Dunedin we are staying with [family friend] Joan Garrett & I visited Roger Hall, Tony Richardson & Rawiri.†

15 November 1981

Well things have gotten away or whatever that word is & am now in a motel at Te Anau with Mum & Dad after an interesting drive along the bottom of the South Island. Have some thoughts about a new play – about consumption & destruction; the first act totally about food & the second about destruction when no food is left. And not just about food but involving tons of food – tea & biscuits, roasts, sandwiches, pies, fish and

---

* **Michael Arthur**, friend and neighbour of RL's from Invercargill days. At the end of their first year of university, in December 1964, the two worked a holiday job on an oil rig in Southland run by a Texas company.

† **Roger Hall**, British-born New Zealand playwright and television writer. **Tony Richardson** (1926–1983), English director recruited as inaugural artistic director of Auckland's Mercury Theatre, 1968–77. He returned to the UK before taking up the directorship of Dunedin's Fortune Theatre from 1980 to 1983. **Rawiri Paratene** (Ngāpuhi), New Zealand actor, director and writer for stage, television and film. Trained at Toi Whakaari New Zealand Drama School, and worked at Mercury, Downstage and Fortune theatres in the 1970s and 1980s.

chips. People cooking and eating and breastfeeding and drinking. To be quite hideous and funny & then in the second act the food, the gluttony has won out and there is nothing left. The people turn on each other and there is considerable violence. How gross. And throughout it all there is an old man on stage telling rambling stories – he sees everything and nothing – he is the conservative heart of New Zealand who can constantly rationalize everything & emerge guiltless.

Must backtrack & elaborate on some of the days so scantily touched on recently. The evening at Lake Ohau turned out to be a major event. Slightly merry when writing in this book I then went back up to the bar & joined 2 bus drivers from Timaru & the bartender for a drink. Was grilled about my life & there were a few veiled comments about my sexuality but it was amusing & became hilarious when we were joined by 2 shearers & a carpenter. A variety of stories, mostly lewd, a demonstration of how they shear – one shearer using the other as a sheep & the two bus drivers doing the same & one pulling the other's trousers down – which everyone else overlooked. And the barman, a young Peter Ustinov, to look at if not intellectually, leaping about waving a lavatory brush – stirring beer with its handle & trying to clean his false teeth with the bristles. Bizarre. Songs. Songs. Country and Western. People pulling out false teeth to reach high notes. The two shearers, good mates, flirt with each other almost. Egg each other on. One of them, Noel, keeps staring at me hard, asks all sorts of questions about New York, wants to show me how to shear. Strange. He takes my address. Politically they all support National but do not have time for Muldoon. They speak highly of Jack Marshall, which surprises me. Anyway, eventually & very drunk I stumble to bed. It was interesting that there was another group in the bar, surveyors, who totally ignored us, which cannot have been easy. The next morning, feeling like hell, I got up for breakfast & we left Ohau quickly & headed down the Waitaki Valley to Oamaru. Past Benmore, Aviemore and Waitaki Dams. Huge projects. One realizes that we have not seen a river or lake on this trip which is untouched by the power department. Dams are everywhere.

We drive from Oamaru to Dunedin stopping for lunch at Moeraki with its wildly overrated boulders. The countryside has continued to be stunning &

spattered with yellow. Rising into Dunedin one gets caught in mist & cloud, very bizarre & then one is there & remembering how steep the city is & how beautiful. I drop my parents off at Joan Garrett's & then go to the Fortune Theatre to meet up with Tony Richardson & Rawiri Paratene. On the way I bump into Roger Hall. We have a beer and I meet his wife for the first time. He has a large Victorian house high above the city and a collection of New Zealand painters which I envy. He also shows me a wonderful book: *The South Island, Scenes From the Road* by Robin Morrison.

17 November 1981

Have arrived at Franz Josef & want a couple of days by myself. Need to bring this up to date & relax. Who knows when? Have been having strange & erotic dreams. The countryside continues to dazzle. My dreams involve New Zealand & New York, very confusing.

18 November 1981

Am in a small room at the Hotel Hampden in Murchison, feel full & bloated after a huge dinner – soup, roast hogget & several vegetables & steamed pudding. Have seen enough scenery these past few days to satisfy most people for a lifetime. Strange here in this corrugated iron pub, I can hear a man belch rooms away & have just farted in response. Think I want to write a Kiwi play & tap this market as I should be able to. Just read that Roger Hall is now 42, which puts him at my age when he wrote *Glide Time* – what vanities I indulge in.

Time to backtrack a little and try to get up to date with my journeys. Drove from Dunedin on down to Invercargill. An easy drive with lunch in a park in Balclutha. The country neat, green & well kempt. Very attractive. The strange phenomenon of watching distant storms & never connecting with them. A magnificent wide open sky. Arrived late afternoon in Invercargill & met with Mike Arthur at his office. He was unchanged as I knew he would be & we went for a drink with Jim Anglem, who was also unchanged.* Michael's wife Sarah is sensible, attractive, bright – all that one would have wished

---

*   **Jim Anglem** (Kāi Tahu), friend of RL's from Southland Boys' High School. In 1964, as first-year Otago students, they roomed next door to each other at Arana Hall.

for Michael. He has two daughters, Lucy about 5 and Phoebe about 3. Lucy very serious & reserved, Phoebe bright & vivacious. They arise early & are active all day. Mike & I indulged in much nostalgia & laughter – stories are beginning to grow. I'm glad I went to see him. It was warm.

The first night Mike & I & Jim sit up and drink much beer. The next day I look around the city – which I barely recognize – and then we go out for dinner with Tui Fox, whom I evidently kissed when she was 13, she is now married & the mother of 2 & very down-to-earth & raucous as well as beautiful. She & Sarah & Jenny, another friend, talk about the tribulations of breastfeeding. Everyone asks me about drugs & social life in NY. It all sounds exotic to me as I relate it. Sunday, Fred Miller, now 77 & once a local reporter & poet, visits. He admires me because I am a creative writer & that makes me feel silly.

The Lords then set off & drive to Riverton, where the sea is a wondrous translucent blue as it crashes on the rocks – & on to Tuatapere on the south coast before following the Waiau River up to Manapouri & Te Anau. We pass the road to Lake Hauroko, where Mike & I tramped once, we pass a bridge under which Mike & I slept. Mike, during my stay, has alluded to tramping, our tramping, appearing in *Meeting Place*. He seems to have forgotten we talked about this in Dunedin in 73 & he asked me then if there was a theme of homosexuality & I, drunk on Southern Comfort, said yes. He & Sarah chide me for not being married. What are they thinking? I don't know.

We stay the night at Te Anau, which is somewhat changed by dams & so forth but not too severely, & the next day drive to Queenstown – a thriving commercial village – & on through wonderful Otago to Wanaka past Cromwell, which is soon to be flooded by a new hydro dam. Wanaka is a joy but I am tired. There has been too much scenery – & all of it magnificent. The following day, yesterday, we go to Hawea, another wonderful & desolate spot, & drive alongside it, then back to the shores of Wanaka & up through beech forests into the Haast Pass. Incredible rain forest, jagged mountains, rushing rivers & waterfalls. I've not been here before & love it. The weather, which is supposed to be good, is not. Rain & mist abound. But this is exciting – it clings to the bush & heightens the feeling of remoteness.

Breaking out onto the West Coast the world changes again & is now somewhat rumpled but still entrancing. We drive up the coast & visit Fox Glacier – seen in the distance through rain but thrilling nonetheless & then on to a motel in Franz Josef. This morning a look at Franz Josef Glacier, which reflects blue of the sky. Yesterday we also visited Lake Matheson, which is seen reflecting Mt Cook in all the photos – it was shrouded in mist but the walk through the woods entranced. Today we drove up the West Coast past old gold & coal mines, past huge empty beaches & strange brookish swamps, over wide stony rivers. Wild & entrancing country. We stop at Punakaiki & see the Pancake Rocks, we cross back east through the Buller Gorge – a wonderful mountain pass with bush-clad hills – & now we are at Murchison. We were here once before, in 1960, & looked tonight at the camp where we stayed then. Have thought of Jay a lot these past few days & wish he was with me as these travels unfold. But it is not so.

20 November 1981

Not a very good night's sleep in Murchison left me tired & edgy all yesterday. We drove to Nelson, where the sun was incredible – lots of pleasant dream cottages along the way. Went to Tahunanui Beach, where we had camped on the family jaunt of 1959. Quite sexy here – people seem to look better, maybe it is the sun. And they are hiding out in the dunes. Then we drive to Picton round the Sounds, stopping briefly by the Pelorus River – one of the perfect spots on the 59 vacation – & then for a beer in Havelock, where I see a group of 3 one-eyed men playing billiards. Have about 9 days to go in New Zealand & feel the experience has been worthwhile, want to write more plays about life here & am determined to crack this market. Need to do it for my head as well as my bank account. The thought of a couple of days in Wellington is not enticing but being with Alan & Val is. Will make an effort to see Roger Hall's play – think I should & also to contact Ginette & Sue & Ross [Jolly].*

---

* **Ginette McDonald**, New Zealand stage and television actor, director and producer. **Susan Wilson**, New Zealand director and actor, and one of the founders of Wellington's Circa Theatre.

Meeting Place, performed at Downstage Theatre in 1972. From left to right: Tony
Ditchburn, Nonnita Rees, Susan Wilson and Craig Ashley. Photograph by Terence Taylor.

I'm writing this on the Aramoana between the islands, a grey day but a still one. Dad has not been very well these last few days. Angina and tiredness & I wonder if it all has not been too much for the old boy. However, he will be able to rest up in Wellington & the journey is ¾ over. I'm now in Wellington again, where the sun is, thank God, shining & the Svendsens are here so I feel at home. Arrived early mid-afternoon & nattered with Val, catching up on the last month's travails. She is now working away & I've been phoning a few comrades. Spoke to Bruce Mason, who was a little distant but we do what we think we should.* Anyway his career is going well and he is happy with that. Spoke to Ross Jolly, who has received a copy of *Family Portrait* from Non – who is very 'on the ball' so maybe something will happen with that. Would be good. There seems to be a lot on here – with Circa doing *Bullshot Crummond*,† Downstage *Fifty-Fifty* & a revue on at the Opera House. All most exciting. Wrote to Reg Livermore, whom I do adore & wish I was going to see in Sydney.

21 November 1981

Have been thinking all day about a new play set during a New Zealand Christmas. Heat. Hot food. Christmas pudding. Family. Three or four generations.

24 November 1981

Last night in Wellington went to see Roger Hall's play *Fifty-Fifty*, which I did not enjoy – basically a good television show – but neatly written & with some touching moments. Amazing how in tune it is, or Roger is, with what an audience wants & and as Alan Svendsen said, looking at the audience, these people have not seen a good film, read a good book – they think they are getting their culture here. So it is sad to see that Downstage is now what we never intended it to be – a very competent version of the old amateur groups doing plays which seem to be daring but which really are not. I find

---

* **Bruce Mason** (1921–1982), New Zealand playwright, actor, critic and writer.

† *Bullshot Crummond*, 1974 play by Ronald E House and Diz White parodying the British pulp-fiction hero Bulldog Drummond, and later made into the 1983 film *Bullshot*.

it rather sad. And it makes me wonder about placing *A Family Portrait* there & I think I'd rather not – do not want that audience, want to go further than they want to go & cannot be bothered pandering to them.

On the first night in Wellington, Ginette McDonald came up for a drink & we reminisced about 26 Clifton Tce. She is now directing *Close to Home* – of course she wanted me to stay on – but for what? The people one meets are all in couples & are all cosy in broadcasting or TV or commercials – worlds not really open to me. Both days in Wellington the weather was superb & the city did look beautiful. On the second I drove about with Alan & we picked up some pot plants, visited a friend who is opening a nightclub, an extension of Il Casino, & hung out at Oriental Bay, where I looked at the local talent & was not much impressed. After the play that night we went home & had drinks with Ross Jolly, Sue Wilson, Ginette, Colin McColl & others.* A bit of talk about theatre & some chat about staying on. Interesting to see Colin, who has spent several years in Australia & is now trying to readjust to New Zealand parochialism. Late night, winey night. Up at 9 in the morning and Mum & Dad collected me at about 10.30 & we set off for Havelock North.

Then on to Te Puke & the family – much beer, drinking & laughter & total exhaustion on my part. Have recently begun to think that Dad lacks adequate intellectual stimulation – which is why the long discourses, the intense concern about money, business & politics. The intensely close scrutiny of every paper. And anyone who lives on a diet of NZ papers is sure to become intellectually troubled. And he is naïve – which is charming – almost innocent. Today is a glorious summer day & the house has been mine for most of it. Mum & Dad, Hilary & Renais went to school to see Nathan's school sports. Have another thought about Dad – he is role-playing Grandpa & not being himself. At least that is how it seems to me. Have continued my thoughts about the new play – family Christmas – and want to start on it – the son returning, others trying to put parents in a home, a son long dead remembered. Good strong elements.

---

* **Colin McColl**, New Zealand actor and director. Co-founded Taki Rua Theatre in 1983; artistic director at Downstage 1985–93 and Auckland Theatre Company 2003–21.

25 November 1981

I feel rested, at last, but have that empty feeling again. Want to start the new play but wonder if I should wait & get an uninterrupted stretch of time when I return to New York. Richard has a property I want to look at. A small beach cottage on the ocean for $20,000. Sounds a good price but I can't afford it. Feel that within the next year I must make a decision about my life. About what to do with the next however many years. At least between New York, Sydney & here I do have options.

27 November 1981

It's about 6pm and am sitting on the deck in the sun. All is quiet & rather peaceful. Went shopping & bought a couple of books by Maurice Gee, including *Plumb*, a novel everyone speaks highly of. Wanted to get Robin Morrison's book but at $65 it is too expensive but Mum has said she might get it for me for Christmas. Then visited Jonathan Hardy at Greenlane Hospital where he is recovering from a heart attack. Felt as if I was attending court – Jonathan leaping about the place, his beady eyes barely settling for a moment on any one of his guests (& there were several), his eyebrows bushy beyond belief. He trotted out a series of slightly lewd comments about hospital life, masturbation, food etc – all with a distinct homosexual tinge – an edge of gay defiance which seems scarcely necessary & a touch neurotic. All great drama. Marcus Craig sent him a cable: 'I hear you're on your back, my dear, only divas are on their backs'– or some such, the point of which escaped me.* I'm getting anxious about the Christmas play – must start it before it escapes me.

8 December 1981

I am now back at 250 West 85th Street and feel at home. The feeling of emptiness that hovered in my stomach during my time in NZ has gone. For the first time I feel happy in this apartment and feel I am in the right place. I also feel a new dedication to my work and that is a major relief. Have the *Owl*

---

*   **Marcus Craig** (1940–2013), New Zealand actor, singer and entertainer best known as Diamond Lil, who popularised drag to a mainstream audience in the 1970s.

& *Pussycat* project to work on, the *Roger* play, GJ's book and many ideas.* If I can establish now a healthy daily work pattern then I will be happy.

Penny & Robert had an election night (Sat. 28th) party to which I was invited but Jan ['Willy'] & I watched at home & I was appalled at the brash arrogance of Muldoon. He does give the appearance of strength but it is a sham. Rowling, on the other hand, seems weak but I am told he rules the Labour Party with an iron hand.

Tuesday I flew off. It was not as sad a parting as I had thought it might be. I know I'll see both Mum & Dad again & feel that we all had a good time & that I was value for money. Quel conceit. But Sydney. Was met by Craig [Ashley] & there started a strange & beautiful encounter full of more love than I knew existed. Feel our relationship is now on a truly exalted plane and that what we have is so special, right & pure that we are indeed chosen. It is not sexual & it is complete. I have not known such feelings before. There is the emotional intensity I felt with Jay & a rightness & perfection that will always last. We will always be there for each other & the strength amazes me. We drank too much, we talked for hours, we went out dancing, we went into the country, I met his friends. Everything & nothing happened. I flew all the way back in one go – some 20 hours with brief stopovers – a total of 30.

14 December 1981

One week since I returned & a strange one. Feel removed – at a distance from the nonsense while I participate in it. This week I went out with Jay, who is anxious for me to go to his Bible group & who is adorable. Saw Jack Hofsiss a couple of times but ours is a relationship truly bizarre & will never be relaxed – or not until Jack becomes more humble & open, which I think is a long way off. Must regain my sense of humour about Jack & NYC & be able to laugh at it. Feel I am being a bit severe in my judgements.

---

* The *Owl and the Pussycat* adaptation exists in outline and sample draft form (MS-2438/166, Hocken Collections). 'GJ's book' was the autobiography of RL's great-grandfather GJ Garland, an early Auckland businessman and councillor. RL was transcribing it with a view to using it as the basis for a novel.

16 December 1981

Monday night I saw *A Place In The Sun* for the first time – watched it at Jack's with a few others, including John Dolf, who has just returned from filming *Best Little Whorehouse in Texas* with Burt Reynolds & Dolly Parton. Anyway *Place* was brilliant as Gilbert has always told me – a major film and so well filmed & imaginatively put together – some scenes almost surreal – one shot of Liz's back & another of the jetty with radio going. And so sexy too – Liz & Monty quite extraordinary.* Strange evening, lots of theatre folk – Ellen Greene arrived in a state of tension re her new musical – *The Little Prince*. Tuesday was lousy weather – rain – and I puttered most of the day & saw *Dreamgirls* with Gilbert that night. 3 million spent most conspicuously & looking wonderful but the story somewhat like an old Betty Grable flick or a Jacqueline Susann novel but without the sense of camp. Very, very, serious – which is a pity. Great acting throughout but all very manipulated & for a show with so much talk about soul it had very little of its own. But what can I tell you – it's a hit.

16 February 1982

How time flies! Wish I had the discipline to work on this daily – but will keep trying to do it. A lot has happened & very little has changed since last writing. Have completely redecorated my apartment, which entailed throwing out much garbage, painting (white & grey), getting floors sanded & then waxing them white & polyurethaning. Bought some new pieces – like a bed – & now have a clean and somewhat sparse abode with the living room set up as an office. This work has occupied most of January & stopped various projects dead in their tracks. Of course as I was working I had countless schemes for writing & then when I finished about a week ago I could think of nothing to do!

17 February 1982

A rather unsettling day as I've had to reconcile myself to more real estate work, which I do not want to do. However, must pay the rent.

---

* **Elizabeth Taylor** and **Montgomery Clift**, stars of *A Place in the Sun* (1951).

18 February 1982

Sex for Robert & Jack seems to be a status symbol. The constant cruising for one thing – but we all do that – but then the constant talking about it & the letting know who they have slept with. Jack, for example, told me the other night he had slept with Doug Watts – a piece of info I can easily do without. It comes back to 2 things. 1. other people understand or interpret things differently than I do – what they construe as a come-on I see quite differently. 2. Sex is not sex in the sense of sharing but an affirmation of one's status, looks, so forth. This should be the subject of a play. I am so easily satisfied – let me read & write & fuck me twice a month! Of course if I had it would I want it? It is imperative that I give up smoking & drink – that latter exhausts me & I'm recently quite paranoid about my liver & am scared I am going to get hep. again. A mood brought on by a recent visit to The Saint where I was speeding my tits off & pigged out on the balcony – slut that I am. Current mood associated with a desire to return to NZ – but I think that is an escapism – if I had some financial security it would be easier. Now I have the apartment I have to get on with work. Later: By the way, I've lost weight. Writing reinforces writing – the act is necessary, it reinforces. Like speaking in tongues.

19 February 1982

Am horny – really, at my time of life, it doesn't make sense. Spent a frustrating day getting real estate together & then a more enjoyable time typing another 10 pages of GJ's biog. Some wonderful relationship material & then some political bumpf & the old boy was an ace Tory. Several problems exist – what tack to take – what voice, perspective & so forth. How to merge the political background with the personal world, how to incorporate a vision of a country played out – which I think is the final verdict. Hofsiss has buggered up his reservations for theatre next week & that has confused my own theatregoing. C'est la vie. As much as many people who surround Jack are star fuckers – that is how he knows he is a star.

23 February 1982

Have just eaten at the American & feel bloated & also horny but the latter has nothing to do with the food. Have been involved in real estate & there is a client who is interested in buying a house at the Grove – which would be a plus. Oh, to have some cash to put away! Am having trouble with my sleeping patterns & cannot get to sleep at night & then cannot wake up in the morning. Life! Curious! Interesting! Etc!

3 March 1982

Had a good day doing real estate on Sunday & made about $1,200. Hopefully this will continue. My ebullience seems to have faded. Was in too good a mood last week. Hudson Guild wants to do *Family Portrait* & we are trying to find out if B Hughes & G Fitzgerald are available* – means starting rehearsals in 10 days or so. Who can tell. I want it to happen. Do not want it to drag on to next season. I need the fix now – need a nice production with respectable reviews & am praying that will happen.

23 March 1982 or thereabouts

Have recently come into contact with, again, Jason Ford, whom I first met in Toronto but first saw on Fire Island late in the summer of 1978 while I was on my knees washing the stairs of an absurdly modern house & he was being filmed walking down the boardwalk.[†] He was making one of those porno pics for which he was quite well known at the time. I don't know who gave me his phone number but in the winter of 78–79 I was in Toronto working on *Well Hung* & came into contact with him again. Jason came from a formerly wealthy family – I think a particular brand of sliced bread carries the name – but grandfather had frittered away most of the cash & by the time Jason's generation had reached maturity there was nothing left. As for his personality, he was & is effusive & he never does things by halves. Never. En route to Toronto Jason would stop off in NYC & avail himself of the various homosexual hideouts & indulge in all kinds of activities. Through

---

[*]   **Barnard Hughes** (1915–2006), American stage, film and television actor. **Geraldine Fitzgerald** (1913–2005), Irish-American stage, film and television actress.

[†]   Name has been changed.

Robert at home during the 1980s. Photograph by Mike Knudsen. Nonnita Rees collection

these contacts he came in touch with some film-makers & eventually successfully auditioned & began a career in porn films. I should also add that he was a grad of a university with an MBA. As he made more & more movies he became more & more interested in acting & so used his money to put himself through 3 years of acting school. His film career had put him in touch with such unlikely people as Sir John Gielgud. Jason & I had a brief but tender affair & then I left Toronto abruptly as the play was a disaster. I wrote to him a couple of times but he never replied. About a year ago I bumped into him at Hurrah & then a few weeks ago on the subway. The porn career is apparently over.

A great deal has been going on lately & I'm not at all sure that I'm pleased. Up until last Monday I was working quite happily on my children's musical & doing some real estate at the Pines. The real estate scene has become ludicrous, there are now over 20 persons hustling to make a buck & it is all rather distasteful & for me the time to bow out. Have made some bread, enough to keep me out of jail. But need now to find a regular income. Anyway, Sunday a week ago *Poor Little Lambs* opened at St Peter's directed by Jack & a fun party at La Coupole afterwards & on Monday Jack, Gary, Keith arrived here & we began drinking & a spree lasting 36 hours was underway & the end result is I now have murals painted on my living room walls & I have not yet come to terms with that. The spree was followed by days of weakness, remorse, guilt, only somewhat alleviated by a party in Jack's honour at Studio on Thursday to which I took Greg Martin. Who is Greg Martin? A very handsome young English actor, son of George, the record producer & boyfriend of Gretchen Cryer.* He is here to become a star, to take *Mass Appeal* to London, & to fall in love with NY while I fall in love with him. Actually I like him a lot & our relationship reminds me of Craig's & mine.

8 April 1982

Too much has been happening in these past few weeks & there has not been enough time to write. Have been very busy with real estate & have not made enough money so I am in shit street financially. The weather has been bizarre with heavy snow 2 days ago & violent storms all around.

10 May 1982

Have just spent some 10 days out on FIP & am glad to be back in town once more to return & work on Gilbert's house – but have had enough of the real estate & am not making enough out of it – must find some other form of income & just write. How many times over how many years have I said that? Received 3 typed pages from Mother about her early years – most moving they are. Have so much to do – am glad to be in my apartment again & like the way it looks. Will not miss the beach or the life out on the island.

1 June 1982

Have spent the day very quietly, thank God, after too much carry-on for too many weeks. The rituals of island life with the naggings of clients &

---

* **Greg Martin**, British writer, producer and actor. **George Martin** (1926–2016), English musician and record producer, sometimes known as the Fifth Beatle for his extensive work with the group. **Gretchen Cryer**, American actress, playwright and lyricist.

my rather ridiculous inability to be immoderate have worn me out. Three weekends ago I did acid for the first time in years (read months) & danced all night & then hung out at Bruce Heim's house & listened to extraordinary music on his extraordinary sound system & watched the clouds & the woodgrain move & a gladioli came into flower before my eyes & the next day had to walk with Michael Stuart to Water Island. And partying seems to have gone on – including a dinner for Mother Buckley at Café Society where Peter didn't arrive & it turned out that Wendy Hanson, who was to have brought him, lost the address & misunderstood the intention & so he went home to be summoned very late & so we dined as anxious dancers waited for us to finish so the floor could be cleared & we ended up having dinner surrounded by men in jeans & t-shirts gyrating.

It strikes me as I write that the people I know, my friends, are all immoderate. That is what we have in common & why we indulge each other. We are fortunately given to our immoderations at disparate times & do not all, except occasionally, go crazy at once. As one alternates between fear of death & failure & joy & infinity one realizes that really this is where I am to be for the duration & a continually expanding happiness to accept this. Jay has left these parts for the world to spread the word of Christ & we missed a final meeting which saddened me, & him. Spoke on the phone, he in Boston.

Saturday night the Club [Hurrah East Hampton, Robert Boykin's new club] opened & looked good but hard-edged music & no dancing. We got a tad high. Sunday the Five (Harv, Jack, David, Marc & I)* went to Taylor's house, a gross & tasteless extravagance with gold & marble bathrooms, padded needlepoint walls etc but with a pool & lawn of beauty & Greg Osborne present with Kevin, a hooker/hustler or maybe a record producer. And preparing delicious butterflied lamb for dinner. Marc always a puppy, always curious & excited. I saw my first chipmunk & drove a great deal. Sunday night at the Club was wonderful. More cooking, more housework, more money laid out & I slept in a different bed every night. Too much.

---

*   **Harvey Kirk**, a publicist for Studio 54. **Marc Jacobs**, American fashion designer; at that time a student at Parsons School of Design and the partner of Robert Boykin.

15 June 1982

Feeling strange & strangely put upon. Wonder if I might be unwell but I
look good & am tired, which is not really a symptom of anything. Well.
What happened since last writing? Recovered, if not financially, from the
Memorial Day exigencies in East Hampton. The following weekend I went
out to FIP with Andrew Perry* & it rained most dreadfully but we cooked &
slept & all in all it was charming but had repercussions beyond the pale – I
didn't realize that Andrew's roomie Jordan was really his lover or thought he
was his lover or something like that – anyway Andrew has been told to leave
the apartment with much drama & upset. Quel Nasty. And I have gotten
somewhat fond of Andrew but cannot tell if he is really fond of me – it is all
a little vague & no one wanting to expose(?) themselves. Andrew also has
contracted some infection & his glands are swelling up. And I do not like
being 'in love' or whatever that is. I am only too aware of how blindingly
debilitating it is, as the feeling rises in the pit of your stomach you can sense
the blinders cutting down your vision & you know your behaviour is based
on a narrowed view of the world. So, reexperienced that. Feel blah!

Jack, Mother Buckley & [Eddy] Betz & I went to the disarmament rally
in Central Park & it was rather incredible – something like a million people,
which is staggering, & very orderly & quiet, too. I continue to transcribe
GJ's autobiography, which has become meandering & rambly & deals at
length with his various roles on local body committees. Don't know how it
will end up but obviously I have to devise a through line of my own for the
early years. All in all I consider my life to be a failure. GJ saw his as a success.
It was.

26 July 1982

Oh gosh & golly gee, well over a month has passed since writing last &
poverty has become almost as oppressive as this extraordinary July heat.
Today moved all my furniture – just about – into the bedroom so can work
in some modicum of air-conditioned comfort. Have spent most of the time
since last writing (except July 4 weekend when I went to the Hamptons)

---

* Name has been changed.

Robert (right) and a friend on Fire Island. MS-2438/223/020, Hocken Collections

in the city writing *Roger the Travelling Squirrel* – have Act One done, am
also sketching out a couple of other projects. Have also been seeing many
films, which is good because I don't often go to movies. Have checked out
E.T. & *Poltergeist* & *Raiders of the Lost Ark*, all good, *Victor/Victoria* good,
Whorehouse bad, *Smash Palace* very good & *[The World According to] Garp*
which was excellent & quite devastating.

Have celebrated another birthday. My many friends gathered in Riverside
Park & surprised me royally. And we all got drunk – or at least I did. Seeing
Garp has made me feel special about writing & also wanting to retreat to the
country. In August I'm off to Maine for a Lord reunion so while there will no
doubt fantasize about a place by the sea.

Good news is that apparently Nancy Marchand has read & likes *A Family
Portrait* – & will do it if the dates can be worked out.* Hope so. She wants
her daughter in it as well – but Bob Balaban has cast Joyce Reehling.† Oh
God, I want that play to happen & to happen decently but am determined
to have 3 scripts ready by the time it goes on the boards – *Roger*, *Owl &
Pussycat* & a play about [great-aunt] Flo & [her daughter] Pat which I've
done a little work on. If only the money side of things can be worked out.

28 July 1982

Am very very broke. No money at all & no food. Horrors. Really do not
know what to do & Gilbert is out of town so can't talk to him. Feel alien.
Have been thinking of trying to write about 26 Clifton Tce, which might be
fun, especially when one thinks of the cast of characters – Craig & Erola,
Netty [Ginette McDonald], Oscar, Bill Stalker & Beaver, Alex Frame, Tim

---

*   **Nancy Marchand** (1928–2000), American stage and television actress best known as
    Livia Soprano in *The Sopranos.*

†   **Bob Balaban**, American stage and film actor, director and producer, best known for his
    appearances in films by Christopher Guest and Wes Anderson. **Joyce Reehling**, American
    stage, radio, television and film actor who appeared in many readings, workshops and
    productions of RL's plays in the US.

Bros [Brosnahan], Gerry, Owen Hughes & dozens of others in & out.* The
Afghanistanians. Parties. Tony Poynton downstairs.† Vivienne Du Bourdieu
upstairs.‡ The fire. The copper. Police etc. And let's not forget Willy The
Knife, Michael & Fiona.§

2 August 1982

Spent the weekend with Steve Durham & Melvin Bernhardt in Upper
Black Eddy in Bucks County, PA. Suburban environment – houses close by
etc – noise a little, but good trees & the Delaware River & Canal nearby.
Sunday Steve & I floated down the river in inner tubes for a few hours which
was pleasant if not exhilarating. Am somewhat irritated by the problems
surrounding putting on *A Family Portrait* – now it seems delayed until
spring, though that I could not tolerate. Really am fed up with my lack of a
role in theatre & with my poverty & general frustration.

---

*   RL lists a mix of flatmates and frequent visitors at his Kelburn flat in the early 1970s.
Tenants at the house also included Jeff Kennedy, then a drama student and later café
owner and coffee roaster; Tony Martin, painter, curator and director of Artspace in
Palmerston North; and Geoff Chapple, author and journalist, who founded the Te Araroa
walking trail. **Erola Whitcombe**, Red Mole actor and then girlfriend of Craig Ashley.
Oscar was Craig's dog. **Bill Stalker** (1948–1981), New Zealand television actor, who
also worked in Australia and moved there in 1979. **Beaver** (Beverley Jean Morrison,
1950–2010), New Zealand jazz singer and occasional actress, was Stalker's then partner.
The couple met through Bruno Lawrence's music and theatre act Blerta in the 1970s, and
had two daughters together. **Alex Frame**, New Zealand barrister and legal historian, now
Honorary Professor of Law at Te Piringa/Faculty of Law at the University of Waikato.
Gerry Meister, Swiss-born academic in the English Department at Victoria University of
Wellington; later a musician based in Tauranga. **Owen Hughes**, New Zealand producer;
worked as production manager for John O'Shea's Pacific Films and at Downstage before
establishing Frame Up Films in 1977.

†   **Tony Poynton** lived with his wife Lois (1939–2001) in the downstairs flat, which was
connected by a trapdoor.

‡   **Vivienne Du Bourdieu**, neighbour who worked at Radio New Zealand.

§   **Jan 'Willy' Williams**, neighbour and RL's friend. **Michael Keir-Morrissey**, New Zealand
actor, and **Fiona Buchanan**, his then wife, who worked at TVNZ.

3 August 1982

Continue reading K Mansfield; the volume is apparently chronological & it would seem I'm reading the *In a German Pension* collection. Am wondering if I could perhaps fashion a play out of them. Very nicely turned stories – KM obviously hated German men & is very prickling & revealing about their pomposities.

21 August 1982

Have just returned to NYC after a night in New Hampshire & a day at the Lord family reunion. Have just reread *Roger* play, which I finished last week & gave to Gilbert, & Gilbert is reading it now & we are to talk about it later tonight. I just don't know what to think about it. Haven't got a clue. Some parts seem to zing along but it wouldn't surprise me if Gilbert is not happy. Must not get too depressed about it. Must keep my mind open & hope that I can salvage something out of it all. We shall see. Looked at a couple of KM German stories & fiddled with them for the idea of a play – think it is good but I don't see it clearly yet. Will work on & off at it for a while.

Poverty sucks. Got some cheques this week – total $800 & it all went on a few bills! Horrors! And with the economy in shit street. Will life improve? Richmond Crinkley & Stephen Robman are both reading *Family Portrait* aka *A Hint of Scandal* this weekend so perhaps we'll get some movement on that front.* Nancy Marchand definitely hot to do it but has another play, but has a two-week out so will be available if & when. Would be good if it happened. Have been having very creepy ghost dreams & waking up thinking people are in the apartment. I do not need such madness. Stayed in the worst motel in New Hampshire – the Spartan in Dover & slept over a dance floor, très noisy. Life is a bitch, n'est-ce pas?

23 August 1982

Gilbert liked the play.

---

* **Richmond Crinkley** (1940–1989), American theatre producer; co-produced *The Elephant Man* (1980). **Stephen Robman**, American theatre and television director and producer; artistic director of the Phoenix Theatre 1980–82.

Robert on the Staten Island ferry, with the World Trade Center in the background.

MS-1907/11/049, Hocken Collections

9 September 1982

Have just returned from an exhausting 11 days on FIP with Jack Hofsiss, Peter Buckley, Doug Watts, Larry Smith, Jim Rosen, Peter Fonseca & Patti & Buddy Ferraro.* We had a new 4-bed pool house which shook every time someone breathed & the pool, about 3' deep at best, leaked. Lots of drugs & disco & a little sex, strange emotional vibrations as our lives intermingle and I became very close to Peter Fonseca, but it is really Jim I desire & guess I have since first we met. Ah, what is to be done. Six of us drove to the beach with 20 pieces of luggage! While there went to several parties including a

---

*   **Jim Rosen**, lawyer friend of RL's, then studying for the New York Bar Exam.

bal masqué which never really happened & a benefit for SAGE hosted by Harvey Fierstein & produced by Tommy Tune & Jerry Herman.* Had a lot of fun & grew close to Gilbert again, who joined in the madness. Returned to NYC to the news that David Juaire was killed in a fire in a Holiday Inn – fell 14 floors to his death.† Oh, I am so poor! But at least I am alive.

21 September 1982

Things go from bad to worse. I'm now absolutely penniless & have the IRS on my back for both 1979 & 1980. The phone will be cut off tomorrow, I have not been able to pay medical insurance & my rent hasn't been paid for 2 months. Shit. Also feel quite wiped out & exhausted after the past week of incessant theatre-going & nightclubbing. Had a letter from Jay today, who is in Manhattan, Kansas, spreading the word of God, & apparently very happy; he belongs to a 'family', one of whom is brain damaged but God is doing something about that. The intrigues of city life also befuddle – the many affairettes that surround one. Feel I am in for a time of complete recession & solitude but am so broke! Buddy Ferraro has offered me a job in his newsstand in the Village! Hudson Guild have announced a tentative scheduling of my play, but I will believe it when I see it. Have done a second draft of the *Squirrel* play & am arranging a reading of it next week.

23 September 1982

Life is not going as it should & I'm stuck in the midst of a great financial crisis. Feel I will soon be evicted from this apartment as I have no money for rent, phone gets cut off on Monday! Went for a job interview at ABT [American Ballet Theatre] yesterday but that did not seem to go all that well. Richmond Crinkley thinks *A Family Portrait/Hint of Scandal* is light Joe Orton; no news from Hollywood. The whole situation sucks dead dog dick as Jay would say. Last night went to an introductory Buddhism class with David Lawson, which I enjoyed & which seemed to make sense. Then dinner with Alex Ely & Jack. Today quiet, but Jim came in at about 11am very

---

*   **Harvey Fierstein**, American actor, playwright and screenwriter. **Jerry Herman** (1931–2019), American composer and lyricist.

†   **David Juaire** (d.1982), casting director and artistic programs director for the New Dramatists.

drunk, having had what he feels is the final bust-up with Michael! Trauma city. Then Stefan, a German friend of Ken's, came in & he wants to stay here – but he is straight! & I don't know if I want that at all. Continue reading KM & thinking about that play. Tonight dinner with Peter Fonseca.

6 October 1982

Well much has happened. The major highlights of the past few weeks have been Jack's birthday & the New Drams reading of the *Squirrel* play. For the birthday after much discussion, debate & confusion we settled on a small dinner at Buckley's with people coming later which of course seemed to answer Jack's desires for a family event. Of course we were wrong & 2 days later Jack organized his own party at Linda Stein's & had everyone there from Matt Dillon to Robby La Fosse to Fran Lebowitz etc etc.* Champagne (cheap). The dinner however was fun & Buckley got drunk. Jack passed out having done way too much K [ketamine]. And afterwards Fonseca, Jim & I went off to The Saint & that was fun. Jack wanted me to go to a party at Channel B & on to Studio Sunday night, but I was neurotic about my poverty & pissed with him. Left one message & he called back & said he had planned whole evening round me. Later left second message & said I had to go to New Jersey (lie) & could not make it. Well didn't hear from him & Monday started work at Le Magasin at 45 Christopher St (hours 10–6, $5 per hour off the books) for Buddy & Patti – nice news shop & I'm quite enjoying it. Last night, Tuesday, after work I got an irate phone call from Jack – 'Are you too ashamed to call me' sort of thing! Quelle horreur. Could not believe the attitude. J: 'I had to walk into that party alone.' Too bizarre by half & I'm over it in a big way.

Want to get new draft of play done by weekend so Gilbert can read it when we are on FIP. Cappy said she would lend me $2,000 last Thursday & then on Sunday said she would lend me $300 only! Horrors & the landlord on the phone & Becky & I on the verge of eviction. But seem to have smoothed things over somewhat. A group of men in the shop now reading the porn – 3 of the guys are gorgeous & doing mucho cruising. Ah life.

---

* **Matt Dillon**, American actor and 1980s teen idol. **Fran Lebowitz**, American author and social commentator.

11 October 1982

Life as a shop girl continues. Have spent the past 2 days with Gilbert at FIP. Hudson Guild is fucking us over again re *A Hint of Scandal* & now Circle Rep is reading it but we are worried that their charter may preclude 'foreign' plays.

14 October 1982

Seem to be settling into life in the magazine world. Today is Katherine Mansfield's birthday. She would be 94 if life had not been quite so noir. The story of her life is quite wonderfully horrific – the number of homes, the constant distress, the insane cures & the irony of the disparity between Katherine & her persona as purveyed by MM [John Middleton Murry]. Strongly convinced there is a wonderful play in it all.

There is no news on *A Hint of Scandal*. Wish we would learn something positive soon. Regarding *Squirrel*, director problems – who – and it would seem that as we cannot get dates for a staged reading until Dec. 6/7 then I might be able to get Stuart White or David Trainer – I would prefer the latter who has also been very perceptive about my scripts & I've valued his advice.* Have had to write a letter of self-evaluation for New Dramatists.

25 October 1982

Saturday night hung out at Jack's & ploughed through too much white powder! Shocking! Tuesday last got very drunk – had a dinner for Jim's 31st birthday. Have been having stomach/liver pains. Am hypochondriacal I expect. But want to be alone right now. Wish I could finish *Roger*. Wish I had some money. Wish. Wish. Wish. The magazine job is really just maintaining the status quo & I am not getting out of the hole. I need time & a lot of solitude to get my work done.

---

* **R Stuart White** (d.1983), American actor and director, and co-founder with Howard Ashman of the reopened WPA Theatre (Workshop of the Players' Art Foundation, Inc.). **David Trainer**, American television director, producer and writer.

Robert and Becky on Fire Island. MS-1907/011/066, Hocken Collections

26 October 1982

Massive depression continues. Ugh. But there seems to be no way out – the
only way out would be some recognition, some sense of accomplishment.
But where is that? Am tired of phoning the agency & talking to Peter, who
is full of depression himself – but worried about the likes of Beth Henley,
who at least have food in their mouths.* And I am a better playwright. I
just know that. So why am I sitting here selling magazines & feeling as if I
am about to cry? Have the phone unplugged at home, which makes things
easier – I really do not want to speak to anyone at the moment. But I tell you
having no money & no prospects is the worst.

---

*   **Peter Franklin**, theatrical agent at William Morris, later head of the theatrical division
    there. **Beth Henley**, American playwright, screenwriter and actress.

4 November 1982

Spoke to Balaban last night, he is taking the script to the Open Space & the Writers Theatre & I have suggested he has another attempt to get Papp to do it – & he is meeting with Joe next week so that might work out.* Then maybe I will be happy for 5 minutes but probably not. Spoke to Jay on Sunday & he seemed in good shape & there was but the smallest twinge on my part. Promiscuity must go. Oh, if I could get a small cheap apartment & recoup some of my losses – that would be heaven. Am tired of running with the pack – I am not, as they say, getting any younger.

9 November 1982

Actually & without intending just read an earlier part of this journal & a reference to a 1981 meeting with Boykin & *Roger the Travelling Squirrel*. Strange to think I have now a complete script of that & that it is very good. Am now trying to line up a reading of the rewrites of *Roger* next week. Am waiting to hear if David Trainer wants to direct it, also Gilbert has some idea for an LA venue. We shall see. No news of interest in *Family Portrait*, which is frustrating.

Peter Buckley is worried about his health – glands swollen etc & fears he has gay cancer & if he does will not get his teeth fixed – waste of money. I told him to have his teeth out & give the best blowjobs in town. Wish, at this moment, that I could meet some real nice man & settle down & share a life of quasi-normalcy. John O'Shea is in town & I'm dining with him & Boykin/Ardi, which is weird as I don't want to see them but do want to see John, maybe I should just settle for the free meal.† Judy Popkin was just in & we have been planning Thanksgiving – I imagine Jack, Bobby et al will be

---

* **Joseph Papp** (1921–1991), American theatrical producer and director who established both the New York Shakespeare Festival (now Shakespeare in the Park) and the Public Theater (now the Joseph Papp Public Theater), and led the 'Save the Theater' preservation efforts in New York in the 1980s.

† **Dana Ardi**, American entrepreneur and author. RL notes in April 1982, 'Boykin has formed a production company with Dana Ardi & they approached me about working for them but it will not work out – $600 a month plus a word processor – no' (MS-2438/109, p. 94, Hocken Collections).

doing something but I am happy with the NZ tradition. Judy is off to NZ in February, lucky thing. Wish I could afford to go.

22 November 1982

Have been drinking up a storm of late & generally whoring about, which is hardly appropriate for my temperament. I feel I am a split personality. One side quite rational, the other completely neurotic. Tis true.

24 November 1982

Thanksgiving Eve. A long day at the shop. 10am to midnight. Everyone is paranoid about cancer including Harvey Kirk who has reportedly (via Peter) lost 15 lbs & is always tired & can't sleep. Jack & I met with Casey Childs of New Dramatists on Monday evening about the reading of the *Squirrel* play & things are moving along but we do not, as yet, have word from Rubinstein & cannot think of a leading lady.* Everyone I know, without exception, is nuts. I cannot think of one 'normal' person except perhaps Gilbert Parker. Is this a normal life experience? I mean, had I stayed in NZ would I be surrounded by mad people? Probably. I keep wondering if I should go back & teach there if nothing happens here soon. There is too much frittered away here. Too many lives wasted & broken & the manifest agony a by-product of indulgence & excess. Ah! To write a play which captured that. That is something worth thinking on. To get out of this bind & spend time each day writing. Have been doing some work on Act Two of the *Squirrel* play & am getting into it again. Am I really talented? Yes. I must be.

2 December 1982

Strangely warm again today – not at all like fall or winter. Want to ask EJ for moola but cannot bring myself to do it. Myvanwy Jenn called last night & is very anxious that the play get on – *Family Portrait* & is talking about us all

---

*   **Casey Childs**, actor, director and producer of theatre and television. Artistic program director for New Dramatists 1981–85, and founded Off-Broadway company Primary Stages in 1984. Spent four seasons as a director at the National Playwrights Conference, working with Lloyd Richards. **John Rubinstein**, American actor, director, composer, singer and teacher.

chipping in etc & doing it – so I guess I should look into costs.* We seem to be putting together a cast for *Squirrel* – Rubinstein, Pamela Reed, Kevin Bacon, Tom Cashin, Dorothy Lyman† – & am not sure as yet who is to play the agent. I can't help feeling that I must handle all these things rather badly as we are getting into a muddle & I'm wondering if Jack is going to over-direct the event. Am taking Friday (tomorrow) off work to polish the play a tad.

10 December 1982

We read the play on Wednesday night after a series of reverses – Rubinstein & Reed both fell prey to income-producing employment & we did not manage to get a cast until Monday afternoon, Mark Blum, Priscilla Lopez, Kevin Bacon, Richard Cox, Dorothy Lyman & Tom Cashin.‡ Thursday night last went with Jack, Buck & David Carnegie to a dress of *Steaming*, which I quite enjoyed & adored the performance by Judith Ivey in lead role.§ Afterwards a drunken dinner at Joe Allen's with Cliff John & Cherry Vanilla,¶ the latter riotously funny describing her employment – she does erotic phone calls – we were very noisy & some tables left. Afterwards we went to Don't Tell Mama's & sang a little & to Van Buren's where we had trouble at the door as it was a lesbian event, so back to Mama's. Too too silly. Friday I hung out at Jack's. We were both hungover & it took 2 large bottles of red to get us back together. Saturday more casting angst & we went to Greg Osborne's in the evening to celebrate his birthday & later I went to The Saint alone. Peter Buckley very drunk before he got to Greg's. Sunday more casting

---

*   **Myvanwy Jenn** (1928–2022), Welsh-born stage, television and film actress.
†   **Pamela Reed**, American television and film actress. **Kevin Bacon**, American actor best known for *Footloose* (1984). **Tom Cashin**, American model and Broadway actor, later co-director of an interior design firm. **Dorothy Lyman**, American television actress, director and producer.
‡   **Mark Blum** (1950–2020), American stage, television and film actor. **Priscilla Lopez**, American singer, dancer and actress. **Richard Cox**, American stage, television and film actor.
§   **David Carnegie**, Emeritus Professor of Theatre at Victoria University of Wellington and former lecturer in drama at University of Otago. President of Playmarket 1981–88. **Judith Ivey**, American actress and theatre director.
¶   **Cherry Vanilla**, born Kathleen Dorritie, American singer-songwriter, publicist and actress.

neuroses & Jack & I had discussions at New Dramatists in the afternoon before going to Peter Fonseca's. Monday I came to work & waited until we realized that neither Christine Lahti nor Mary-Joan Negro was in town & then at about 4 called Priscilla, who fortunately agreed to do it.* Tuesday & Wednesday we rehearsed & I really liked working with Jack – very simple & easy & no strain & in the time allowed good work & I felt that by & large the play worked. It seemed to me to be well received by the audience, which included Phil Adelman, Ted Ruff, Michael Gottfried, Gil, Buck, Lisz & Clams, Rosen, Monte Merrick, Paul Rudnik, William Ivey Long, David Carnegie, Boykin, Dana Ardi, Buddy & Patti, & some others.† Afterwards Boykin asked me if he could produce it & I said talk to Gilbert & he said he would if I said yes first. So I said if he could get it together then I had no problems. Next day met Jack at 7.30 at Fultons – he had been in a meeting with Boykin, & he told me Robert had made an offer for the play! Strange, thought I, that no one has told me. Went to *Present Laughter* with George C Scott & hated it – over-acted in that awful theatre & everyone moving all the time (I got dizzy) so we left at the 1st intermission & then off to Joe Allen's & dinner & drinks & a lot of good talk about the play & I have ideas now for Act One & think I can pull it off. Jack wants us to aim for a June opening. Can I live so long? Now feel we should aim to do rewrites early in January & want to do some sort of reading late in January of *A Hint of Scandal*, which no one is interested in but I feel if one afternoon we could get Nancy [Marchand] & perhaps George Martin† or Barny Hughes to read it we might get some people in & get some response. Hope so, & if that doesn't work we should then move on without Balaban.

Tonight I have a cocktail party at New Dramatists. Tomorrow I'm going to *Alice in Wonderland*. Actually feel good today, which is a surprise, but the world is weird & who knows when I'll turn funny again. Wish I had a lover.

---

*   **Christine Lahti**, American actress and filmmaker. **Mary-Joan Negro**, American actress; later professor of theatre practice.
†   **Michael Gottfried**, American theatre hair and makeup designer. **Monte Merrick** (1949–2015), American playwright, novelist, screenwriter and producer. **Paul Rudnik**, American playwright and screenwriter. **William Ivey Long**, American costume designer for stage and film.
‡   **George Martin** (1929–2010), American stage, television and film actor.

Becky on Fire Island. MS-1907/11/081, Hocken Collections

By the way, my fatness is no longer funny.

Gilbert just called; evidently Boykin has made an offer & wants to do a workshop to tidy up the play & then move it to an off-Broadway house. Gilbert skeptical but felt better when I pointed out that Brent Peake would probably be involved – he knows & likes Brent. Need to see if Jack wants to be involved & what he thinks about it all. Ran my idea for a New Drams reading of *Scandal* by Gil & he liked it & agreed that if we can't get interest after such a reading we would scrap the whole plan of Balaban directing. Sounds fair to me. David Carnegie enjoyed *Squirrel* & wants to write a piece for *Act* on it & to read *Hint of Scandal* also – so have made him a copy of that today. He feels it could be done in NZ so will send off a copy at some stage to Playmarket.

11 December 1982

Have been thinking about *Squirrel* and it suddenly occurred to me that it is almost a mirror of *Scandal* – the NZ play is about someone rejected by society & the US play is about someone who rejects society. Who knew?

13 December 1982

Have told Gilbert vis a vis *Squirrel* & Boykin: a) I'm not interested unless it is for a decent sum – like $2–3,000 for the option. Otherwise no point. b) while I am happy for Jack to direct I don't feel he is the only possible director & therefore do not want it to be a Jack/Robert package, which would hold production up a great deal. Anyway we shall see what Boykin says. Must say I am strange in that I get upset to hear Jack raving about jacking his fee up (to 300,000 from 150,000 a movie) & going on about his integrity etc when I am basically starving. And to have Boykin say: 'drop by & see my new typewriter, it only cost $1,000, I couldn't resist it,' when he calls me a greedy queen when I suggest I might like to get paid. I guess I'm jealous but I don't think that is really what I'm going through.

Am really on the verge of a change, want to get out of the city – I think – or do I just want to get out of the bind I am in? That would help. But do not

Robert in a domestic moment. MS-1907/005, Hocken Collections

like the social milieu or the goals that seem to be admired. Reading Noël Coward's diaries, which are amusing but obviously were not designed to be read.

Letter from Dad on weekend – he worries about my tax situation. I worry about my income. Mother has a new boat. Also package from Blundells – dishcloth, vegemite & 2 tins of pâté which were damaged in transit & covered in green yuk. I am getting fat & my skin is going to pieces. Also think my sex drive may be taking a vacation, which is a pleasant change. I'm sick & tired of seeing men with their genitals squashed inside tight trousers. Want to be quiet & read & think. Must be very careful about going back to work on *Squirrel*: don't want to leave it too long or I'll never get into it. A check arrived! Refund from tax, so have enough to cover 1 month's rent – we'll worry about the arrears tomorrow – thanks Scarlett. I must continue to believe that some of this will pay off.

14 December 1982

Oh dear, home phone has been cut off, which is a bore, and Heller's office is calling frantically for the rent, which is very upsetting, shall try to borrow some money & get rid of one week's arrears (I mean a month's) this week. Don't know what to do about the phone. Poverty is boring. Really should get a better-paying job but feel guilty about leaving Buddy & Patti. Will talk to them tonight & we shall see what we can do. Just got up the guts to call Heller & said I can pay another month's rent today (lie) & next week the balance. Need a cash infusion of a few thousand to get in the clear. Maybe Jim Lentils can give me some money today & I can borrow from Sally & Don & then perhaps get an advance from here. Hate this situation. Wish that Boykin would shell out something for *Squirrel* but he is a flake & don't want to just take the money & then never see the play done. In the meantime I continue to read Noël Coward's diaries & enjoy them but am of the opinion that diaries should not be published, there is a great deal in them that I'm sure he would not want spread before the world – especially while the subjects of his comments are still alive (Olivier, Mary Martin etc). Coward also very interesting about the American obsession with sex & it is strange in this most liberated society there should be so much concern – though

I suppose that fundamentalism has a far more pervasive influence than I acknowledge. But I for one am sick of porn. Survived yesterday without the demon drink & will try to do the same today. Spoke to Balaban & he is gung-ho to do the *Scandal* reading on the 11th with some rehearsal on the 10th. Sounds good to me.

Later: Got in touch with Gil late in the day & he had talked to Boykin & they had hemmed around how much moola was available & finally Robert had said he would wait for the rewrites – which is fine if Robert realizes he will never see them. Actually it is good because it alleviates working with him and as no money is down there is no need for loyalty on my part. And it is bad – Robert's mouth is too big, why was he so full of largesse about the project & then decided not to put out: how does he expect me to find the time to do the rewrites? And massive confusion in my head – how does he see the play? If I was to take his interest seriously, & if I was supposed to rewrite to his requirements, what would I do? I have no concept of how he sees the show. So I'll never be able to deliver what he wants.

16 December 1982

A few days later, much calmer, but still a buzz of anger at the core. So, have talked to Balaban & January 11 at 3pm we will read *A Hint of Scandal* with Nancy Marchand, which is good, told Gilbert so he can jolly well get some people there. Then talked to JT,* who is all 'up' about *Squirrel* & wants to workshop it & to have Melvin [Bernhardt] direct. He says Melvin is very enthusiastic about it. So JT is to talk to Gilbert on Monday & we will start putting the whole thing together next week. Hope the money is still there. Oh God, it will be hysterical. One will have totally alienated Robbo & possibly Jack & will have to deal with Melvin's madness – or is he mad? Have a feeling that I am a neurotic bitch & that these pages will bear testament to that. Oh dear. I'm not really, just confused, insecure & broke. It will be wonderful not to have to work with Robbo & then see if we can be friendly. I enjoy not having a phone. Everyone is shocked.

---

* **John ('Joey') Tillinger**, Iranian-born and UK-raised US director and actor. From 1975 to 1997 he was literary consultant for the Long Wharf Theatre in New Haven, CT.

20 December 1982

Have learnt the hard way that no phone is a no-no. Mum was trying to get in touch as Dad is in hospital having bad heart trouble & things looking grim. Spoke to home on Saturday & after a bad night he was evidently a little better but the doctor says his condition is precarious. In addition to this, after talking to his brother JT finds that there is no money available at the present so that is a pity, but maybe in January. Flip flop in moods at an alarming rate. Dad doesn't want me to fly home because of his illness but I can't help feeling that maybe it is time to return. Will get the phone back on this week, which will make things easier. Spent Saturday night with Peter Fonseca – I fell asleep in front of the television. Friday night had dinner with Fonseca, Buckley, Hofsiss & Betz. Later: Not having a phone I realize how much useless time I spend on it. Like now, waiting for Gilbert for dinner, I would probably yak to all & sundry & fritter time & money.

27 December 1982

Another Christmas come & gone. Money spent. Liquor consumed.

28 December 1982

Where are we & what is happening? We are in the shop, that is where we are, & after days of not writing, of champagne & caviar, of intrigue & joie de vivre, I am trying to get back to the nitty gritty. Finally finished the Noël Coward diaries. Am also reading Ted Morgan's biography of Somerset Maugham, which I am loving.

What would I give for a lifestyle where I could write 3 to 4 hours a day, swim, & read? What would I give? A good question. Do I need to continue to receive the stimulation of NYC, would I stagnate in NZ? If it were possible to get, quite soon, a grant for a year to write there, then I could find out. I think I need to do that. In the meantime I am sorting out my financial mess here aided by a generous ($500) bonus from Buddy & Patti, a refund from the IRS, $350 from the Hamilton Operatic Society for helping get rights to some shows. Have, thankfully, at the moment no interest in sex & this is something I would like to see continue.

A great deal happened over Christmas & let me see how much I can remember. Letter from John O'Shea, who wants me to continue with the Boykin film project but I am not taken with the idea – or rather have yet to find my way into it. Do not want to write another film that I do not feel is right for me. Hate not being in control of the material. Ghastly & demoralizing situation. Since the volley of phone calls have not heard from the family so presume Dad is recovering or at least holding his own. Apparently he was on the verge of dying & was given no chance of survival & this has gone to a 1 in 10 chance then to a 3 in 10 – last time I heard. Hope that if he has to die soon then it is quick & painless, the thought of his lingering & suffering is not a happy one. Christmas Eve I went to several parties. Lee Linderman, who often comes into the shop, asked me to a party with him, which of course fluffed my ego (me who has given up sex) & made me feel better about myself, but I feel he is lonely, having just broken with a lover, & I do not feel I want to risk rejection by making a pass & so am happier just to jolly along.* Anyway we went to Jack's for champagne with Julie & Gary, Julie draping the tree in her fashion & padding about in a state of calculated confusion. Forget, night before this I had gotten drunk with Sally & discussed life & art. Called by Jack's on the way home & greeted Julie who'd just arrived & she gave me socks & a red union suit. From Jack's on Christmas Eve we went to Doug's, where everyone was suitably impressed that I had a date. Doug gave me 3 pairs of Calvin Klein undies, being apropos because of the *Squirrel* play. Many there, none of whom I knew well, lots of champagne, turkey etc. Much silliness. Larry Smith shocked to see Lee with me (he has a crush on him). Anyway Lee & I departed & went to some friends of his in a residential hotel on 57th St for dessert & champagne & that was very boring. Very fuggy & the suite painted a hideous lobster bisque. The desserts were numerous & rich. Then to Sally's where, of course, everyone was drunk but it was fun especially as Jim & Michael, John Dogg & Gary Crist were there. Doug arrived & was highly miffed to see John present & would not stay in the same room. Larry passed out. Lee mingled. It was all silly. Julie Weiss cooed over [Sally's] baby. Julie & Jack

* **Lee Linderman,** Broadway ensemble actor.

were supposed to meet Boykin & Ellen Greene at her abode but did not make it & they refused to come uptown, so much discontent sown there. Lee went home & I wandered home with Jack & Julie & we bought eats in a late-night deli & found ourselves in the middle of an 'incident' but we ignored it. Christmas Day – opened the shop for an hour in the morning & then went to visit Buckley, who had a major fever & flu & was worried about himself, & then to a very amusing dinner with all of his family (mother, father, sister & her 2nd husband & 2 daughters, great-aunt & uncle). Huge meal – pasta with meatballs & rolled beef. Stuffed artichokes. Salad. Fillet of beef. Pastries. Then home & Becky & I went to Fonseca's, where Jack & Julie joined us along with La Fosse & some others & that was fun except I wasn't ready to eat again. Then on to Couri Hay's for champagne & caviar & I felt slightly ill-at-ease as I always do there.* Then to Studio, which was hideous, & I went home & they all went to The Saint. Madness. Jim Rosen gave me trousers, Jack a beautiful shirt, Jim Lentils scotch, Gilbert a photo of Becky, Peter Fonseca magic glasses & a nightgown. Sunday I had brunch with Boykin & Weiss, which I'm afraid to say bored me. In the evening had cocktails with Jack, Julie, Ethan Silverman & Cheryl his girlfriend, who is an actress & very bright & has spent a great deal of her life in Sydney so we had things to talk about.† I was quite amusing, I think. Mother Buckley came by for a visit & looking much better, thank God. JT has phoned & I am dining with him tonight. Must work on *Squirrel* this week. Have also been thinking of maybe writing a novel. I'm always thinking of maybe writing a novel, but I am thinking now of something like *The Kite Play* set in the Clifton Tce apartment & doing it very New Zealand, trying to sketch in the social pressures, the hideous attitude to women prevalent in the late 60s–early 70s & the general sexual/emotional confusion we all enjoyed. Tone is always the key. Hit the tone. Do not see why I should not be able to do this. Maybe while reading the Maugham I will find the inspiration. Peter Fonseca just dropped by – we have agreed to avoid New Year's Eve.

---

* **R Couri Hay**, American publicist and gossip columnist; started his career at Warhol's *Interview* magazine, and worked at the *National Enquirer* 1976–83.

† **Ethan Silverman**, American director who specialised in directing new plays; later also a filmmaker and academic. RL's friend and later roommate; directed 1989 Primary Stages production of *China Wars*.

2 January 1983

Well another year has begun & I expect I should have either some witty remark or at least a list of resolutions. But no. Escaped NYC on Friday night & came by bus to Upper Black Eddy, where I am guest of Melvin & Steve. Got fed & drunk on Friday night, dressed in my Brooks Brothers nightie & Wayfarer glasses to watch the ball fall. Do feel good that 1983 has begun with the rent up to date, & at least something paid off the bills. Wish I wasn't so pudgy though. Thursday of last week I went to the Joffrey Ballet with Jack & his new friend Patrick – a dancer with the Feld company – & Peter Fonseca. Wednesday I dined with JT. Down here I have slept & continued to read Ted Morgan's excellent biography of Somerset Maugham, am now about halfway through & find it fascinating. What an odious shit he was. And how cleverly veiled, screened, whatever, the lives of the famous were/are. Yesterday we cocktailed with some friends of Melvin, the husband is father Ryan in *Ryan's Hope*, I did not point out that I had once written for the show. Guest of honour, Bob Randall the playwright.* Pleasantly eccentric house with a pond & tennis court. Many lesbians in attendance. Have not done any work on the play, which is causing me to feel anxious. Have to meet with Balaban & Casey Childs 6.30 Monday about reading *Hint of Scandal*, don't know if the boy is cast. I would very much like Kevin Bacon to do it but think Bob does not regard him very highly. Phone call from home on Friday & apparently Dad is much better. Thank God.

Later. Just arrived home after a surprisingly short bus trip from Upper Black Eddy to find a letter from home which has not exactly thrilled me. My mother is quoting from my father: 'Dear Rob, while I have been ill I have been thinking a lot of our family matters & you in particular – to be frank it gives us no joy or pleasure to know you are perpetually hard up & now & again you mention you have financial problems, which indicates to me you could be in debt. To be in debt is a disaster unless one has firm arrangements to clear the debts.// We also must be blunt when we say that your career as a playwright is not being a success – financially I mean.// I have a suggestion to make. You are still young – why not take a break from

---

*   **Bob Randall**, born Stanley Goldstein (1937–1995), American screenwriter, playwright, novelist and television producer.

your New York life & come back home. We have just repainted the den &
had it waterproofed & it looks very comfortable. You could come back here
& work to your heart's content in that undisturbed atmosphere. Gilbert
must know you well by now & I am sure he could attend to your work by
mail as easily as the personal approach. You certainly by now must have the
experience & ability to work this way.// Should you do this I am sure Richard
would find little difficulty in getting you seasonal work in the orchards of
the Bay of Plenty & there must be other types of work around.// Robert at
your age it is time you established a little independence & you should be
able to do it in this way without discarding your life's work.// I know this
will be a very difficult decision for you to make but you can always inform
your critics & friends that you are coming home because of the health of
your parents.// Now I don't want to upset you but I have been very ill lately
& with my heart anything could happen suddenly & I can have no regrets
as I have had a lovely life with a wonderful wife & family.// Now, think this
over – the last thing I want to do is to interfere with anyone's career, but if
you are interested in acting on this suggestion & come back home for a 3–5
year period to let things get sorted out I would be prepared to pay all your
debts & provide your air fare home. In all fairness to Richard, if there is any
substance in your debts your mother & I would treat the expenditure as an
advance from the legacy you will inherit when she too passes on. Think it
over very carefully my boy – it will be your decision. God bless you. Dad.'

3 January 1983
Well, was quite upset when I received the above but have cooled now.
Strange the confusion of emotions that have been going on these past weeks
especially about family. And as much as one thinks about a return to New
Zealand I cannot really see myself sitting in the basement & typing away, as
a matter of fact I can feel now the tensions & stirrings which I know would
become part of my life. It is, of course, very upsetting to have scorn dropped
on one (does that make sense?); realistically a 3–5 year return to NZ would
put an end to any possibility of a career as a dramatist, I would move out
of touch in more ways than one & heighten the cultural confusion that I
am finally coming to terms with. I could not expect Gilbert to adequately
represent me from such a distance, indeed I can only believe I would be

Robert typing in the apartment. MS-1907/011/04, Hocken Collections

shuffled into an even more remote corner than the one I occupy now. So to return would mean to give up. I'm not ready. If I do return it must be on my terms. It's all so truly hateful. Later: Feel wistful, melancholic, want to be in love, to be young, passionate, committed. Ah, shit. It is noisy in the shop. Balaban just called, cast seems set – Nancy Marchand, George Martin, Joyce Reehling, Dan Hedaya, Kevin Bacon.* Hope that it can work & that there is some rehearsal time.

7 January 1983

A strangely topsy turvy week emotionally. Started out feeling great but ran out of energy. Dinner Tuesday night at Odeon with Fonseca & Rosen, expensive but fun. Thursday night collapsed early. Today a doctor's visit & a chat about gay cancer & blood test, I feel there is nothing wrong with me. Tonight dinner with John Wilson & others, which I'd rather not. Tomorrow have to go to movies with Lee Linderman, which I'd rather not. I'm just a girl who can't say no. Plans for the reading of the play continue apace, Brent Spiner† is replacing Dan Hedaya, who is making a movie somewhere. Finished reading the Somerset Maugham biography, which is excellent – in the last years he suffered senile dementia, sometimes sane sometimes not. Alternating between reasonable behaviour & the irrational. The presumption is, of course, that he doesn't mean what he says when he raves. Interesting to think that he is perfectly sane at all times, we often contain 2 or more reactions to a situation but allow one to dominate.

8 January 1983

Love time alone! Saturday. Nice sleep in. Putz about. Walk dog. Write to Craig – oh I miss him. Now another walk & shop & then home for a read maybe. Am supposed to go out tonight with Lee Linderman. As much as I like him would rather stay home and work. Am reading Katherine Mansfield's diaries &, although we are dealing now with the early years, I cannot help wondering if it is naïveté which is such a point of connection for me. Growing up in New Zealand one cannot help but be naïve. God knows

---

*   **Dan Hedaya**, American film and television actor.
†   **Brent Spiner**, American stage, film and television actor best known as 'Data' on *Star Trek*.

it is the most obvious thing about me. If Buddy & Patti are agreeable I could go to Vermont on the 15th Jan & return on the 23rd, which would give me 7 full days there, surely enough time to polish up the *Squirrel* play & get my head together. Feel that I cannot leave Le Magasin, yet, as they have been too good to me but have to find a way to get some money and also to write without being constantly exhausted. Have been thinking about the letter from home & feel that the best thing is to ignore it, or at least only an acknowledgement. Obviously I cannot go back in the way that is suggested.

12 January 1983

Yesterday had a reading of *Scandal/Portrait* which seemed to go well. Jack very enthused about it. As a cold reading there were patches that didn't work and sometimes the play seemed to meander, but I think that given a rehearsal period this could be solved. Did think, though, that the railway station material wears a little thin by the time we are into Act Two. That should be simple to solve. Need to give Bert, Maisy & Tom a few more moments each. There must be a ton of business. Cooking etc. Tubs. Running water. No one is ever idle. Except Bert at times. Maybe I should put in material re driftwood. A hobby of his. Or bird feeders. Maybe Grant polishes driftwood. I think these things will heighten the second act. Last night phoned home & spoke to Lorelle, evidently Dad is still in hospital & they are trying to stabilize him for a coronary bypass operation.

13 January 1983

Thinking about the New Zealand play. Am wondering if I could turn it into a novel with a Thomas Bergeresque style. Feel the piano must be used, if not then opportunity is down the drain. Getting flack from Jim re Gilbert, who he thinks is not doing enough for me. He really should be calling people about this play now – though I tend to feel nothing is going to happen as a result of this reading, which is a pity. Letter from home yesterday including a clipping of Bruce Mason's obit, he must have died just after Christmas. Also a clipping from some paper claiming Sam Hunt has sold his poems to an American publisher for $500,000!* Sounds too bizarre & improbable for words.

---

* **Sam Hunt**, New Zealand poet, known for his public performances of poetry.

Maisy (Alice Fraser) and Bert (Grant Tilly) in *Bert and Maisy*, the eventual title given to
A Family Portrait, at Circa in 1986. Photograph by Justine Lord. MS-2438/019/004, Hocken Collections

14 January 1983

On Sunday I will go to Dorset, Vermont for a week & will work on both
Portrait & *Squirrel* plays & do some reading & work on the novel perhaps.
Must write. Must write. Yesterday met with Balaban & talked over some
ideas for the play (*Portrait*) which I will attempt. He seemed quite enthused
but I need some action. I need to think about how to live the rest of this year
– in other words, do I continue the 5 days a week grind or cut it down to 3 or
4 & so get more writing done. Also must write home next week.

17 January 1983

Dorset, Vermont, pop: very small. One store; Peltier's (pronounced 'Pelchers'
through some strange corruption of the original French) which sells wine,
beer, food, & just about all one needs. A small stone congregational church,
2 ancient inns & a library which seems to have an unconscionably large

selection of murder/mystery novels. Dorset also has several inches of snow on the ground & a summer stock theater to which this rambling old house in which I am staying belongs. I have an overheated, underdecorated but comfortable room & lots of quiet, which is what I want. Other residents seem pleasant but I am staying to myself. Bussed up on Sunday, some 5½ hours through the wasteland of New Jersey sprinkled, & looking better for it, with snow; into New York State as snow clouds thickened & on to Albany where, from the disadvantage point of the Greyhound Terminal, I saw the incongruous Empire State Plaza lording over the more established red brick

Maisy with exotic stranger Tom (Jon Brazier) at Circa in 1986. Photograph by Justine Lord. MS-2438/019/005, Hocken Collections

& the extravagant chateau-style architecture. Then through snow falls to
Manchester, CT, where John Nassivera collected me & drove me to this retreat.*
So far I have accomplished nothing but have finished *The Hermit of Peking*,
which did not inspire me to write a play, & also *The Dog Beneath the Skin*, which
Jack thinks should be adapted for David Bowie. Tomorrow I will start in earnest
on *Family Portrait*, which I hear Circle in the Square are interested in. Friday
I took Peter Fonseca for dinner at Burgundy, where the hostess asked for Lee
Linderman's number! Saturday drank Courvoisier with Jack in the afternoon,
visited Jim & Michael & dined with Peter & David & David & indulged in
Special K & got quite wrecked. Folly. My stomach is playing up.

18 January 1983

Am not being quite so lazy today & was up & about before 10. What would
they say back home when any man worth his salt is up by 7? Wandered to
the local shop for the *Times* & found it not in. So have been dipping into the
Evelyn Waugh & *Silas Marner* & find in the first paragraph of the latter work
much that is pertinent to *Family Portrait*.

19 January 1983

Woke up this morning in a foul mood feeling my full 37 years & something
of a failure. I wonder if the letter from home, to which I responded yesterday,
is having its effect? Resolved to enrol on a graduate course at NYU so if push
comes to shove I can teach in NZ.

Have actually commenced work on *Family Portrait* and am pleased with
what I am doing – strengthening Tom & giving him personality and at the
same time beefing up Bert. Am also trying to escape the Pinteresque echoes of
the opening, the sparse dialogue which speaks volumes etc etc. And feel now
Bert probably can't stand silence – like Dad – and would always be talking. The
sound of his voice is reassurance. And Tom has a sense of direction & purpose,
even if it is crazy – a motorcycle tour of the Indian sub-continent. So he ceases
to be a tool & becomes instead a person. My God, if this doesn't solve the play
& get it on! Evidently Circle in the Square are interested now.

---

* **John Nassivera**, American author, playwright and college professor, and founder of the
Dorset Theater Festival in Vermont.

20 January 1983

Dazzlingly beautiful day, perfectly clear sky, sun & snow & bloody cold as I found on my trek in pursuit of the *NY Times*. Had a good day yesterday on *Family Portrait* – rewrote Scene One & commenced Scene Two. Hopefully today will get well into the second act. Evening sat around with other residents & talked about very little. One boy here reminds me of Russell – his hair, his skin, his eyes, even the way he wears his clothes. C'est la vie. A thought has been running through my mind all day. It relates to the New Zealand play & to Nonny Mann talking about what one misses from not staying in the same place. A texture of life is hidden from. I imagine it but cannot feel it. And it's too late now. I'll never be part of the weave. I think of Sandy & Warwick [Williams] & other family, who are living all their lives in a proximity & in an adherence. I have denied myself that pleasure, believing other things are more important. I am not unhappy & do not regret this but I must admit, have to admit, I have denied myself a pleasure (and a pain).

A rowdy first night back & of course regretted it & got bitter & twisted. And my mood was not improved by learning that Bobby Christian had died of gay cancer & that Stuart White was back in hospital – all this is quite depressing & causes one to have healthy/unhealthy moments of introspection.* It all came to a point last Friday night when Jack, Peter, myself, Sally & Donald went out for dinner & got too drunk & silly & complicated, especially with Sally, & who knows what that means if it means anything. So I had to take to my bed for Saturday & Sunday & did not answer a call. Everyone thinks I am weird. Which I am.

18 February 1983

Have not been able to face this diary for a long time. Was extremely depressed by Bobby Christian's death & the dinner with Sally & Don mentioned above flung me into a funk & I took to bed for several days & refused calls, which pissed everyone off. Jack when we finally got together forgave my madness & since then have tried to keep everything on an even

---

*   **Robert Christian** (1939–1983), American stage, film and television actor, known for his 1982 performance as detective Bob Morgan in the soap *Another World*. RL mentions seeing him at the O'Neill in his 1974 diary.

keel. Had a reading of the rewrites of *Family Portrait* last week with Doris Belack, David Margulies, Christine Ebersole, David Rasche & Brent Spiner.* Everyone very impressed & the play much improved. A beat round the climax needs tinkering with & have been doing that & yesterday I discussed it through with Gilbert. Was going to do it last night. Will do it this weekend while Becky is with Gilbert.

Last weekend Jack, Mother, Doug and I had brunch then proceeded to party all Saturday. Naughty but fun in a snow-covered Village. The Friday night I had gone for dinner to Patrick's (Jack's friend) & we had a goodly time & 20 inches of snow fall & I slept with Patrick's roomie. Earlier that week in a moment of madness I phoned Russell Craig in London & told him why I was cross with him & that I loved him still & we should get together. A few days after that I told Jim Rosen that I thought the two of us should be lovers & we are supposed to discuss that. Then a truly gorgeous man came into Le Magasin & I swooned – Eric Robertson, a Zoli model,† I have yet to work up courage to ask for a date & I probably won't. What does all this mean? Simply I'm nuts. Dad seems to be recovering, which is good, & the operation was successful. Mum sent a photo of herself with Hilary & Nathan in her new dinghy, made me quite homesick. I've decided I want *Family Portrait* to be a great success & make me a mint & I will buy a farm in NZ which Rich & family can live on & I'll build a house there. Must be on the sea. I'll also buy a building in New York & start a theatre. Travel to Europe, have a lover, raise a family etc etc. Dream on.

1 March 1983

Went to the White Party at The Saint & found it to be quite an instructive experience – learnt I never want to go there again. Was shocked at the amount of drugs people still take & the fact that they still carry on in outrageous ways upstairs. I think Dad is home from hospital now, which

---

*   **Doris Belack** (1926–2011), American stage, film and television actress. **David Margulies** (1937–2016), American stage, film and television actor. **Christine Ebersole**, American stage, film and television actress and singer. **David Rasche**, American stage, film and television actor.

†   The Zoli Agency, a New York modelling agency in the 1970s and 1980s, featured in the 1980 documentary *Model*.

On holiday with Becky, probably on Fire Island. MS-1907/004, Hocken Collections

is a great relief. If I do go down I will then apply for some sort of writing fellowship for 1984 – by that time I should have at least something happening in New York. Russell called me last night from London but I was out – at least he was thinking of me. I have triumphed over Eric R – or rather over my infatuation with him.

3 March 1983
Tuesday night a New Dramatists cocktail party at Zilla Lipmann's, which was moderately amusing except I do not really like my fellow New Dramatists – a somewhat dowdy group.* Wednesday night mahjong & dinner. And we all fell about & were silly. Yesterday met a Basenji dog named Beaver who was in the shop and true to form she could not bark, evidently she can yodel and is very agile with her paws – can climb a chain link fence. Want to get one of her pups when she is mated for Peter Fonseca. Have had an idea for my Christmas play – set on Christmas Day but over 40 years (1945–85) – but action on a single day so there may be some plot but the characters will age and change. If it works it could be wonderful, intend to take notes on it today. And must proceed with the *Squirrel* play and get some action there. No news as yet about *Family Portrait* but that is to be expected. Want to get thinner – am really piling it on at present & look quite gross, so should diet & exercise. All too tedious.

4 March 1983
I am entering one of my I hate the world phases. God. I am sick of all the nonsense & bother. There is too much to do & not enough time. Original thinking, eh boy?

27 March 1983
The fact that I have been unable to attack this diary for over 3 weeks, the fact that I was never able to come to any accommodation of Bobby Christian's death, the fact that I cannot look at the mountain of bills or

---

* **Zilla Lipmann** (1904–1999), script reader, producing associate and philanthropist who co-founded New Dramatists and helped the Museum of the City of New York establish its extensive theatre collection.

bring myself to read a letter from my father. What is the problem? It is obviously, only & solely thwarted ambition. The gnawing, twisting knowledge of failure – & the total inability to confront such a situation, to be a 'man' if that is what is demanded. Let us analyze. So the *Squirrel* was written & sits on a shelf. The play needs some tinkering. Then work on *Family Portrait*, & very good work, which took some time & which was delivered to Gilbert at least 3½ weeks ago to be sent to all those places who had expressed further interest & to date no response from anyone & Gilbert announced he would call everyone this week but obviously has not, which prompted an abrupt treatment of Peter Franklin & then an apology. Sometimes when bitchy & neurotic, I think Gilbert only cares about me because of Rebecca, but that is too cynical.

7 May 1983
Well, here I am on the deck of Gilbert's house at the one & only FIP enjoying glorious sun & contemplating leaving for NZ in another 3 weeks & so this book has nearly come full circle. Have been here since Monday last with Jack Hofsiss, whose recent efforts on Broadway garnered a crop of nasty notices & a run of one night & also, I must add, not a few tears. Jack ran the gamut, as they say, of the emotions, this time from Y to Z. I do not seem to be in quite the mess I was in the last entry here but am still frustrated, though have come away from this week with some ideas for the *Squirrel* play, which Gilbert & I have renamed *All About Ego*. I'm looking forward to NZ for a change of pace as much as anything else & for the chance to work in a theatre again.

29 May 1983
For the first time since leaving Le Magasin last Wednesday I am sitting at my desk & writing; writing if not my *Squirrel* play, at least this sentence. I'm beginning to feel the pleasure of putting pen to paper. Have been wondering if I can, if I have descriptive powers, the ability to describe. Why do I wonder this? I have been reading PD James, Edmund Crispin, Antonia Fraser & am now on to Barbara Pym – & all these writers have descriptive abilities I find rather staggering, but I wonder also if practice & thought

may not help. Mike Nic is coming to see me any minute, in town on some press junket. It will be good to toss some ideas around with him. I have an itinerary set out in front of me for NZ/Australia but do not have the $US970 to buy the ticket. The play is now to be called *Unfamiliar Steps* & I don't know if it makes any sense at all. Strangely I am seriously & nonneurotically considering moving back to NZ at least for several months next year. Even spoke to Jay Funk about it, suggesting he might want to come with me & take up potting – but why try to open that can o worms, Robert will you never learn? Sex, of course, is a major problem these days because one dreads having it – the plague being forever in the spotlight. One cannot help but think there will be some hideous backlash soon – the *Post* has already run an op-ed piece going on about homosexuals turning their back on nature & now nature is getting back at them!

30 May 1983

Last night's dinner with Mike N was very pleasant & I may see him again this evening, he is very anxious that I should get back to NZ for the play & must call Playmarket & make them pay for the trip. So will try that today. Just flipped through a few pages in this diary & really I do come across as a hideous neurotic. I am generally quite stable. At least at the moment.

I am always hesitant in passing judgement on the plays of others largely because I am insecure about my own work & do not know if I am right or wrong. I can feel my mind adjusting to settling back in New Zealand.

31 May 1983

Got drunk last night, which was reasonably pleasant but now I am sluggish today. Going to a lot of theatre with Mike N – *42nd St* tonight, *Dreamgirls* Wednesday & *Nine* on Friday.

1 June 1983

Last night went with Mike N to see *42nd St*, which seemed to have become cornier – by which I mean everything was hit over the head with a sledgehammer & everyone shouted. But the dancing etc was good. Walked home. In the early evening we had a beer with Lindsay Shelton of the NZ Film Commission.[*] More & more I seem to be gearing up for my NZ trip.

12 June 1983

I have been writing away at the *Squirrel* play. The first act of which we read Thursday & it seemed okay but needs some nipping & tucking, which I am about to do. Friday had a reading of *Family Portrait/A Hint of Scandal/ Unfamiliar Steps*, which I now want to call *Bert & Maisy* – nice casual feel to that title & not too pretentious. Reading was at W Morris & was for McCann/Nugent – Joel Martin also present as was Gil, Peter Franklin, Jack H, Ethan & Peter Fonseca. I thought it went well.[†] Good cast – George Martin, Kate Reid, Chris Curry, John Glover, Suzanne Lederer[‡] – the first act is too long, need to get rid of 5 if not more minutes from the first scene & another 5 from the other scenes in that act. Hard to tell what Liz or Nelle thought. Completely stonyfaced. Joel laughed. I laughed. We shall see. It would be great if they optioned it. Or is that asking too much? Probably. Other news is that Ethan, searching for a one-act play at a festival at the Ark Theatre, read *Balance of Payments* & is trying to get it on there. We shall see.

• • •

[*]   **Lindsay Shelton**, former journalist, film festival director and the NZ Film Commission's first marketing director 1979–2001.

[†]   **McCann & Nugent Productions**, theatre production company set up by Elizabeth McCann and Nelle Nugent, which staged many award-winning Broadway shows from 1976 to 1986. **Nicholas ('Nicky') Martin**, born Joel Martin Levinson (1938–2014), actor, and later director and theatre academic; played the Dormouse in *Alice in Wonderland* on Broadway, probably the production described by RL.

[‡]   **Kate Reid** (1930–1993), Canadian stage, television and film actress. **Chris Curry**, American film and television actor and writer. **John Glover**, American film and television actor. **Suzanne Lederer**, American stage and television actor.

Robert did not write any diary entries between June 1983 and August 1984. He visited New Zealand in July 1983 to see the premiere of *Unfamiliar Steps*, the play that would become *Bert and Maisy*, directed by the Australian Aarne Neeme. It was performed by the Court Theatre at the Christchurch Arts Centre.

1984–1985

Jay Funk, 1986. MS-1907/005, Hocken Collections

10 August 1984

My moody, intense, neurotic & depressed state has continued unabated & with no end in sight. I have managed to tidy the apartment & rearrange the living room. Have not yet commenced to paint it. Work brings me some pleasure. Are diaries an act of narcissism or self-torture?

Richard Porteous – a friend of John Glover's – seems interested in my play *Bert & Maisy*. If nothing seems set in my career by the end of this year I will leave New York. In the meantime I will complete the new play, rework *Squirrel* & do another final scene for *Bert & Maisy*.

20 August 1984

In a terrible continuing state of ennui. Am frustrated by everything – plays written & unwritten. The job. The health. The heat.

24 August 1984

Am somewhat fired up & plan by summer to have:

a) completed final rewrite on *Bert & Maisy* – with a reading or two thereof – this to be done in September, early October.

b) have a couple of readings & a rewrite session on *Squirrel* prior to going to NZ so will have a good clean working script before rehearsals start in February.

c) in September & off & on thereafter rework *Cop Shop*, calling it *The Used Car Salesman* or *How Not To Sell A Car* – the former I think. Want to tighten the script very much, way too long. Herb DuVal gave me an insight when he said the play is about selling a car.* Need to trim & remove some of the excesses of the Toronto script – have an innate dislike of the farce element – problem is resolving the pregnancy problem.

d) complete the neighbourhood play.

e) write *Café Society*.

---

* **Herb DuVal** (1941–2022), American actor, director, teacher and playwright.

The last two I should have in good draft form by spring, if not complete. Wish, plan, to do a reading of 'neighbourhood' at ND [New Dramatists]. *Café Society* in January. Want to have the apartment redone & spotless by midwinter in preparation for the visit of Mum & Pam & hopefully Dad.

But the key is to complete work on the five plays – in the hope that there might be an interest in my writings.

7 September 1984

A somewhat hectic & dishevelled time of late. A Labor Weekend on FIP which had moments of elation & depression, drunkenness & sobriety. I continue my love/hate relationship with myself. In the meantime the apartment is getting done, with Jay doing the painting. It looks great with a pale grey & blue & white living room & a white & grey bedroom. Will finish the floors again soon & build a couple of basic pieces of furniture – like a headboard & bedside table. Am also, finally, getting my teeth done at NYU & hope by early 85 to have a squeaky clean mouth. Work [typesetting] is work & not too dull or too exciting.

Received a letter from Aarne & a copy of *B&M* with copious notes about passages to be reinserted.* It was good to have someone taking my work seriously. Am off to Vermont on the 16th for 2 weeks to finish off this stage of the play & to complete draft one of *China Wars* as the new play is called (now). Will have readings of *B&M* & what I have of *CW* before I go up.

17 September 1984

Dorset, Vermont.

1 October 1984

NYC Depression.

5 October 1984

Do have several things lined up at ND – a reading this week of *Squirrel*, then the *B&M* – the following week a reading of the first draft of *China Wars* if I

---

* **Aarne Neeme**, German-born Estonian-Australian theatre and television director involved in several Australian productions of New Zealand plays.

can get it all down & after that *Cop Shop*. Have to keep busy. Have applied for a Guggenheim & will next week apply for the NY State Fellowship. Financially am nearly out of my hole, owe a couple more thousand (3) but hope to have all that gone before the end of next year. Jay has painted living/bed/hallway, Martin Zimmerman is doing the bathroom with faux marble walls & clouds on the ceiling! Have found a glass-panelled door for the living room & hope to have that installed soon & then will tackle the kitchen myself. Still going to the gym & hope that is making some difference to the outline of my body. Next week will find out if I get a free tkt to Sydney but kind of doubt it – & in a way don't mind – stay here, write & make some money.

When applying for the Guggenheim I outlined 2 projects, one *Christmas Play*, the NZ epic which slightly daunts me but I think I know what I want to achieve – a NZ *Ah Wilderness*, the other *Café Society* which I think will become a play about Jack & as such should be funny & tragic. Denis Blundell died last week. Heard from Pam who is in LA. Write to June. Sad, an era is ending.

12 October 1984

Friday, actually about 4am, Saturday, of an action-packed & rather thrilling week. Wednesday had a reading of *Squirrel* which was most helpful. Act One worked very well & just needs some pruning. Act Two, after about 10 minutes (page 12), took a nosedive & while sporadically amusing was obviously not working according to plan. Socialised somewhat Wednesday night – a video club. Thursday the dentist beginning to work on root canal. Friday – today – a reading of *Bert & Maisy* to hear rewrites. Basically loved them but need some fluffing. The style is so important – it is a comedy of manners – it works on a real level but not if played on that level. Each beat must be played for the reality of that beat – myopic absorption in detail.

For *Squirrel* David Roche, I thought, made a very appealing Bart – Tillinger doesn't see it quite that way.* Glenne Headly was a delight as Jane, not spot on but daffy & appealing.† John Glover perfect as Terry & Stockard

---

* **David Roche**, American actor.

† **Glenne Headly** (1955–2017), American theatre, television and film actress.

Channing revealed the weaknesses of Julie – and it takes a good actress to do that.* Tom Cashin, Joyce Reehling, Nicky Martin were delicious. *B&M*, Nicholas Saunders was a charming befuddled Bert.† Saylor Cresswell excellent Grant.‡ Victoria Boothby & Nick repeated from last time & Jeanne Cullen was interesting as Shona & grew during the reading.§

24 October 1984

As usual no news which is not good news. No free ticket to Australia. No producer &/or production for *Squirrel*. Am working on *B&M* & on *China Wars* – want Ianthe to have had a lesbian affair with Hal's former wife.

30 October 1984

Jay was here for weeks. Now the apartment looks clean but unfinished. Bathroom walls & ceiling are done but I need to do the finishing touches & need more linen etc. Have a feeling that I'll come to the end of this year & have earned some $30 thou & have nothing to show for it. Of course many bills have been paid off, but … if I have to keep working (please, God, no) then this time next year I should be better off & probably insane.

3 November 1984

Having not had a drink or cigarette or tense moment in several days, having finished work early last night & gone to bed at a normal hour, having walked Rebecca long & hard, having vacuumed, tidied & rearranged, I feel quite content with myself. With Martin out & the place to myself for two weeks & with none of my friends calling me. Then I can deal with life. Am sure I

---

* **Stockard Channing**, American theatre, television and film actress, best known for her role as Rizzo in *Grease* (1978).
† **Nicholas Saunders** (1914–2006), American theatre, television and film actor.
‡ **Saylor Cresswell** (1939–2000), American stage and screen actor.
§ **Victoria Boothby** (1930–2009), American theatre, television and film actress. **Jeanne Cullen**, American actress.

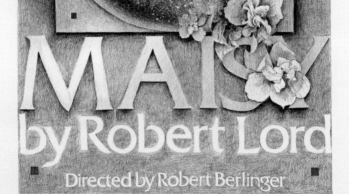

Cassius Carter Centre Stage
Nov. 30 – Jan. 12

BERT &
MAISY
by Robert Lord

Directed by Robert Berlinger

RUSSEL REDMOND

OLD GLOBE THEATRE
SIMON EDISON CENTRE FOR THE PERFORMING ARTS
© 1985 R. REDMOND

THIS POSTER WAS MADE POSSIBLE BY A GENEROUS GRANT FROM Gibraltar MoneyCenter, Inc.
Member Gibraltar Financial Group™

will end up a miserable recluse (wreck/loose) but on my own head. Martin had his marbleizing photographed today, he hopes it will result in other jobs. Have decided for the present to concentrate on *China Wars* & fiddle with *Cop Shop* on the side. Feel *Bert & Maisy* is now down & the *Squirrel* is in such a state of flux it needs intensive care which I can't offer. *Cop Shop* is structured, except for final beat, as I want it to be & it just needs to be trimmed right down. *China Wars* wants to have this 'nice' suburban couple haunted & charmed by insidious mass murderers.

15 November 1984

Have rewritten Act One of *Cop Shop* – last 26 pages – threw out Mrs Hawkins & replaced her with Hortensia Herrick, novelist & thespian. Am proceeding with Act Two & with creating Wally/Adam Lynette/Hortensia as roles for 2 as opposed to four actors. Have a reading Tuesday so a busy weekend ahead. Over Thanksgiving Weekend I intend/hope to complete a first draft of *China Wars* which I will then submit to the O'Neill. December must be given over to a new draft of *Squirrel*. This is the chosen life & I am happy. Seem to be on track with everything but *Squirrel* – do want to commence *Café Society* in January & get that rolling. *Bert & Maisy*, which I think I've exhausted, goes into rehearsal in Sydney today. It hardly seems likely I'll get there as I've no money & none in the offing. Feel that if I was there then some publicity would result & that my non-appearance looks like a cop-out. Also feel that my presence might jinx the project & third feeling is that after 2 successes the critics might want to sharpen teeth on yours truly. Am reconciled to not going. Spoke to parents tonight & they seem okay.

My reclusion basically continues. I enjoy it. Am impressed with the regularity with which I am now going to the gym. Strange but feel that now I am old & there is no hope of my ever being gloriously gorgeous then I can work at my body for real reasons – like I enjoy it – & not as a means to a sexual end which I could never sustain belief in.

20 November 1984

Had a reading of the revamped *Well Hung/Cop Shop* today & liked it – have not quite got to the end but the reading was excellent in determining what works & what does not. Most of Act One is fine though I think we can get rid of a couple more pages. Having heard the characters I think I can do some refining.

Today during the reading I had that hideous paranoia sensation that everyone was indulging me & that my play was dreadful! Fuck. What a bore. I overcome a desire to flee. It's hardly surprising I'm this crazy when one examines my lack of success.

21 November 1984

A pleasant day. Was exhausted last night after work on *CS* so slept late & then puttered about, picking up repaired TV, shopping etc & finally cleaning the house & doing laundry. Did not get to the gym which is frustrating. A pleasantly busy night at work.

Was gratified to get phone calls from Joyce Reehling & John Glover, full of enthusiasm for my work, which went some way to allaying the paranoia of yesterday. Joyce is compiling a list of producers she knows & is anxious to do another reading of *Squirrel* to get support/backing. She, John & Fritz evidently talked about me (or my work) after the reading & agreed something must be done.* John is anxious (anxious is the wrong word) – he thinks *CS* is very funny & there is a market for it.

29 November 1984

The month rolls to a close & we have no plans for an antipodean excursion. Have completed a draft of *Cop Shop* & have lost enthusiasm for it. Controlling the conclusion is, I fear, beyond me. So much needs to be quickly resolved. Not easy. Also I find difficulty in maintaining the brio of the dialogue. Must enliven all this. Oh my dizzy & dismal career – but there is nothing worse than a farce that runs out of steam before it should – the soufflé should have risen to its peak just as the lights go to black. Not every question needs an answer.

My financial woes – today cashed paycheck & shopped & paid bills – have $28 to last the week. Still owe $2700 – credit cards & Dramatists Guild. The

---

*   **Fritz Weaver** (1926–2016), American stage, film and television actor.

next 2 paychecks will go for rent. The third in line should cover phone/gas/ xeroxing, the fourth part payment of bills & then 2 more for rent. Should I get a second job? I seriously think I must either opt out of theatre & try to live or – ? I don't know. A letter from NZ – trouble remains rampant in Te Puke. All very sad. What can I do? Return & become a hausfrau?

30 November 1984

Am deeply frustrated right now – what else is new? Odd to realize I will never have a love/sex life. Work is peculiar, very mixed emotions & strange things happening there. Wish I could leave.

3 December 1984

A day of decision is almost upon me. Tomorrow morning, actually in an hour or 2, Aarne will call with news of a passage to Sydney. There are several misgivings – if I go I will be out of pocket – may have to pay my own roundtrip to LA (minimum $400), then there is rent here & bills & missing 2 or 3 weeks work. If I leave Friday 2 weeks would take me to Christmas weekend – if I get back to commence work Friday 21 I would get paid for the following Monday & Tuesday which are days off work, but naturally I would like to get to NZ to see family for Christmas! Oh dear. I could leave Christmas Day NZ and get back here for work on 12/26. What should one do? The trip would set me back about $1000 if not more. Further, I run the risk of missing Craig Ashley in both hemispheres. Of course work could refuse me time off, then I would have to quit. Shit, if I don't go then I will miss out on the opportunity of seeing the play in rehearsal & perhaps correcting some errors – talked to Grant Tilly & he indicates the Aussies are rather heavy-handed & I want to ensure the lightness of touch is found.* Further, some publicity might result from my presence. Also, I think I might need a jolt, a total break from the work/writing pattern of the past 18 months. Found out today I did not get an NEA grant, which is a pity, but had no reaction of disappointment at all – guess I am inured now.

---

* **Grant Tilly** (1937–2012), New Zealand actor, set designer, teacher and artist; helped establish Wellington's Circa Theatre in 1976 and appeared in many of Roger Hall's and RL's plays.

Alex Ely in his New York studio, 1985. Alex took the photographs shown on page 201.

MS-1907/001/003, Hocken Collections

'Martin Zimmerman, faux artiste, at leisure', Robert's apartment, 1985.

MS-1907/11/001, Hocken Collections

5 December 1984

Well it seems that I'm off to Sydney Friday but through a catch-22 of ticketing will not visit NZ. Most odd.

25 March 1985

There is no way this diary can provide a cohesive narrative of the past four months. The prospect of flashback covering the past is too daunting. We shall just begin again. And fortunately today I am feeling quite well & the sky is blue & it is all somewhat springlike. If only I can get over my current malaise & confront the typewriter but depression keeps intervening. I find the rigors of the job too much & it takes all weekend to start feeling normal again – as a consequence it is only for a few hours every Monday that I feel up to scratch & ready to write. What a bitch. Have completed a reworking of *Cop Shop* & have formulated a new final scene for *B&M*.

26 March 1985

Drove to Princeton last night for a reading of a play by Jan Paetow, arrived late, could not get in, drove home.* Very boring indeed. Missed work. Took in last hour of the Oscars. Very boring indeed. Life.

2 April 1985

Not too much has happened. Am working & bored with it. Need to sleep for a week & get my head cleared. Must make some sort of effort re *China Wars* – need the energy. I have to place, locate, fix, the play in some mythical America. This must be clear. The play is about dead dreams/the pursuit of individuality as opposed to the common good – which is the ultimate American anarchy.

15 May 1985

Dorset, where it is perfect. Glorious weather & after arriving Monday afternoon I am now relaxed & ready to start work. Wish I could stay here. Really love it here – quite perfect. Probably the most beautiful valley I know of. Went for a long cycle today – about 20 miles & got lots of sun. Am very worried about the *Squirrel*, I just can't seem to get into it. Managed to read it

---

*   **Jan Paetow**, a playwright friend of RL's who lived in Bogota, NJ.

Part of a proof sheet from a New York studio shoot, 1985. Photographs by Alex Ely.
MS-1907/006/007, Hocken Collections

today. Find sections amusing but some lags, especially in Act Two. If I do the restructuring suggested I'm not too sure if I can end up with a whole play. The trouble is getting into the skin of the play again.

27 June 1985
Life goes on. Completed a rewrite of *Squirrel* & we had a reading for the producers, who turned out to be rude, insensitive yobs, which is par for the course – & I continue to doubt if they will get the play on, though of course they insist they will. Did a good job on the play – am not sure how but deadlines put life into one.

Work bores me but I am going to learn to type properly courtesy of the company. Am approaching the end of my dental programme – another $900 & 6 caps & we're done. Thank God I get some back. Had Mike Nic & Mike Houstoun to stay & enjoyed that. Ross Jolly visited.

Am I lonely? I don't think I have time to be. But why the question? Life has an aura of sadness. Which I think is not uncommon. Went to a shrink. Very interesting. There are distinct problems & I acknowledged these –

family being one I have of late, through guilt no doubt, denied. May continue to go to shrink if it can be worked out. Just feel that though working all the time I am not at 100% of what I should be. I am unacknowledged & therefore incomplete. Can I make *Bert & Maisy* more touching without being sentimental?

Between now and July 15 rework *Squirrel* – do bulk of this by July 7 – have Joey set up a reading in week after 7th for me. Then go over *Bert & Maisy* – very important – get any rewrites, opening up, etc done before end of July. Complete *China Wars* during August.

28 June 1985

Strange, or not strange. Have been living in the past a lot today. Remembrances of Granny Lord, Rose, Papa Bert, Granny Cooke & others. Saw Alan Carlsen – a blast from the past also.* And reading scripts for New Dramatists. How dreadful most plays are – & how they sit on the page. Want to reread *Bert & Maisy* & will do this weekend. Open the wellspring of compassion. Whoops. Who said that? Structurally it is difficult. Scene One must leap out from a vacuum & create relationships from the iceberg. Opening Scene Two must show the iceberg beneath the water. Want to get well into *Squirrel* Act Two.

17/18 July 1985

My birthday. Who knew I'd survive so long & so strangely. Seem to have successfully eliminated close friendships. Warwick Williams died last week. Dad has been in hospital & Mum suffering with flu.

The *Squirrel* producers evidently hate the rewrites so much they fired my director. I meet with them again tomorrow to announce I want out of the marriage. Hope it doesn't cost too much. Am most exceedingly irritated – Gil has other producers on a list but I fear we are going from bad to worse & my dreams of a theatre career fade fade fade. It's all too weird.

---

*   **Alan Carlsen**, US actor, director and theatre academic.

Am going to Betty Owen school & learning to type correctly. Go with Glenn from work & it is all rather odd & amusing & I am not good at it at all. What a curse. But I will triumph at the keys if not the stage.

22 July 1985

Jack [Hofsiss] dove into a pool at Fire Island & broke his neck. Gary L & Brian J, who were with him, managed to get him out & restrain him during a seizure & then panicked. Jim Rosen arrived at that moment & administered mouth-to-mouth & revived Jack. Eventually he was taken off the island to a hospital where he is now in traction – it is hard to know if he will fully recover. Reports vary & the same stories keep returning in slightly differing forms. It seems quite possible he will suffer some permanent paralysis below the waist. The worst aspect is the way in which some of those behaved around him – though I expect panic, reaction, shock & fear have a lot to do with it. It will be some time before anyone knows what is happening. It is all rather depressing but makes my miseries of age seem minor. Am still confused about *Squirrel* & need a breakthrough.

9 August 1985

Feel uncommonly good this early a.m. – just in from work which I enjoyed for the first time in months. I actually seem to be doing something challenging – or at least worth thinking about there. Think this change of mood must be due to having a minor breakthrough with *Roger [The Travelling Squirrel]*. I begin to see it now – & more important – have the end in sight. I must devote my energy to the plays & get out for a while. Interest is shown at Geva, Rochester, NY in *Country Cops* – would dearly love to have another production this coming season.* Apply for NY Arts Council grant!

• • •

---

*   Geva Theatre Center, Rochester, NY, founded in 1972 and the most-attended regional theatre in New York State.

There are no diary entries for the period between August 1985 and April 1987. Aarne Neeme directed *Bert and Maisy* as part of the 1984 *Oz Duz NZ* season of New Zealand plays at Sydney's Stables Theatre. Robert went to Sydney for the last week of rehearsals. The play was subsequently directed by Robert Berlinger at the Old Globe Theatre in San Diego, California, in 1985, and staged at Wellington's Circa Theatre in 1986. A proposed radio series titled *Bert's World* was never produced, but a television series was filmed in 1987 and screened the following year. Robert was awarded the University of Otago's Robert Burns Fellowship for 1987 and made plans for a year of writing in Dunedin. *The Travelling Squirrel* was performed in the winter of 1987 at Long Wharf Theatre in New Haven, Connecticut, directed by John (Joey) Tillinger, and Robert attended rehearsals before he left for New Zealand.

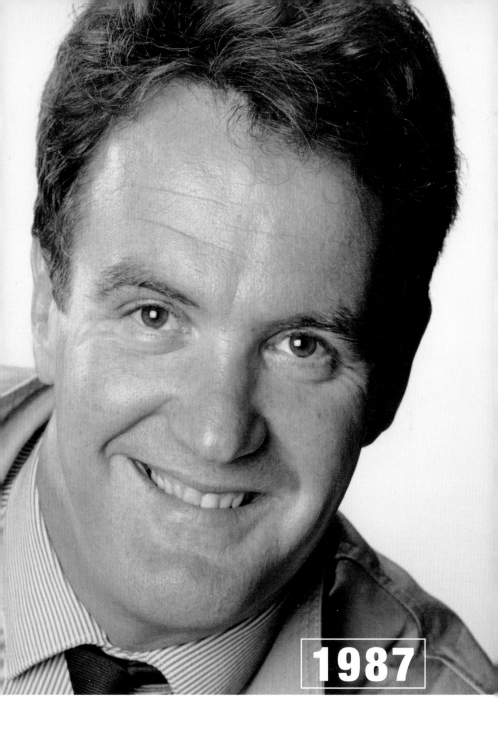
1987

Robert's publicity photo for the Burns Fellowship, 1987. Photograph by Reg Graham.

MS-1907/006/001, Hocken Collections

16 April 1987

The day before Good Friday. Restless feeling on campus all day which has very little to do, I think, with Christian worship. More liberation, for a day or two, from the routine. This is the end of my sixth week in Dunedin as the Burns Fellow. Have been thinking off and on of writing a diary about the life and Roger Hall today suggested it.* And it is something that should be done. Over the next few days I will go over my appointment diary and work out what has happened. The major events, apart from arriving and acquiring quite quickly a bike, a video machine, a cassette player and a king-size bed with duvet, have been the completion of a new radio play (*The Body in the Bathtub*), the first draft of two episodes of *Peppermint Twist* [a New Zealand version of *Happy Days*, set in the 1960s] and the first episode of a half-hour radio comedy series based on *Bert and Maisy*. Have also had several radio, television, newspaper interviews and leapt into the thick of new friendships. And have managed to key *China Wars* into the new computer in preparation for revision, have also gone through *High as a Kite* and cut two-thirds out of it looking for the heart and am going to use it as the starting point for a new play (*The Affair*) which I might direct at the Globe.

As much as I have been busy writing I have also had several professional frustrations. *China Wars*, which should by now be a week away from opening at Circa, has been postponed till October, which really irritates me as they have been planning to do it for ages and should have been better organized. Additionally, *Bert and Maisy*, scheduled for production here in July, has now been postponed till November at the Fortune. Don't understand this. Campbell Thomas has been very busy since I arrived with both *Objection Overruled* and *Billy Bishop* in rehearsal so it wasn't till last week that we actually met in a relaxed situation (his house for dinner) but the meal did not give rise to any conversation about the play and this week I rang to see if there was any news about director, cast etc and was surprised to learn the new dates.† Am saddened by this as November is not the academic year,

---

*   After his Burns Fellow year in 1977, Hall taught playwriting at the University of Otago until the mid-1990s, when he moved to Auckland.

†   **John Campbell Thomas** (1935–2019), theatre director, designer and artist. Artistic director at Dunedin's Fortune Theatre 1985–99.

students will be gone, my tenure will be almost over and any excitement surrounding a professional production of one of my plays in Dunedin will have gone. The Film Commission has finally and pretty thoroughly given the thumbs down to the movie of *Bert and Maisy*, which frustrates me also.

Ah, but I have Jane Waddell staying at the moment and as she said yesterday the world can't revolve round me.* Fuck it, why not?, I sometimes wonder.

Dunedin definitely belongs to a different time and has an aura of simplicity and naïveté which is charming and appealing. The long main street looks for the most part as it must have done for the past forty years. The hills surrounding the town are, now, tingeing yellow, red and copper. Mount Cargill, which rises above the end of George Street, excites me every time I look at it. Sometimes clouds pour over the top like slow-moving surf. The climate is sensational in its variety. What the day will be from one moment to the next is anyone's guess.

And there are people from the past to delight in. Jane Nimmo (née Macmillan), who has a husband and three children and is an amazing ball of energy.† Claire Matthewson (née Watson), now divorced but with three children and about to marry again.‡ And new friends: Karen Best and her husband, David, the vicar (and their four children).§ Michael Wooliscroft, university librarian.¶ Marc Metzger, young playwright.** More details on these later.

---

* **Jane Waddell**, New Zealand actress. She was then married to Mike Knudsen, and is referred to by RL using both names.

† **Jane Nimmo** was a family friend of RL's from Invercargill days and worked as a nurse at Dunedin Hospital.

‡ **Claire Matthewson** was a school friend of RL's from Invercargill days. She worked in academic administration both at the University of Otago and internationally, and is a trustee on the Robert Lord Writers Cottage Trust.

§ **Karen Best** (now Karen Elliot), actor and later director at the Fortune Theatre. Her then husband David Best was vicar of All Saints Church in Dunedin 1983–97.

¶ **Michael Wooliscroft** was Dunedin city librarian 1978–87, and university librarian at Otago 1987–2005.

** **Marc Metzger** is now Michael Metzger.

I am feeling a little homesick for NY, especially for Becky who is having a minor operation next week. Have written to dozens of American friends and no one has replied. But one understands, their lives are busy. I am the one outside. Fortunately I have a good schedule and manage to get to the office between 9 and 9.30 most mornings and stay around till 6ish at night. Roger Hall is next door and the walls seem to be made of rice paper and we do hear most of each other's conversations.

18 April 1987

Today, as with yesterday and probably the day before but I can't remember, the weather has been spectacular. Bright, crisp and the green hills splashed with yellows and reds. I'm conscious of the weather as I am reading Denis McEldowney's book *Full of the Warm South* about his time in Dunedin in the early 60s. He records the weather changes meticulously. Doubly interesting to read, for me, as it covers the period when I was here as a student and he worked in the Phys Ed Dept. where my beloved Raewyn studied – and also he associated with the literati of the period (Brasch and various Burns Fellows – Mason, Shadbolt, Gee were here then; somehow I don't see myself as belonging to the same species).

Jane Knudsen is staying with me, arrived Thursday afternoon and departs this evening. She is four months pregnant and that is rather exciting. Last night Tim Bartlett, who is so good in *Bill Bishop* at Allen Hall (which no one is going to see), came for dinner with Lindsay, the administrator of the Fortune.* Much hilarity, watched viddys (*The Long Good Friday* which I liked and *Purple Rose of Cairo*) and played 500, which I haven't done in 15 years. In the afternoon we strolled through the gardens and observed drunk students shambling through the streets (the most amusing being three Asians singing 'We are the World'). Dunedin really is peculiar and makes me feel melancholic. It seems to be not of this world and it isn't. It's like visiting your grandmother. But I like it and I like being surrounded by the youth and vitality of the students (but one does notice it when they disappear – as for Easter).

---

*   **Tim Bartlett**, New Zealand actor and 1980s *Play School* presenter. **Lindsay Shaw**, business manager at the Fortune Theatre.

This afternoon Jane has Robert Pollock (Fortune actor) and I am here at the office and hoping to do some work. Didn't do any work yesterday which upset me and which means getting back into the rhythm again. Always have trouble with who one writes a diary for, I have trouble not imagining it read by another, which means, I think, I have trouble finding a natural voice for it. If it was just for me I wouldn't have to explain certain things, etc. When I have kept diaries in the past I have never gone back and read them myself.

In the following weeks I met with Lisa Warrington, who runs the Drama Programme at the university. She runs a good programme and seems to have a loyal following of students. Also dined with Claire Matthewson and with Roger Hall and family.

Had two trips to Wellington. The first one stayed with Michael and Jane and saw, among other friends, Donna Akersten and Michael Houstoun and worked with Susan Wilson and Philippa Campbell on *Peppermint Twist*.* Visited Playmarket. The second trip to Wellington I stayed with the Svendsens and the weather was lousy so I rested but did get to Tony Groser's farewell from Broadcasting which was fun.† He is off to Scotland for six months. Had meetings re TV and radio.

Then Melanie Read called from Auckland.‡ She is a producer/director (film) and wanted me to write a screenplay for a 72-minute telefilm to be co-produced by her company with TVNZ. Wanted me to sign an

---

* **Mike Knudsen**, stage and film lighting designer and builder; then husband of Jane Waddell. In 1984 he spent six months living with RL in his New York apartment while working on the *Te Maori* exhibition. Mike and Jane built a basement room at their Brooklyn house for RL to live in when he was working in Wellington. **Philippa ('Pip') Campbell**, actor, stage director and script editor; more recently known as a film and television producer. She and Susan Wilson were both script editors at TVNZ's drama department.

† **Tony Groser** (1922–2002), UK-born New Zealand actor, director and radio drama producer.

‡ **Melanie Read** (since the 1990s, Melanie Rodriga), writer and director, whose *Trial Run* (1984) was the first New Zealand film to be written and directed by a woman. The project discussed here became the 1988 film *Send a Gorilla*.

PROVINCETOWN PLAYHOUSE

PRESENTS

I'LL SCREAM IF I WANT TO

THE WORLD PREMIERE OF A COMEDY BY
ROBERT LORD DIRECTED BY MARSHALL OGLESBY
AUGUST 23 THROUGH SEPTEMBER 4 MONDAY -
FRIDAY AT 8:30 SATURDAY AT 5 AND 9
487 0955

exclusivity contract for three months and gave a list of deadlines and a scene breakdown (3 girls work in a singing telegram company in Wellington – based on experience of one of the girls and with improvised dialogue etc, which I love). Didn't like it. Can't understand how they can be all ready to go on a project and then suddenly realize they have no script. Then discovered it was to be shot in 16mm or maybe 35mm and released theatrically overseas and I should write this for $7,700? Come on. Netty [McDonald] very upset Melanie had approached – felt she was stealing me away. The upshot, nothing happened. But I am angered by this madness when something like *Bert and Maisy* gets kicked in the teeth all the time. Am trying to get some production interest in *Bert and Maisy* down here.

At Roger's Lunchtime Video show saw Alan Bennett's *A Woman of No Importance* and an excellent *South Bank [Show]* documentary on Bennett. Dined one night with Jane Nimmo at the Staff Club – good, and another night with Rowena and Claire at 95 Filleul [restaurant].* Went to a dreadful Stop AIDS meeting, which I thought would be political but turned out to be a consciousness-raising session encouraging people to abandon unsafe sex practices (which is not much trouble in my case). An attractive man, Hamish, drove me home and came in for a drink and I should've, I guess, lunged for him but instead chatted away like a madwoman and all the while felt a butterfly shed its chrysalis and flutter its wings inside my chest and I was reminded of the possibility of love. A reminder I could do without. Kathy O'Shea called from London and was wonderful and I have managed to slip into a routine of daily work.† Here endeth the second entry.

21 April 1987

Easter is just about over, though the university is grabbing its extra day and I am quite discombobulated. The whole festivity has managed to throw my rhythm quite out the window. When I left the office on Saturday

*   **Rowena Cullen**, director and performer at the Globe Theatre, Dunedin; later Emeritus Professor of Communications and Information Management, Victoria University of Wellington.

†   **Kathy O'Shea** (1951–2010), New Zealand-born and London-based film editor, and the daughter of John O'Shea. RL described her as 'one of my dearest friends from Wellington days' (MS-2441/054, p. 42, Hocken Collections).

afternoon went home and met with Jane and Robert Pollock and off to the pub for too many beers, then Karen came round and we watched videos and finally Michael Wooliscroft and a friend from Christchurch dropped in quite late and so Sunday was spent in a state of malaise. Did nothing during the day but rummage round and watch *Splash* and *Zelig* (the latter I thought excellent). That evening to the Bests' for dinner (roast pork) with Wooliscroft, John and Martin, another Christchurch friend of Wooliscroft. Excused myself shortly after dinner and trundled home for a reasonably early night but managed to sleep in again on Monday morning. Monday afternoon went to the beach with Wooliscroft – wandered along wild Andersons Bay (I think) in the shadow of the crematorium. Wonderful getting fresh air.

Thought yesterday for the first time, or so it seemed, of what it is to be a creative artist, if that is what I am. I end up with something tangible. Something which is, for good or ill, mine. I create something. Was thinking about an article for Aline Sandilands for *The Otago Graduate* when this popped into my mind.* Have also been thinking about the rather strange process of writing and resting and just how necessary one is. Today for example, came to work and knocked off 17 pages of *Bert's World* Episode Two and am now back again to do more. Will probably have a draft of it sometime tomorrow. Over the past few days I couldn't bring myself to think about it even. Was it percolating away in the left hemisphere all this while?

After a slow start it has turned out to be quite a productive week and am pleased to have completed first drafts of episodes one and two of *Bert's World*. Mum and Dad arrived last night and seem to have settled in quite well. Dad old but not too bad. Mum has half-a-dozen projects with her as always. Have rented a car for the week they are here. Tonight had Roger and Dianne Hall, Jane and Peter Nimmo, Rowena Cullen, Claire Matthewson, Aline Sandilands and Giora, Jane Waddell and several children round for drinks. It was fun and went over well I thought. Managed to take Mum and Dad up to Signal Hill and out to Port Chalmers as well as into town this

---

*   **Aline Sandilands**, Fortune Theatre administrator and later chair; later worked at TVNZ in Auckland.

afternoon. Picked up framed Marilynn Webb and 'Je suis un kiwi' prints, good. In the a.m. I'm off to Wellington and return on Saturday afternoon. Have had a thousand profound thoughts, none of which I will relate here as I can't remember them. Gilbert rang today to say Becky is okay after her operation. Also Doug Watts is fading fast. I wrote Doug what I hope was an amusing letter and also dealt with other correspondence.

27 April 1987

Had a busy time in Wellington and was pleased with the *Peppermint Twist* meeting. Also visited Radio Drama and dropped the first two episodes of *Bert's World* off to Ron Mikalsen.* Spoke to George Webby, who seemed pleasantly abrasive as is par for the course. Then to Downstage for a drink with Tony Taylor and George Henare† and later to *Hooters, Trumpets and Raspberries* by Dario Fo – a pleasant enough exercise but one which never really sparked, but there was a flutter in the second act. Next morning to Christchurch and I popped into the Square for a quick look around and then on to Dunedin. Michael Wooliscroft was on the same flight (next seat) and he and John drove me home and we had a chat covering everything from the need for a Department of Media Studies at the University to my identity crisis. Actually had an idea for an article for the *Listener* perhaps about my current cultural confusion. Yesterday came to the office for an hour or two and caught up on the mail from the States (which includes a letter from the IRS, who are auditing me again. Shit). Today must start on *Peppermint Twist* revisions. There is just too much to do and I'm getting worried about whatever it is I'm going to do for the Globe.

29 April 1987

Yesterday the two large mail bags arrived from the States. They are sitting now in my office looking rather grubby. The wisdom of bundling the contents was considerable and I now forgive the hour and a half Mum and I spent on the floor of the Planetarium Post Office repacking.

---

*   **Ron Mikalsen**, script editor at Radio New Zealand.
†   **George Henare** (Ngāti Porou, Ngāti Hine), New Zealand stage, television, radio and film actor.

Roger Hall (left) and Robert (with Becky) in Central Park, New York. MS-1907/002/002,
Hocken Collections

In the morning, yesterday, I met with Campbell Thomas over the *Bert and Maisy* scheduling and there appears to be no easy solution. He can move it into the end of October, a bad time with exams etc, or do it during August which is also bad as the students are away. He displayed the year's calendar and suggested that if I could find a slot for it then he'd go along. But there is no slot.

Then I went to lunchtime video and saw *Jewl's Darl*, a NZ film about transvestites, which I quite liked, and had lunch with Michael Wooliscroft after a quick meeting with Roger Hall and Michael about the State Literary Fund. Completed my article 'Who Am I Anyway?' and sent it to the *Listener* and had a meeting with Rowena Cullen about the Globe production. A young man came to see me who wants to be in the Globe play, I asked him what he did, he's been on dole for six years!? Managed to turn some of my mind to *Peppy Twist* in the afternoon and in the evening took Mum and Dad up to Jane Nimmo's for dinner with Jane's mum and aunt. A lot of fun. Have thought of a couple of articles I want to write – one about our national negativity, the other about the Arts Council becoming an anti-arts organization. In attempting to direct the arts it usurps them. When the bureaucrats make artistic policy, artistic policy ceases to exist.

30 April 1987

Yesterday managed to get stuck into *Peppermint* and broke the back of Episode 25. Must not do many more of these as they take too much time. Wish it were my own series. Perhaps one day. Today Mum and Dad depart. I will drive them to the airport and then come back to the office in the hope that I can polish off some of the television.

1 May 1987

Mum and Dad left yesterday and I spent the rest of the day feeling a little frazzled and irritated, think I was a little tired. In the evening saw *Whatever Happened to Baby Jane?* at the Film Festival, first time I have seen anything but the opening of it (which I watched once with Mason Wiley who wanted to show me Bette's daughter).* Great Grand Guignol and the epic scale is wonderful, and also the off-center sense of humour (Victor Buono and his mother). Pity that the Joan Crawford character is not more interesting, too wimpy and I guessed the ending. But great Bette.

Began to wonder as I shaved this a.m. if I have given up on the States from a career point of view. The frustrations of *Squirrel* are almost too much to carry and I am not happy with the attitude over *China Wars* – everyone seems to be hedging their bets and giving themselves an out. Made me a little despondent but I guess I will get over it.

Roger Hall has departed for Britain with wife and kids. I think he is more anxious about international success than I am. He seems to have more faith in his work than I do in mine and gets really upset when it is spurned, rejected or ignored. It has happened so many times to me that I don't even think about it anymore.

---

*   **(Robert) Mason Wiley** (1955–1994), American author who co-wrote *The Official Preppy Handbook* and *Inside Oscar: The Unofficial History of the Academy Awards.* He lived in a studio apartment on the same floor of RL's building. Bette Davis's daughter **BD Merrill** played the part of the neighbour's daughter in *Whatever Happened to Baby Jane?* (1962).

The cast of the February 1987 Long Wharf Theatre production of *The Travelling Squirrel*, a New York-based story about relationships, the entertainment business, ambition and fame. John ('Joey') Tillinger, third from the left, was the director, and Joyce Reehling stands on his left. Nicholas ('Nicky') Martin, second from the right, later became a famous director, and Robert Lord stands next to him. MS-2438/222, Hocken Collections

3 May 1987

Am in the office after lunch at Arana Hall. Hectic few days trying to complete second drafts of *Peppermints* 25 and 26. Finally done and am now xeroxing. Yesterday worked all day, saw a student production of *Alice* based on the André Gregory (excellent)* and watched *Play It Again Sam*, which

---

* **André Gregory**, French-American director, actor and playwright, best known for the 1981 film *My Dinner with André*. His 1970 Manhattan Project Company adaptation of *Alice in Wonderland* was very influential on American theatre.

made me laugh a lot. This a.m. Nimmos came round and borrowed TV and video for the 10 days I'm away. Friday I lunched with Aline Sandilands and Lorraine Isaacs, who is head of TVNZ for Dunedin. Talked about the possibility of doing TV comedy out of Dunedin given the restrictions placed on the station here. Very positive meeting and I am following it up with a meeting with Ruth Harley in Wellington on Monday.* Joyce Reehling called this morning from NYC and announced she is coming to NZ to make a movie in June. Great. She will spend a few days with me after her shooting is over. Am really pleased and it will be a breath of fresh air. Gorgeous day here today. Clear blue skies, but have been inside working – such a relief to have 25 and 26 out of the way.

18 May 1987

On the evening of the 3rd I went to Michael Wooliscroft's for dinner to meet the famous Rodney Kennedy.† It was most amusing. Dinner was caramelized pork which had a black gloss and looked odd but tasted good. Kennedy was intriguing and I hope to meet him again. Obviously a man of taste and discernment and strong opinions. On the 4th I flew to Wellington and had script meetings about episodes 31 and 32 of *Peppermint Twist*. It would be a challenge to try and write one of the episodes as the producers would like them written. Also met with Radio NZ about *Bert and Maisy* and with a couple of minor quibbles they seem happy with the first two episodes. Out in Avalon I met with Ruth Harley re the television version of the same series and she seemed interested but had doubts about the viability of a Dunedin production body. On the 5th I sketched out a scene breakdown of 31 and 32 and rushed them off. On the 6th I met with Mr Little the tax accountant and am now getting that together. That evening Alex Ely arrived from Sydney en route to NYC. It was great to see him, he looked gorgeous (as always), really handsome but a little too thin which, coupled with his upset tummy, caused

---

* **Ruth Harley**, New Zealand theatre, film and television executive. After being theatre and dance officer at the QEII Arts Council, from 1986 she was commissioning editor of projects and television series at TVNZ. Inaugural chief executive of New Zealand On Air, then CEO of New Zealand Film Commission and later of Screen Australia.

† **Rodney Kennedy** (1909–1989), Dunedin artist, art critic and drama tutor.

me to worry about him for a few days. But he seemed to get better and when he left for NYC yesterday he was in good health. The Svendsens, Alex and I flew to Picton next day on the Skyferry and drove to Westport. Before we had done 40 kilometers we had made three stops (one for champagne at Le Brun, one for coffee and one for a drink). Lake Rotoiti was the highlight of the day. Westport, a strange and bedraggled little town with an appalling restaurant with hysterical wine service. We saw the building which was Alan's father's pub.

The next morning drove out to where Alan's grandparents had lived and where his mother is buried before going down the coast to Punakaiki, Greymouth and Franz. Kept bumping into 2 American guys and an English girl whom chance had thrown together and they were doing the quick tour. In Franz we wanted to get the plane to the glaciers but the weather was bad, instead we walked to the foot of the glaciers and picked up a chunk of ice which we stored in the trunk and used to chill the drinks. On the 8th we walked to Lake Matheson (picnic of chardonnay, du Comice pears, Evansdale cheese), then through the Haast, where we stopped to get water from a fall to go with the scotch, and on to Hawea and Wanaka. Great day for visuals and Alex got some wonderful photos. Excellent hotel at Wanaka (Lakeside Resort) where we had adjoining rooms.

The next day we flew to Milford and took the launch out on the Sound and saw dolphins and seals and much else before flying back to Wanaka and driving to Queenstown via Arrowtown (and stopping to fill the car with armfuls of wild thyme). In Queenstown Alan and Val checked into an overpriced hotel and Lex and I stayed with Mike Knudsen (who was there on the Disney film). That night we dined at The Roaring Meg, which was good. The next day we drove up to Glenorchy after checking out the town and returned to have pizza with Michael at The Cow. Later that night Michael ripped the phone out of the wall and threw it across the carpark after an argument with the motelier. What a feisty lad he is! Tuesday was maximum activity day with a trip on the Earnslaw on the lake, a jetboat trip down the Shotover and taking the chairlift to the top of Coronet Peak. All wonderful. Next morning drove to Kingston and took the steam train before driving to Dunedin via Lumsden and Gore.

Thursday I flew to Wellington for difficult stage 2 meetings over episodes 31 and 32 and wish even more fervently that I had never decided to do them. None of my ideas can be made to work within the parameters of the series, or so it seems. My hangover didn't help. Neither did holding the meeting at Avalon. Also met with Ruth Harley, who seems to be positively impressed with the TV idea and we are proceeding. She has grave doubts about the possibility of doing it in Dunedin but has some producer ideas and when I have done a tele version of one script we'll send it off. I am encouraged.

Friday we drove out to Taiaroa Head, which was very pretty. Visited Glenfalloch (a swizz) and Larnach Castle (tacky). That night we had dinner at the Staff Club, where Alan was impressed by the wines, and then Lex and I went to the Captain Cook to watch the drunk youth carry on. A strange and aging experience. We saw one slob pee on the carpet while sitting down. Saturday drove out to Aramoana and across the Blueskin and made a wrong turning. Instead of going to Evansdale and the cheese factory drove back to Dunedin. We visited the Art Gallery then dropped off Lexi before heading back to Evansdale for a look at cheesemaking and a cup of tea. That evening went to the Otago Art Society opening (awful, though the Svendsens bought two pictures), then a beer at the Captain Cook to show Valerie how bizarre it is and home for fish and chips. Alan has got the fire going well and turns the dining room into a laundry with clothes drying everywhere. Sunday out to the airport and the Svendsens leave at 12. Lex and I drive round for an hour or so and he leaves at 3. Lex did a roll of headshots of me out by the airport. They are being developed today. I head back to town, tidy the house, do the laundry, feel lonely, panic because I've got too much work to do, worry about Lex being thin etc etc.

19 May 1987

It has rained steadily since Sunday evening. The laundry on the line is saturated. Yesterday I purchased a drying rack and last night managed to dry off a few things in front of the fire. It was quite fun and the highlight of a hideous day. Managed to get to the office early after a battle with the rental car people, who wouldn't give me a break over the cassette player which I had specifically requested. The manager informed me that while all their cars had cassette players this did not guarantee the cassette players worked.

Then threw myself into the bills and letters and managed to get up to date before turning to *Peppermint Twist*. Oh shit. Why am I doing it? It makes me feel incompetent, useless, etc etc. One of the problems is I really believe they expect way too much for directorial instructions. Everything spelled out. Anyway, went through the copies of episodes 25 and 26 which Pip Campbell and Sue Wilson had edited and obviously have to do third drafts of both. There is an enormous amount they want.

I don't particularly enjoy writing within the safe conventions of the series. In order to be challenged by it I have to try and dredge up something really hard. But last night went through the scripts again and think I have come up with acceptable stuff. Today am determined to get them done and out of the way.

Some of Alex Ely's headshots of Robert, May 1987. MS-2438/224, Hocken Collections

21 May 1987

Thank God I managed to get 25 and 26 of *PT* into the mail yesterday and can, hopefully, forget them. Pip Campbell, my script editor, rang up to see how I was getting on with 31 and 32. I told her I hated them and didn't want to do them, she reminded me I'd signed a contract, told me she thought I was tired (charming, I hate being told I'm tired – though I was hungover at my last meeting with her). Anyway, forced myself to look at the plot outlines for the episodes and seem to have a decent shape worked out for 31 and 32, is beginning to come together so perhaps it won't be too painful. If I can do some more on the outlines today and mail them off tomorrow then TVNZ might leave me alone for a couple of weeks so I can think about *The Affair* and get that properly underway. It has been raining solidly since Alex left, which could perhaps be an omen but is probably just bad weather.

22 May 1987

Am returning the second stereo to Paterson and Barr, which is a slight embarrassment but what the hell, and am buying a carpet sweeper. That vacuum cleaner is a joke. Had a letter from Gilbert today, Becky's paw was broken when someone slammed a taxi door on it. Poor thing. She is in a cast and staying with Gilbert for the duration.

Yesterday found the preliminary work I'd done some years back on the Katherine Mansfield *German Pension* stories and the idea of the play came flooding back and it is good. This morning I picked up the collected KM, several diaries, biographies, etc. Why not throw another log on the fire? As there were actually patches of sun today I rushed home at lunchtime and threw some clothes in the washer and now, as they dangle from the line, the sun has gone, the clouds are greying and it looks like more rain. Fortunately the little patches of sun managed to lift my spirits, which had been down a little – probably in reaction to the sudden letdown after two weeks of busy busy.

23 May 1987

Had an excellent night's sleep last night, which was greatly needed, and this morning did not throw my legs out of bed until 10.30, when Michael Wooliscroft rang to confirm my going there for dinner tonight. Yesterday selected my third stereo and found it to my liking and celebrated today by buying the most peculiar selection of tapes at Nathan's. Ron Goodwin conducting the NZ Symphony Orchestra through such hits as 'Picnic at Rotorua'. And Sinatra, Nat King Cole and Crystal Gayle collections, a pop compilation entitled 'Outrageous Hits' and Prince's new album, which Lexi had been playing and which is excellent. Hard to believe I went downtown thinking I'd buy some opera to listen to. This morning as I fluttered round the house doing laundry, fluffing the carpet with my new carpet sweeper ($45 from Briscoes), I played some Talking Heads and then the Boss [Bruce Springsteen]. Why a grown man of whatever advanced age I am would start crying on a Saturday morning (a beautiful Saturday morning, I might add) while listening to rock is beyond me. Actually it isn't, the Boss is a consummate performer. He has also, concealed beneath his hard rock edge, a heart which is almost sentimental. And he's sexy.

The Affair – I keep getting excited about it and hope I can pull it off. Last night in the Robbie Burns talked to John Dickson who, as always, talks about writing and, as always, sounded very interesting.* I hate talking about writing, I make it sound either very boring or very pretentious. I'd much rather just write. Anyway, John in his ramblings was suddenly talking about S&M in New Zealand writing – or, actually, the lack of it. Well, I mulled this through a bit. John said he thought the plays were coming closer to dealing with this than other forms and mentioned *Well Hung* and *Foreskin's Lament*. I realized then he was talking about the ambivalent violence at the heart of the good keen man, there is a love/hate based on a personal insecurity (which is possibly why, as a nation, we simultaneously accept and reject the USA). All this was of value in thinking about *The Affair* for I think it should end violently. After watching four people sitting at a table and talking, to have one of them stand and slap the other and for her to suddenly spit blood would be très dramatic (especially if followed by a symphonic rendition of 'Now Is The Hour'). But it also reaches the heart of what I think I am trying to say – there is this unresolved violence in this country. The ads in the daily papers: 'Men, is anger hurting your relationships?'

---

* **John Dickson** (1944–2017), New Zealand poet and 1988 Burns Fellow.

24 May 1987

Last night dined at Michael Wooliscroft's at St Leonards. Most pleasant, especially as I was in a good mood, the work on the play going so well. When I got back from dinner I played tapes on the stereo, which I really do like. Next weekend Michael W and I are supposed to be going to Stewart Island, should be interesting.

26 May 1987

Made reservations for the Stewart Island Lodge yesterday and it sounds good, $99 a day for a single room. Flying over from Invercargill on Friday afternoon, returning Monday afternoon. Don't know if I'm looking forward to it or not. It will be good if I can get the first draft of *The Affair* done before I leave and can just relax.

Would like to be able to take *China Wars* to Stewart Island and start working on that. In the next two weeks I am going to have to polish up *Bert and Maisy* for the radio and also to do the *Peppermint Twist*. Seem to be pleased with the direction *The Affair* is taking but go off and on very quickly. Last night ended up liking it.

Stuart Strachan brought over twenty brown cardboard boxes yesterday and into these I will place the bits and pieces of my life.* What a strange feeling. I see them in a line on the floor and they look at once big and little. But it will be a nice feeling to have it all done and put away. Wish I had more stuff published but I don't.

27 May 1987

Did a good day on *The Affair* yesterday, mainly implementing the previous night's notes on the previous day's work, and so it goes at rather a snail-up-a-way speed. Have finished the second movement with Robin and Frank, the couple having the affair, deciding to live together.

Alex called from NYC and I loved chatting with him. I slept in till about 9, which I needed (my brain by yesterday evening was fried). Had a peculiar dream where I was rushed to this beach and walked past this long, long, line

---

*   **Stuart Strachan**, Hocken librarian 1985–2008.

Robert at Milford Sound in 1987 with Val and Alan Svendsen, photographed by Alex Ely.

of peoples of all nationalities, of gibbons, apes and chimpanzees holding hands with natives in loincloths. We then walked past Livingstone and Stanley and other explorers until we finally reached a railway carriage (turn-of-the-century style) where Gilbert was waiting for me. It turned out that I was about to be married and I was wearing white. My husband was wearing a pale grey suit, I don't know his name, and seemed to be an executive in the advertising industry. He had arranged the walk past earlier as he 'wanted me to see everything before I wed'. Gilbert was giving me away. I seem to have had no qualms about the wedding, or about the fact I hardly seemed to know my fiancé. I remember taking some huge (about 1" square) blue cufflinks from a bowl and putting them on. I was then woken by my house being shaken by what sounded like a locomotive – which would hardly have been possible as I'm miles from a train track. It got louder and louder and a flashing light cast shadows in my room and then it faded into the distance. It was either a street cleaner machine or a UFO. I decided not to get out of bed and look, I didn't want to limit the possibilities. Today the *Listener* are coming to take my photo and I hope to break the back of *The Affair*. Last night *Pictures* was on. I recorded it but was wise enough not to watch. Now that I have the tape I can threaten myself with it from time to time.

29 May 1987

Last night Michael's friend John phoned to announce Michael was unwell and the trip to Stewart Island was off. The news came as a relief as well as a frustration. I really want to go but have far too much work to do. Still have not finished *The Affair* and all yesterday afternoon I was telling myself I shouldn't go as I wouldn't get the damn thing done. However, now have the long weekend to break the back of it and I'm pleased about that. Hope it comes together. It is coming together in my mind, though that doesn't mean much. Last night went to a large social function at the Art Gallery associated with a conference on Health Care In Old Age. I had to wander about and speak to people, about what I'm not too sure.

30 May 1987

Managed to get some work done yesterday after dashing off to check out a couple of auctions with Karen Best and to see nothing of value or interest at all. Then went back to the office and advanced the play to page 50. The most difficult thing about the play is the elusive nature of what I am trying to do. I know it when I hit it but I can't work out intellectually how to get there until I arrive. I have to keep plodding on and on on each page till it comes. In the evening I took Karen to the Staff Club for dinner, after which we returned to [my house at] 77 St David Street and watched the movie *Blood Simple*, which is really very clever and awful.*

Claire Matthewson dropped by and she and I are going to dinner with Rowena and Michael Cullen.† Should be interesting. Saw two huge salmon in the Leith yesterday and some smaller ones. Quite impressive. No gossip on the theatre front other than Grant Tilly, Michael Haigh, Alice Fraser are unable to do *B&M* were it to be done in Dunedin.‡

31 May 1987

Last night dined with Michael and Rowena Cullen and Claire Matthewson and Peter Methven.§ Michael Cullen had cooked salmon. Most enjoyable even if the conversation tended to spin circles round me. Lots of political stuff, which was hardly surprising, and talk about elections, possible cabinet roles for Michael and so on. Then a long discussion about cot death and an intense one about [Keri Hulme's novel] *The Bone People*, which Claire and Rowena defended and which, of the men, only Peter had been able to finish. Finally got home about one, which was far too late. Today have a stiff neck for some reason and a slight sniffle. It is hard to believe it is the end of May already. So much to do.

---

* Robert's rented house stood where the university's Centre for Innovation is today.
† **Michael Cullen** (1945–2021), New Zealand politician. Former MP for St Kilda, Dunedin, and Labour deputy prime minister and minister of finance. Lectured in History at the University of Otago 1971–81.
‡ **Michael Haigh** (1935–1993), New Zealand actor and a founding member of Circa Theatre. **Alice Fraser** (1934–2004), New Zealand actor who played Maisy in both stage and television productions.
§ **Peter Methven**, then partner of Claire Matthewson.

1 June 1987

Well, still have not finished *The Affair* and have been very frustrated. Inner feeling that something is not right, something in the direction I am following – and this accompanied by a feeling that I know nothing about writing for the stage, television or anything. Too tedious.

Have decided I am just too fat and must do something. Have been contemplating not drinking for a month, jogging and dieting. It will be interesting to see if I take any of these routes. But something must be done. I should weigh myself. That might be a good start.

5 June 1987

I knew it had been a couple of days since I wrote in this but not so many. Since last writing I have completed casting of *The Affair* (Stephanie Millar, Susan Brady, Nic Farra, Philip Grieve) and have had two rehearsals but still have not finished writing it. I was getting so boxed in about getting it finished I couldn't do it. Now am getting a decent feeling for the end and hope to have it done by Monday. Rehearsals are at home (it is bloody cold these days and at least at home I can have a fire). First rehearsal was simply a read-through and chat, today we went over one page about 10 times. Tuesday night went to a party launching Prof. Jones' book on NZ criticism and Ruth Dallas' *Collected Poems*.* Drank too much white wine, went home and drank more and watched *The Breakfast Club* with Karen (mildly amusing but insidious, the only way the kids can come together is through drugs). Wednesday had a thumping head.

Friday attended Roger's writing class – he returned from London this morning – and talked about the frustrations of my career. I think it was interesting. Joyce Reehling has called a couple of times and will come south for next weekend, I'll whip her up to Queenstown. Wish she had longer here. I'd love her to watch part of my rehearsals. If we have gotten far enough along the way we might do a bit for her later Friday morning.

---

* **Lawrence Jones** (1934–2022), US-born academic in the English Department at the University of Otago.

6 June 1987

A grey day and a restful one. Woke about 9, fell back asleep and got up round 11. Cleaned out fireplaces, set fires, had breakfast, answered boring mail (bills), returned last night's video (*The Paradine Case* – undistinguished Hitchcock) and then to the office. Have just finished (having begun last night in front of the tele) sorting through receipts for my tax return. The sort of activity which always makes me feel very virtuous when I've finished. Kind of complex this time due to overlapping US and NZ tax years and being in both places. Should have done some work on *The Affair* but have procrastinated again. Have promised myself I'll have revamped Episode 32 of *PT* by Monday. Hope I make it.

Yesterday talked to Roger Hall's class about the saga of *Well Hung/Country Cops*. An interesting story. I wouldn't mind doing some sort of biographical work concentrating on different plays. One episode on *Well Hung*, another on *Bert and Maisy* and a third on *The Travelling Squirrel*. Maybe I will. Have started sorting out papers. Came across pieces of a diary which made me cringe. Don't know if I can force myself to read it all.

7 June 1987

Dinner last night at Jenny Uren's house (she is engaged to John Dickson). Very pleasant and a rambling old house on Opoho Road just below Knox College (actually realized where Knox is for the first time). Idle chatter, good food. Slept extremely well after a false start followed by a dream in which I had a heart attack. This morning the beautiful day inspired a load or two of laundry, resulting in flooding the wash house, while in the kitchen I boiled the kettle over and burned the milk I was heating. Life is nothing if not full.

9 June 1987

Thank God I have managed to get some more done on *The Affair* and am pleased with it. Yesterday completed the penultimate scene. Read it this morning and it seems to flow well, though we may have to do some trimming. Have now reached the point where the affair is over and Robin is pregnant. Have now to write the final scene and also need to do some tidying up in the opening scenes. Rehearsals are going quite well. Today had a lunch meeting with Rowena, Janeen and Hugo and they seem to have most things under control.* Watched *Rumble Fish* the other night, what an amazing film. The technique and style are boggling and masterful.

15 June 1987

Every entry this month must start with 'still haven't finished *The Affair*' and this entry is no different. Joyce Reehling arrived Friday and we headed off to Queenstown. A good drive up but weather in Qtown was awful, however the drive back through Lumsden and Gore was great. Reading LM's memoir of Katherine Mansfield (we are now entering the final stages of Katherine's life). Can there be any NZ writer who does not identify with KM? During the lousy weather in Qtown we watched *Sleeping Dogs* on the video. I had never seen it as I'd tried to get John O'Shea to produce it years ago. The film is very disappointing. It is exceptionally well put together and very cinematic but does not satisfy on emotional or intellectual levels. We are not told nearly enough about the revolution, we have to presume the government is bad and the rebels good. We simply don't know what is happening. The emotional line of Sam Neill's estrangement from his wife, affair with Donna, remeeting with his wife who has taken up with Mune, and then Boy's Own heroics and attempts to save a wounded Mune don't make sense either.[†] Pity. But obviously an important movie in its time establishing as it did the careers of Roger Donaldson and Sam Neill (who looked so young!!!)[‡] Tempus fugit. Joyce tells me I must tell the Fortune to fuck themselves over *Bert and Maisy*. She's probably right and I probably won't.

Wish I had Becky here. Miss the little angel. On the way up to Central did stop at St Bathans, a truly quaint little village on a lake formed after gold sluicing which, in former times, was a strange milky blue colour due to some chemical property. In recent years much rain has altered the chemical balance and it is now a muddy milky green, which is a shame. But a pleasure

---

* **Janeen Grieg**, production secretary for *The Affair* at the Globe; also stage-managed the 1988 production of *China Wars*. **Hugo Vlugter**, actor and director at the Globe.

† **Sam Neill**, New Zealand actor. A frequent visitor to the Clifton Terrace flat, he also appeared in Downstage productions in the early 1970s before launching his film career. **Ian Mune**, New Zealand character actor, director and screenwriter.

‡ **Roger Donaldson**, Australian-born New Zealand film director, producer and writer.

to visit the village and have a beer at the pub. Might be a nice place to escape to for a weekend to write but no open fires which is a bore.

16 June 1987

Oddly enough there was an item on the radio this morning about the St Bathans pub, which has evidently recently been purchased by a group of locals – there are only nine houses in the town. Yesterday managed to plough through to an end for *The Affair* but am not really pleased with it and don't know if I can reshape it. But will spend today trying to do so. Keeping the emotional line tight and the focus clear is not easy but should be possible. There is a dusting of snow on Mt Cargill and other hills surrounding Dunedin. I managed to get to work just after nine and want to go right through the last twenty-plus pages of *The Affair* before rehearsal this evening.

18 June 1987

We read the whole play including the end at rehearsal on Tuesday night and it all seemed to make sense, which was a vast relief. Wednesday morning rehearsal started going through the first scene very slowly and ironing out problems. Read ending again and I have made some adjustments. Last night began listening to music and thinking about lighting. Slowly it is all falling into place. Was very pleased with the performances at the Tuesday rehearsal (in the Globe – what a peculiar theatre, so tiny). Have got to start doing some exercise. I am the size of a whale and it is most unattractive. Also seem to have acquired a plethora of grey hairs in recent days. All too humbling really. This morning an article in the *ODT* about Alan Ayckbourn, apparently he writes his plays in a week. Perhaps I should start setting such constraints. Also an article about David Mamet, whose *American Buffalo* opens here on Friday.

21 June 1987

Sunday afternoon at the office. Have been going through the play checking on the script. We finally seem to be getting through it during rehearsals. Yesterday, thank God, we got through the cocktail party scene and I think it will be funny. Hope tomorrow morning to get to the end of the play so we can then start blocking it tightly on the set and throwing in technical things. After rehearsals we watched the final of the World Cup Rugby, which disappointed me a little – not as dramatic a game as France/ Australia last week. The captain of the NZ team was very impressive in success. Friday went to the Regent Theatre 24 Hour Book Sale. Great. Aisles and aisles of books and people browsing. Quite an event and I picked up several volumes of plays. Saw Tim Baigent there and he bought nine volumes of the collected speeches of Lord Cobham.* I'm reading a play by Clemence Dane, which is quite interesting but makes me realize how quickly fashions in theatre change. Watched the Tonys on tele last night and felt a little homesick. Very hard to know how I feel about NY. Do I feel I've failed, haven't quite made it yet? Am I frightened, does the city hold too many memories? I need to come to some sort of acceptance of it before I go back.

Having got the script of *The Affair* tidied up I have turned my mind back to the odious *Twist* and have done another outline for Episode 32. If they find this unacceptable then I will pull out of both 31 and 32.

23 June 1987

Glorious clear days with frosty mornings at the moment, which makes life quite jolly. The afternoon sun floods into the office and is too warm but who can complain? The play is muddling along with Phil out sick and everyone a little on edge realizing it isn't too long before we open. I am sick of being overweight and unattractive and tried to go jogging again last night. Today phoned the Les Mills people and am seeing them on Thursday for an evaluation. Apparently if I go in the afternoons there aren't too many people there. Suits me. Work in morning till 1. Lunch. Cycle to gym. Work in late afternoon till 6ish. Have completed work on Episode One of *Bert's World* and am about to start ripping into Two. Am delaying work on *PT* until I get

---

*   **Tim Baigent**, university student involved in productions at the Globe; sound operator
       for *The Affair* at the Globe, and designed logo and poster for the Allen Hall season.

some reaction from TVNZ, which I expected yesterday. Spoke to Campbell [Thomas] yesterday and he announces he is doing *Bert and Maisy* in September from the 11th to the 25th in the main theatre. I asked him about the casting of Bert and he said rather vaguely he was working on someone really wonderful for that part, which could mean anything at all. Hope to God it is someone I have as much faith in as Campbell does. Have been working on my playwrights' workshop, which I would like to do round the 18, 19, 20 of September. Tony Taylor is agreeable to direct and if Playmarket can come up with the money then all should be well.

30 June 1987

Well, several days since the last entry and much has transpired. I am pleased with the script of *The Affair* but am having a little trouble with the actors, who are not working hard enough. People say I should be tougher, throw a tantrum etc but I don't see the point in such behaviour. We open Friday and I just hope they knuckle down to it. Last night had something of a technical and we seemed to make some progress on that front. Yesterday quite a good interview in the *ODT* with me and on Saturday *South Tonight* filmed me wandering round the theatre. Hope it is an interesting piece. Front man, Alan Brady, is father of Susan in the cast.

On the weekend had dinner with Bests on Saturday and with Wooliscroft on Sunday (plus Shona MacTavish and Louise and David Petherbridge).* Friday night was the gala opening of Roger's *Share Club* at the Mayfair. It was all a bit much but a great success and the play worked well. Unfortunately afterwards Rex Simpson was involved in a car accident and he lies now in a hospital bed with broken bones etc.† Saturday night I was nearly clobbered by a car on George Street by the Regent Dairy – going about 100mph it snapped off a power pole and crashed into a house. I don't think I would have survived had I not leapt out of the way. Saturday also

---

*   **Shona Dunlop MacTavish** (1920–2019), New Zealand dancer, teacher, author and choreographer. **Louise Petherbridge**, New Zealand actor, director and producer, and her son David.

†   **Rex Simpson**, TVNZ Children's Department director and producer. In 1988 he moved to the new channel TV3.

Stephanie Millar (left) and Nic Farra in a 1987 production of *The Affair* at the Globe Theatre in Dunedin, the city that provides the setting for the play. MS-2438/034, Hocken Collections

edited a tape with credits etc for *The Affair*. Have written five pages of notes today for a talk tomorrow morning at the Dunedin Travel Club (at the Savoy) about my life in art. Hope I can pull it together.

Sunday lunched with Roger Hall and others to honour Davina Whitehouse, who later in the afternoon spoke in the Fortune Lecture Series at the Union Hall. An awful hall, an amusing anecdotal speech and not a very good crowd (200). Am busy arranging the workshop and readings of new plays and hope we get some action soon. I quite anticipate that Playmarket will decline to fund it. They have no imagination anymore. Too sad for words.

10 July 1987

Obsessed with guilt that I haven't written in this diary thus far this month but have been extremely busy with *The Affair*, which is now running at the Globe and packing them in and got great reviews. All in all a very positive experience and I'm so glad that I finally directed one of my plays and 'got it right'. Feel now that I can get *Squirrel* right too given half a chance (which might come up as Casey Childs evidently wants to produce it at his theatre in NY). I really do believe there is a way to do my plays in which all those words become palatable to the audience and amusing for them. If you do the play with lots of business etc then I think you undercut it. However ... Have also been very social. Last weekend both Friday and Saturday nights the cast came round and stayed till all hours and again last night. Had my first session at the Les Mills House of Beauty and Pain yesterday and don't feel too bad today. Managed to nearly knock myself out in the shower there! Fool. Today looked at houses. Nice to fantasize. Saw a neat old place up in Roslyn which I loved (65,000). This week I had readings of Casson's, [Marc] Metzger's and Turner's plays at the house and all had good and positive qualities.* Also got the 'go' from Playmarket and with Karen am trying to raise some more money so the workshop can go on longer. It seems to be falling into place. Cannot believe that I actually finished *PT* 31 and 32 this week. Sat at the computer and went hell for leather until they were done. What a relief. Duncan Smith called this afternoon to announce episodes 13 and 14 are two minutes short each and I have to write more stuff for them over the weekend.†

Have just returned to the office after two or three hours wandering round town with Tim Baigent. Such a serious boy but very nice. Met his Dad and younger brother on the street. Tim has pulled out of French and is now devoting himself to photography. Booked a ticket for [Mike] Knudsen for tomorrow night at *Affair*. It is nearly sold out. Yea! On the 23rd I'll fly to Auckland for two days and then back to Wellington. *Affair* may move to Allen Hall next week at late night, which could be good for the kids to make some money.

---

* **Mark A Casson**, New Zealand playwright and television writer. **Brian Turner**, New Zealand poet and author.

† **Duncan Smith**, New Zealand actor and director who was then working in script development at TVNZ.

Mike Knudsen in New York. MS-1907/11/003, Hocken Collections

Spoke to the Dunedin Travel Club last week and that seemed to go well. Was a bit nervous to start but everyone said they liked it and some people came along to the play and now I've been asked by the Toastmistresses Club to speak to them. Next week have to do half an hour on 4ZB. Last week did a stint on 4XO. Quel success.

Doug Watts died yesterday and I feel too depressed to deal with the reality of his departure. [Peter] Buckley will be shattered and I'm sorry I'm not there to help him. It's funny how I don't grasp death. Maybe the distance has something to do with it.

I like Dunedin at the moment. Except for yesterday when the wind was unbelievable the weather this week has been balmy. Such a pretty town. Maybe I will find a nice house here. I think I'll stop this entry, which is too scattered anyway, and wander down to the New World and shop. Fab!

13 July 1987

True to my word I did go to the New World and had a good shop. Also stocked up at the Robbie Burns and generally prepared for the arrival of Knudsen. Such preparation was almost undone by Friday night when, after the play, several of us went to the Robbie and then the Staff Club and then to my house, where people talked for hours.

Mike K arrived Saturday and I popped him off to the theatre that night and afterwards a boozy party at my house till the wee hours. Sunday we slept half the day and then watched videos, which was pleasant. *Howard the Duck* was my favourite. Today I've done very little other than answer mail, help Rowena get the TV monitor from the Globe to the rental company, and go to the Les Mills House of Pain. Consequently it is now only 5.13 and I feel buggered. Too much high living I fear. The cheque for 31 and 32 of *PT* arrived, which was amazingly quick, and also letters generally saying how pleased they are with the drafts. Tomorrow I have to pick up the revised versions of 13 and 14 of *PT* and comment on them. Have not started work on *China Wars*, which is naughty of me I suppose but will tomorrow. Sent off a copy of *Affair* to [Robert] Berlinger [of the Old Globe, San Diego] and one to GP [Gilbert Parker] and one to Sue Wilson. Am now trying to get the play on all over the place. Just called Raymond Hawthorne (not in) and left a message, both he and McColl are going to be in Christchurch this week, it would be good if they could come further south and see my play and Roger's.* Oh, for an active life in the theatre.

Knudsen has gone off to spend the evening with the Rogano people.† I will have a quiet night. I hope. Though with my luck anything could happen. Want to watch video of my serial *The Detective* and mellow out a little. The cast gave me a beautiful crystal and a gorgeous earring and now I have to get my ear pierced!

---

* **Raymond Hawthorne**, New Zealand actor and director. Director of Auckland's Theatre Corporate 1973–81 and Mercury Theatre 1985–92.

† Rogano was a restaurant in Princes Street, Dunedin.

14 July 1987

What quiet evening? Got home and did a mountain of laundry which I couldn't hang out because of the rain. Then prepared a little dinner and was just relaxing in front of the fire and watching *Matlock* when Chris Mangin came round with a six-pack and stayed till after midnight, quite disturbing my intensive telewatching and catching up on *The Detective*.* Karen and Marc Metzger came by about 9.30 and stayed an hour or so. They'd been to a rehearsed reading of *Merchant of Venice* which was apparently one of the worst things either of them had ever seen. This morning I managed to get the laundry on the line and be domestic and then was about to go to TVNZ to pick up *PT* 13 & 14 but it has yet to arrive because the courier man is in a meeting! How bizarre. Last night wrote a long letter to Gilbert suggesting I might stay here longer. It will be interesting to get his response.

16 July 1987

Gilbert rang yesterday telling me of Doug Watts' memorial service, which sounded tragic and moving. I'm not sure how to deal with it all. Feel very grumpy today and nothing seems to be going right, which is probably some sort of reaction. Also reaction to all the highs and carry-ons of last week. *The Affair* starts at Allen Hall tonight. Have spoken to Mike Arthur and there is a chance his company will underwrite a two-night season there [in Invercargill] in a couple of weeks, which would be rather jolly and could make us all a few dollars. Last night watched the GOFTA [Guild of Film and Television Arts] Awards on television and truly disgraceful they were too. Hardly anyone showed up, everything went wrong. John O'Shea did receive a lifetime achievement award, which was the only decent thing. Seem to be in the midst of a great frustration. Am having a hard time working on *China Wars*. Also today received a letter from Pip Campbell about *PT* 31 and 32. I get especially irritated when ideas they suggest are incorporated and then they tell me I can't do them. Am changing my plans and not flying up on Sunday after all. Will wait till Monday night before leaving. This way might be able to get started on *China*. It's too frustrating right now. So much to do!

---

* **Chris Mangin**, general manager of Royal New Zealand Ballet, and later CEO of Creative New Zealand.

20 July 1987

The play fared well at Allen Hall over the weekend and while the actors seemed a little unsettled the audiences seemed happy. Not an easy play for the cast to sustain their concentration in. Plans to take it to Invercargill have gone astray, which is probably just as well. Too much work involved and I, for one, don't have the time. Both Friday and Saturday nights the cast came back to my house and so the weekend was a bit of a waste but a pleasant waste and much celebrating due to my birthday. Tonight I'm off to Wellington, and on Thursday Auckland. Will have meetings about *PT* and then dinner with Mum and Dad. *China Wars* has fared badly of late due to a malfunctioning computer disk and as a result I have gone over the same material three times and keep losing it. Not very pleasant. But seem to have it licked now, though don't want to tempt fate. Have just reapplied for the Burns and it will be interesting to see if I get it and if I accept it.

29 July 1987

Back last night from several days in Wellington and two at home with Mum and Dad. Wellington managed to put me in a snit at first, those script meetings with *Peppermint Twist* always do. However, we battled through and now I just have to remember what I said and do it. Good news from the trip was that Downstage will do *The Affair* from April 15th to May 28th next year.

Also had meetings with John O'Shea re *Te Rua*, a new project being written by Barry Barclay, Wi Kuki Kaa, John and now myself.* Am not sure if it is going to be a hell of a lot of work or not. Probably. Have written to John to ask him to clarify the financial situation so I can see how much money is involved. Seem to have a huge amount of work on my plate right now. Today I have been getting up to date but must, this evening, work on the script of *Cops* for Kip Gould.† I think I need to make a big list of priorities, etc. Radio NZ is buying *Body in the Bathtub*. The first episode of *PT* screened on Sunday and it was pretty dreadful. Hope it gets better.

---

* **Barry Barclay** (Ngāti Apa, 1944–2008), New Zealand filmmaker and writer. **Wi Kuki Kaa** (Ngāti Porou and Ngāti Kahungunu, 1938–2006), New Zealand actor. *Te Rua* (Pacific Films, 1991) was a German/New Zealand co-production.

† **Christopher WD ('Kip') Gould**, founder of Broadway Play Publishing.

6 August 1987

Have just returned from Air New Zealand Air Cargo where I popped the second draft of Episode 32 of *Peppermint* on the night flight to Wellington. This means that after so many months of frustration I am finally rid of it. Of course, having said that, I realize that the phone will go sometime tomorrow and they'll want more changes. God, I hope not. Now I can concentrate on *China Wars* and get that in the mail to USA by Monday or Tuesday I hope and later next week the second draft of *Bathtub* should be dealt with. Saw four films at the Film Festival: *Raising Arizona* (good), *Touch of Evil* (not as good as I remembered), *Death of a Salesman* (wonderful) and *Prick Up Your Ears* (a major disappointment that didn't come to grips with the subject matter – it proposed the biographical quest as looking for an answer but the question was never really posed). Great weather here at the moment. I'm going to a Drama Ball at Allen Hall with Stephanie Millar tonight. Have cancelled my trip to Sydney – I was supposed to go on Saturday but knew if I did I wouldn't get the *China Wars* rewrites done and I just have to make headway on that front. This week I also had meetings with Campbell Thomas and Richard Finn and Margi Mellsop about the season of *Bert and Maisy*, which is my next headache.*

8 August 1987

After writing the above I headed off to Air NZ and popped Episode 32 onto the plane. Of course as it turned out Pip Campbell (my script editor) was up in Auckland on another job and when I rang yesterday afternoon no one was sure if 32 or 31 (sent two days beforehand) had actually turned up. When I got home I found the tape of episodes 7 and 8 had arrived and watched it before Stephanie Millar came round to take me to the Drama Ball at Allen Hall. 7 and 8 are awful! So much worse than I had imagined. What is left of my scripts after the slashings of the script editors is so badly performed that no wit is apparent. It is too sad to contemplate what people will think of me for, as I well know, the writer is so often blamed. But it isn't just the performances, it's the way the episodes have been tackled. You cannot see what you're watching. The sound is dreadful.

---

*   **Richard Finn**, associate director at the Fortune. **Margi Mellsop**, marketing manager at the Fortune.

Anyway, off I went to the Ball. Most of the university thespians were there and, lo and behold, who should turn up but Hamish Blennerhassett. We had a strange little chat which seemed, to me, charged with a certain electricity. Later in the evening we chatted further. I asked him to come home. How uncharacteristically bold of me. Anyway, a few minutes after I got home he arrived and the evening looked dangerously like repeating the pattern of our last encounter when we sat chaste on opposite sides of the room and nothing happened. But on this occasion it wasn't long before we were reclining on the bean bag in front of the fire in a position of relative intimacy. It was so strange. I kept thinking that Hamish couldn't possibly be interested in tired, middle-aged me but the evidence seemed to refute this. He had arrived at the house under his own steam and did not display great signs of disdain when intimacies occurred. Very confusing. He finally left about 6am and I had a few hours' sleep before trotting off to the Staff Club for a meeting with Rowena Cullen and Karen Best re the workshop. All seems well on that front. There was a strange, spring feverish malaise spread upon the campus. The early budding trees, the warmth of the day, and the dwindling numbers of students – they seemed to evaporate before one's eyes, no doubt to soon rematerialize as skiers in Queenstown or beach bums in Fiji. Rowena, Karen and I each had a glass of wine. We wanted more. No one wanted to go home. We were uncharacteristically strong and behaved ourselves. In the afternoon I met Richard Huber and gave him a copy of *Heroes and Butterflies* and talked to him about the Katherine Mansfield project.* Then Karen and I headed for the New World, where I managed to spend $100+ on goodness knows what. After that to Flint, an upmarket menswear shop, where I bought 2 pairs of trousers, two shirts, four pairs of sox and two belts. Then the aforementioned viewing of *PT* and subsequent humiliation followed by trying to watch a damaged tape of *Howard the Duck* which no one else found amusing.

Then Metzger and I headed off to a gay and lesbian dance at the Maori Hill Community Centre. I was dressed in some of my new finery. Unfortunately the new sox were of the thinnish variety and I was petrified a shoe was going to fly off as I boogied and strike a lesbian on the head and

---

*   **Richard Huber**, New Zealand director, actor, teacher and playwright.

Suzanne Bacon and Alex Trousdell in a 1978 performance of *Heroes and Butterflies* at Downstage. Photograph by Stephen McCurdy. MS-2438/090/001, Hocken Collections

thereby cause a riot. That very tall, very young librarian, Dougal, danced with me. He has peroxided his hair. I'm not too sure if it is an improvement. Michele, my instructor from the Les Mills House of Pain, was there, as was Stephen, the greengrocer from Mataura, who is also Marc's sometime lover. A man came up to me and said he'd heard me on the radio and I was brilliant. There were pieces of chicken [young men] on the floor and I didn't stay long. Mum called last night while people were at the house and I don't think I sounded much fun. I will call her again tomorrow. I've heard of a house I want – a three-bedroom place on a four-acre farmlet at Portobello. It sounds perfection. I really must try and see it. This a.m. the paper boy arrived and woke me up as usual (at midday), he was shocked. I then did laundry and tidied the house before trundling over to the office, where I must now throw myself into *China Wars.*

10 August 1987

Frustrated in this morning's attempt to see the farmlet at Portobello. The Bests' family vehicle was trapped inside their garage tighter than a sardine in a can and we didn't have a key to pry back the door. Oh dear. Yesterday wrote a number of letters mainly to the States but also to Kathy O'Shea telling her to think about returning to New Zealand. I also wrote to Casey C, Gilbert and Joyce R about *Squirrel* in NYC next year and came to the office and went through the pile of drafts, winnowing it down to about 10. Last night started reading one labeled First Draft and dated 1982. It has a wonderful opening but seems to run off the tracks. I am now quite looking forward to reading them all and with Karen Best doing the same we might be able to get somewhere and create a decent play.

14 August 1987

Have had a couple of conversations with Ginette [McDonald] over *Peppermint Twist* and have asked for my name to be removed from all the episodes. Don't know what will happen. Last night Phil Grieve and Susan Brady came round for dinner. In the morning I'd gone to Portobello to look at a house for sale but at $150,000 it was out of my league. However, have decided that I do want to live on the Peninsula if I want to live anywhere here and have got a realtor looking up places for me and we are going looking next week. Tonight cocktails at Cathy Fitzgerald's.* Tomorrow, the election. Everyone getting a little worried that National might squeak in. Wouldn't surprise me at all. Oh dear.

I am battling with *China Wars* and have done the first scene of Act Two. It is a slow process. Am also commencing work on *Squirrel* by reading all the drafts. I have just read the first draft and liked the simplicity with which it began. It seems more focussed and genuine than later drafts. But will reserve judgement till I have gone right through the pile. In the first draft I have people walking in and out of scenes they are not in in reality and also commenting, through asides, on scenes. In a sense it is not unlike the technique used in *The Affair*. To me this gives an element of excitement and

---

*   **Catherine Fitzgerald**, New Zealand film producer.

I am wondering if there is a way to return to it in *Squirrel* without confusing everyone. As I recall, the reaction to this style in the first draft was mild uncertainty. If I could find a convention to justify it (as the TV studio in *Affair*) then I would be okay.

17 August 1987

The election is over. Thank goodness. It was truly boring. Spent the evening at the Bests' watching the results and managed to make myself nervous. Then Tim Baigent came round and we watched *Subway* on the video, part of my Christopher Lambert film festival (having taken in *Highlander* and *Greystoke* within the last few days). Friday night I had a meeting with Richard Huber about my idea for a Katherine Mansfield play, which was very positive. Have got him interested in a subject he had hitherto thought boring. Want to set the play in the health spa and somehow encapsulate her life and dilemma within that framework. Then to a party at Cathy Fitzgerald's and finally dumped off the *Squirrel* scripts to Karen. Saturday I was highly domestic and wrote several letters including one to Ethan [Silverman] explaining that I want him as director of *Squirrel* but it is not really within my power to demand. Sunday I continued my domesticity but came to the office in the afternoon for about five hours and did draft three of Episode 32 of *PT* which, this morning, I popped onto a plane. That must be the end of it. Surely. Also went to the Les Mills House of Pain for a workout.

18 August 1987

Last night watched *Cousin Cousine*, a delightful movie and somewhat helpful in terms of thinking about my Christmas play – I love family comedy. This morning talked for an hour at Moreau College to a lunch of not very inspired 6th-form girls, only one of whom had ever been to the Fortune. Then went out to Karitane with a realtor who is originally from NY and who talks all the time in a very NY patterish fashion. Was supposed to be looking at a house, but the brother of the owner was in residence and refused to let us in on the principle that his brother should find him somewhere to live before trying to sell. Did see one other house, quite nice but out of my bracket. I am sure this is the house Peter Johnson wanted to show me. Great. Then back to town and to the gym for a workout. Up to the Fortune, stopping off at Sanitarium to buy a bean sprouter and some of the new upmarket version of Weet-Bix. At Fortune had a chat with Campbell and discovered the tour of *Foreskin* closed in Timaru – so will not rob us of an audience in Invercargill after all. Want to make that trip next week with Karen. Then called Michael Nidd, a lawyer who is on the board of the Fortune. Roger Hall had mentioned my idea of a theatre for Queenstown to him and apparently he is hot for it and has mentioned it to interests in Qtown and there is action. He wants a three-way meeting with Roger and me so we'll do that on Thursday. Must jot down my basic ideas. Still battling with *China* but it becomes clearer. Ginette has found a way to remove my name from *Peppermint Twist*, which is a relief. It pays to jump up and down. Everyone seems happy with 31 and 32 so there we have it. Nearly a year after it all began the *PT* adventure is over.

20 August 1987

Yesterday went to my first rehearsal of *Bert and Maisy* at the Fortune. A low-key read-through. In the evening I ripped all the weeds out of the back garden and then had to go and compere a concert for the Logan Park High School Jazz Band. Was a little nervous to start but warmed to the event, which was laid-back to a ridiculous extent. The programme changed several times during the first half and the whole show ran too long and there was not enough discipline in getting bits on and off.

23 August 1987

For some reason I felt I hadn't written in this for ages but I see it was quite recently. What has happened? I have looked at more houses on the Peninsula and it is very beautiful there – one house at Harwood built on a sandhill was very appealing but way overpriced and not a very practical place. Yesterday tootled round with Jane and Peter Nimmo and found a great place – Wickliffe – overlooking an inlet and quite remote but not even half an hour from the Octagon. Attended a rehearsal of Scene One of *B&M* and as I sat there got very depressed, the casting seemed wrong. Then, after a coffee break, they ran the scene and it really worked very well.

Must remember that the San Diego cast had been rehearsing for over a week before I went out there. At Roger Hall's instigation I got very gung-ho again about touring *Affair* and, again at his suggestion, *Bert and Maisy*. Of course when we investigated the situation we cannot go to Invercargill at the obvious time because of the local Rep's production of Roger's play *The Share Club*. An ironic touch, that. Have been getting into the habit of Les Mills every other day but I think it will be many moons before I appear as the Adonis I imagine lies beneath the adipose. Some of the guys there are too fucking well proportioned for comfort. Oh! Have finally battled my way through Scene Six of *China Wars* and am now about to start attacking Scene Seven. We inch forward.

31 August 1987

Keep getting whispers that I'm not going to get the Burns [for a second time]. So I'm set for that. Right now I just wish I could finish *China Wars*. When I spoke to Jane last night she told me the *China Wars* cast – Grant Tilly, Stuart Devenie, Glenis Levestam, Alice Fraser.* Should be good.

8 September 1987

For some reason I'd imagined that I'd done a couple of entries but apparently not. The major things on my mind are, of course, *Bert and Maisy* opening at the Fortune this Friday and *China Wars*, which is still not finished. Have been having a devil of a time with *Bert and Maisy*. The first read-through was okay but as I attended subsequent rehearsals the production seemed to be going from bad to worse. On the 3rd and 4th I saw run-throughs which were dreadful. No one listening to anyone and the play cracking through at a rate of knots with nothing either amusing or touching. There is also no standard of excellence which frustrates me. No one is forcing everyone to better themselves. It's all too lazy. My playwrights' workshop starts next week.

---

* **Stuart Devenie**, New Zealand actor and director. **Glenis Levestam**, New Zealand actress. She played Maisy's sister in the TVNZ series, and also appeared in the television version of *Joyful and Triumphant*.

13 September 1987

The days since the above entry have been very tense and sick-making. *Bert and Maisy* opened Friday at the Fortune and got an undeserved good review in the *ODT*. The audience also seemed to like it. A few of my more discerning friends said they liked the play and had queries about the production. They certainly should have. What we have is a halfway house production. The theatre is very slap-happy and lax. The earthbound set is splatter decorated – no real reflection of Maisy's taste – a random Kiwi Kitsch look. Costumes show a similar lack of thought. However, it does look as if the play will have a successful season for the theatre and I am in two minds about that. I don't think either the production or the theatre deserve the success. The fact that such a mediocre production is a success to my way of thinking helps perpetuate mediocrity. I can honestly say that if I hadn't stepped in when I did the theatre would have had a disaster on its hands.

Plans for the playwrights' workshop are coming along, though it does seem I told two people it was next week last week meaning the week after next, which caused some confusion. But we shall get there (I hope). The prime agitation on my mind right now is finishing *China Wars* – can't believe it is still dragging on. I have finished Scene Eight about ten times and still feel a bit stymied by it.

Last night went to Helen White's one-woman show *Living with the Man* at the Fortune and was intrigued by it.* Opened with twenty minutes of mime and then a poetry reading. Helen said she loved *B&M*, which means it will get a good notice in the *Sunday Times* next week. Today's *Sunday Times* has a piece by me about the playwrights' workshop and it looks okay.

The major news at present is 3 Titan Street. Perhaps on the afternoon of the above entry I got a call from Diane Stevenson (real estate) and she had

---

*   **Helen White** (now Helen Watson White), New Zealand actress, writer, academic and theatre critic (including for the *Sunday Star Times*).

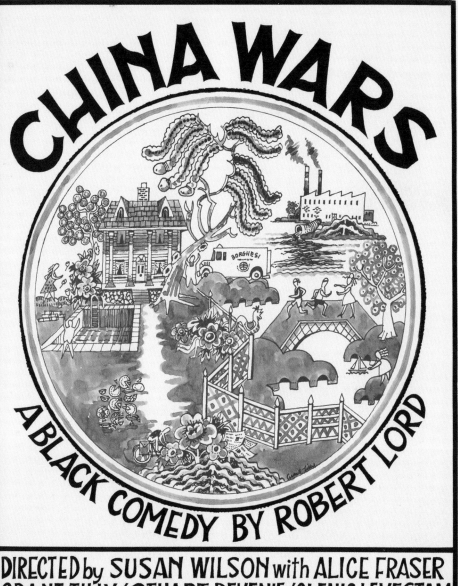

CHINA WARS

A BLACK COMEDY BY ROBERT LORD

DIRECTED by SUSAN WILSON with ALICE FRASER
GRANT TILLY/ STUART DEVENIE/GLENIS LEVESTAM
CIRCA THEATRE From NOV. 7 1987
BOOK : STATE OPERA HOUSE. Ph.850·832

a tenement to show me ($49,500). Karen came along. The house was not all that startling (dozens of people seemed to live in it and it was tiny). On the way home we drove past 3 Titan Street and I said as I looked at the outside 'this is it.' Absolutely tiny. One bedroom. Tiny courtyard out the back. Brick. Old (turn of century). Interior in good shape. Less than 5 minutes' walk from 77 St David and about 7 minutes from my office. While the interior is in good shape the whole place has terrific potential and I have lots of schemes. Asking price $36,000. I made an offer of 32, then 33 and finally 34, which was accepted.

Bruce Aitken got valuer in, who reported back 34,000 (apparently the valuation is usually below the asking price so this is good).* I have 7 days from last Thursday to come up with financing. This morning Mum and Dad phoned to say they will give me 10,000 advance on my inheritance, which should bring the weekly mortgage payments down to a very acceptable level. People seem to think it will rent easily. I want to build a new bedroom where the lean-to out the back is (there is a second lavatory there and also a laundry). With a bedroom out there I could then knock out a wall inside and have a decent open living space. All most exciting and if things go through then I will move in on October 1.

Peppermint Twist is being cancelled, which is good and bad. My last two episodes will never be done. Tonight my second episode is on.

An hour or so later:
Got the word re the Burns for 1988. John Dickson has received the nod, which is great for him as he needs the recognition. Apparently it has been recommended that I get some extra money to stay on for a while but there is no certainty that will happen. This throws me into a quandary as to what I should do. Especially about 3 Titan Street. In the back of my mind I guess I was thinking I would get the Burns and having the money (and residency) for that year would give me a chance to get the house established. Now I am in a complete state of confusion. I must make a decision very soon.

---

* **Bruce Aitken**, RL's lawyer and a Lord family friend from Invercargill days, who later served on the Robert Lord Writers Cottage Trust for many years.

24 September 1987

Very shoddy diary entries this month. God, a lot has been happening and I've ranged from insane to inspired. *Bert and Maisy* continues to play at the Fortune (extended a week). Got a great review in last Sunday's *Sunday Times* which made one wonder about the sanity of the critic. The announcement of next year's Burns has been made (John Dickson), my buying a house is practically a fait accompli and, best of all, I finished *China Wars*. God it was difficult. It was making me feel physically ill. I just knew it wasn't right and it was getting harder and harder to do. Each of the final four scenes was harder to write than the one before. But a great feeling of elation now it is done and we await production, rehearsal and rewriting. Will xerox copies this evening and have them sent round the world tomorrow. Now I must revise *Squirrel* and do something about *Christmas* but first I must fluff up *Bathtub*. Seem resigned to returning to the States in February and will hope we get a few productions and some money.

I feel really good about *China Wars*. Don't know when I've felt this confident about a play. But it is good and silly and interesting and well written. Having survived the work on *Bert and Maisy* one then had to face the playwrights' workshop. I am glad to report it was an unqualified success. All the writers benefitted in various measure and I was very pleased with the way the company meshed together. Tony Taylor was great. We drank too much, had the occasional spat, but otherwise all was well. I feel light-headed now that *China* is off my chest and can't really pay attention to this diary. Perhaps tomorrow after I've done a radio piece at 4XD and talked to a local high school about the play. Ah, busy life.

27 September 1987

Have suddenly gotten a bit weird about 3 Titan Street. It is tiny. Though I don't think I'm mad I have a feeling everyone else will. Don't want Mum to freak out when she arrives and sees I'm living in a rather large dog kennel. To confuse everything Nick Enright is arriving next weekend for a few days so I'll have the 3 of us squashed into the smallest house in the southern hemisphere if not the world. I have started getting my papers all ready to go to the Hocken. So far have got about 16 boxes done and think there will be about 25 all told. It will be a relief to have everything put away and neat and tidy. Now must just consolidate my business matters. Will talk to Bruce Aitken about it. It would seem sensible to have one person in charge of everything – not that there's much to be in charge of. Glorious day here and I am about to go for a cycle, maybe out to Andersons Bay, to see how I get on with such intense masculine activity.

30 September 1987

Plans have changed again for the coming weekend. Mum is not now arriving and Nick is arriving via Christchurch and Mt Cook on Sunday. At least I will be able to move into the house happily on Friday and Saturday and be all cosy when Nick does turn up.

Got over the shock of being rejected by Radio for the *Bert's World* series and now Brian Bell has phoned and is interested in it for television.* Great. He is flying down to meet with me this coming week and discuss what will initially be a 7-part series with perhaps another seven. I will write all the episodes. Called Gilbert about this today and will get him to handle it. Hope it works out and I can make some money. Got a somewhat stupid letter from Radio NZ explaining why they made their decision. Most unsatisfactory. Have begun preliminary work on my new play (Circa) and it would be good to get a draft out of the way before work on the series started in earnest.

9 October 1987

It is becoming clear that I am not a great diarist. The last week or so has been more than usually hectic. Moved into the little house on Titan Street Fri a week ago and am delighted with it. Got everything in (which wasn't hard as I don't have much) and got a lovely kitchen table (scrubbed wood top, cutlery drawer), a chest of drawers, a sofa bed, a wardrobe and a washing machine delivered. Also had locks fixed and chimneys swept. On Sunday, Nick Enright and Hilary Linstead arrived from Sydney via Auckland and Christchurch and we zapped round the Peninsula.† Monday we went up to Queenstown, did a jetboat ride and stayed at Nugget Point, where

---

* **Brian Bell** (1929–2000), journalist, broadcaster and writer.

† **Hilary Linstead** (1938–2022), Australian agent, casting director and film producer.

The real estate sign is still up in the window of the cottage at 3 Titan Street in North Dunedin. MS-1907/008/002, Hocken Collections

we got very drunk. Tuesday drove back to Dunedin and I dropped them off at the airport and on the way back home stopped by Otago Casting and Manufacturing Ltd in Kaikorai Valley and ordered a coal range and a larger (40 gallon as opposed to 25) water heater, which is dual electric and wetback. The current heater is a non-insulated copper one and the water does not get hot and steamy. To buy the heater and the coal range and have them installed will cost a little over a thousand dollars, which isn't too bad. I will then get Jon Waite to put a whole new airing cupboard etc in and will possibly leave space on that side of the room for a fridge.* I will also be getting Jon to redo the kitchen with a new sink, a new window and

---

* **Jon Waite**, actor, set designer and production manager at the Fortune Theatre.

new shelves and I'll have him put some cupboards and shelves in the living room. While there is potential for major renovation and some people (like Karen) think I should be sticking in skylights and knocking down walls, I rather like it as it is and don't want to live in a gorgeously renovated house in the international redone style. My preference is for that which is true to the house and New Zealand. I do think, though, that it will be rather spiffy when done.

Tuesday evening Brian Bell and Steve La Hood arrived in Dunedin and we had dinner and lengthy talks about *Bert's World* as a TV series.* TVNZ wants me to write a seven-part series for the 7.30 time slot. This is great news for it is what I wanted from the word go and to come so close on the heels of radio's rejection is a blessing. I liked La Hood, who will be the producer, and he seems to have a fairly keen appreciation of the show and the characters. David Copeland and Netty will be the directors.† I want Grant and Alice as Bert and Maisy (Steve suggested Michael Haigh – I couldn't see much to gain in that if Grant is available (Grant is short-listed as director of the Drama School)). But there is time before we need to get specific about casting. The schedule is to have the first drafts done by January 25th and the final drafts done by the end of March with a week's rehearsal in late March and shooting starting in early April. This plays havoc with my schedule for returning to America but there isn't much I can do about that at this stage.

Monday it was announced that Roger Hall received the Turnovsky Award ($30,000), which seems to have pissed a few people off. Apparently George Webby had also applied. Oh dear. Roger has certainly done much for NZ theatre. He has, in a way, made NZ theatre in his image. For most NZers good theatre is a R Hall play. This is either good or bad. Rosemary McLeod is in Dunedin at the moment interviewing Roger for *North & South* magazine. Last night Mum arrived and we bought a fridge. Today she is in town shopping for curtains. She likes the house (thank God). I've got Bruce Aitken looking into the bit of land next door – might as well try and buy that too if

---

* **Steve La Hood**, director, producer and documentary maker, and later designer of multimedia museum exhibitions.

† **David Copeland**, actor and director, and later involved in new media and e-learning. He worked on both *Peppermint Twist* and *Bert and Maisy*.

I am going to make money. Had a long talk just now to Jane Waddell, who is delighted about the series and got a little edgy when I reported La Hood thought she was a little old for Shona. I'll just have to write another part for her. What a relief it is to make some money at last!!! This morning there is a letter in the paper saying how awful *Bert and Maisy* was and how snobbish etc. The letter is attacking the critic for an inadequate review. It is hard for me to get angry about the letter as I really agree with it. The play did seem to condescend to the characters, which is why I get so upset. C'est la guerre.

15 October 1987

Have been speaking to Sue Wilson about *China Wars*, apparently the general consensus is that the end is still not right. Now that I've done so much work on scenes 5, 6 and 7 apparently the dynamic does not push through to the end. If I can sit in on a couple of rehearsals then (I hope) it will make sense in my mind and all will be well. In the meantime I am working on *Bert's World* and having fun creating the little town, Gladstone, in which the characters reside. Can't help wondering if 'Gladstone' mightn't be part of the title: *Gladstone's Finest* or some such. Mum is returning to Auckland this afternoon having done the chores she came to do. I think she had a good time and she really does seem to like the house.

23 October 1987

The weekend in Wellington was pleasant. The weather glorious. Clear blue skies and warm – no, hot. At the end of Saturday I suddenly remembered what summer was like. Yes, I thought, I like that feeling. Had a session with Steve La Hood re *Bert's World* and that was amiable and we seem to see eye to eye. Discussed various possibilities etc. Went to two rehearsals of *China Wars* and it seems to be coming along a treat. The problem is still Scene Eight and I am about to redo that today. Strange – in the last writing I got to Scene Eight, started it, it didn't go right and I battled away. It took weeks. I managed to solve the scene eventually by turning a blind eye to the emotional lives I have set up. Now I must get back to the early impulses. Other problems are relatively simple to solve – a beat going on too long, etc. I've redone some of those sections. Of course Stuart Devenie wasn't there so I didn't actually see all the play. One of the problems is everyone on the show is doing 8,000 things. Sue is starring as Aunt Daisy in a TV documentary. Grant is teaching and designing the show as well. Glenys L and Alice F are doing a TV play and Stuart is doing a show in Christchurch.

I was delighted to get back to my little house and it is only just beginning to dawn on me that I'm not really going to have much chance to enjoy it. But the backyard is a suntrap and I bought a sun chaise and beach umbrella and a barbecue (all of which might be asking too much of the Dunedin climate but this week it has been splendid). The new hot water cylinder arrived and this a.m. the plumber came around – he will install the cylinder and attach it to the stove (arriving this week) while I am up in Wellington. The plumber will also install an outdoor shower and move taps in the kitchen. Jon Waite is dropping by on the weekend to see if he can help me with carpentry. The airing cupboard will have to be torn down for the new cylinder. But with that done and a new bench then my tinkering with the house will be over.

Have completed a bible for *Bert's World* with detailed character notes etc and between now and next Friday have to do scene breakdowns for the seven episodes. Shit. Watched *Peppermint Twist* last week (it was a Lord/Copeland episode) and it went well and some of it was funny. It probably had 27 or 28 scenes and a couple of plots but I found the balance between major and minor plots blurred – I was never too sure what I was supposed to be seeing. I must avoid this in *Bert's World* – there has to be a way in which you set up the episode for the viewer and the viewer then puts the pieces together as the show progresses.

A great week for NZ television: *Twist* wasn't bad. *Erebus* was very competent (if incomprehensible to one such as I, who didn't know the background). A short film on Sunday about Stalin in a Catholic school was wonderful. And *Marching Girls* began and it was very good and straightforward and enjoyable. And *Gloss* continues. Not a bad achievement.

Received a call from Gilbert, who feels we will know about *China Wars* in San Diego next week and considers it to be a 50/50 chance – problems being Jack's schedule and Jack's uncertainty as to whether Bob B [Balaban] should do it – I have always thought this might stop the production. But Gil

The dining/living room in the cottage. MS-1907/008/003, Hocken Collections

delighted with my work on the play. Also got a letter from Bob expressing similar sentiments, he seemed to give the play slightly better than 50/50. Hope it happens. It will involve some hectic schedule jumping with TV and all. I worry if I shouldn't be round Wellington for all the shoot of *Bert's World*. We shall see. Also had a letter from Ethan, who had Becky for a few days. Gil arrives here on the 22nd of November.

Last week I received the detailed breakdown of *Te Rua* and I am very much confused by it. It seems like three pictures now with the adventure section tacked on. Not helped by Barry [Barclay] changing styles halfway through, which disorientates one. An underlying anger disturbs me slightly but in a good way. I feel that the commercial direction Barry and John are trying for is wrong. It seems at odds with the film's good moments. The back in NZ material is excellent but tips the balance of the film – it is all about Wi Kuki there. Will have to mull it over.

Otago University Press is going ahead with *Bert and Maisy* and I will be setting the type, which seems to be the most efficient way to make sure it gets done. *Bert and Maisy* and *The Affair* were reviewed in the *Listener* this week and a very nice review it was. However, I feel guilty *B&M* received such a nice notice – that production just doesn't deserve it.

26 October 1987

Labour Day. Have been working consistently on *China Wars* for the past few days. This morning I borrowed the vicar's car and whipped the last ten pages of Scene Seven out to the airport and, this afternoon, they will rehearse them in Wellington. How efficient, if expensive. Was half expecting Mike Arthur to turn up on Friday but he didn't and then caught me off guard by bursting into my office on Saturday evening. We managed to drink too much and to eat well (at Rogano) and on Sunday morning we went out to Wickliffe where we found Alf Birchall's house – great, right on the water. I would love it. Unfortunately Mike drove like a maniac and that coupled with the curving nature of Portobello Road made us both feel a little unwell. Last night I did a lot of thinking about Episode One and did copious notes this morning. I certainly have got into the habit of a working sleep. I seem to, when trying to grapple with a plot or story, wake up every half hour or so with a new shaping of it. I don't take notes and half my night is panicked by the thought I won't remember. But perhaps because of that, I do.

28 October 1987

I wonder how many times in this diary I have announced the completion of *China Wars*? I do seem to have come to the end of it again but this time, deep down, feel that I am really on the right track. That it is there. Thank God. I just had too many details to get through in previous drafts. In this version it is nearly all pared down to essentials and the focus is definitely on Dolly and Ken. It was a great help going up to Wellington last week and seeing those glimpses of rehearsals.

This afternoon the coal range is being delivered. Yesterday had to pick up the painting I'd put a deposit on months ago at Carnegie Gallery – it is huge and quite swamps my little house. Jon Waite has been round to check on my building problems and is able to do it all. Oh dear – will I be able to afford it all? And I still keep thinking about Wickliffe Bay! Quel madness.

November 1987

This is a retrospective entry as it is now December 8th and I suppose some afterthoughts are better than nothing at all. At the end of October the coal range and hot water cylinder were installed at 3 Titan (the bill has just arrived: $700+ for the installation) and I decided to buy an IBM PC from the university. Where is all the money coming from? Then I was up to Wellington for the last week of rehearsals for *China Wars*. The fun and enjoyment I found in rehearsal were lost once we got into the auditorium – this was the fun and enjoyment of the cast discovering the text and they never found a way to relay that enjoyment to the audience. But the cast did love doing the play. We were hampered by problems with publicity – *Bouncers*, the previous Circa production, had had a massive campaign – posters all over town, banners on buildings etc and lots of newspaper stuff. *CW* had practically nothing. I did one radio interview (Access Radio, which no one listens to) and one newspaper one (*Evening Post* – my photo made me look like Robert Morley!) The problem is each production at Circa is a co-op and the publicity depends on the strength of the co-op. In earlier times everyone shared from the pot and that was that; nowadays there is a top-up system so actors get decent salaries and the pressure on the co-op to sell a show is lessened.

My trip up to Wellington for the final rehearsals was highlighted by the loss of my luggage by Air New Zealand – it has still never turned up and I lost much including the delicious coat I bought in NYC and the nice linen trousers I bought about a month ago. Air NZ gave me $100 cash for emergency undies etc and I ended up spending too much money trying to get some clothes together.

I did bits and pieces of work on *CW* and fiddled with the opening. Sadly the play was very under-rehearsed when we opened and did not live up to my vision of it. The audience, though, responded well and we got an excellent review in the *Dominion* and a so-so one in the *Evening Post*. The *Sunday Times* gave it a mealy-mouthed incomprehensible notice and I wrote a letter complaining about it. I am sick of being dumped on. That review spoke of the play in disparaging terms as being 'middle-class comedy', which indicated that the production was not working. Choices, such as Grant's, to play in a conventional farce fashion do work against the play. I must say I am becoming clearer on how I think my plays should be done – but does anyone care?

My second week in Wellington was hectic. I had been staying at the Svendsens' and then moved into Judy Russell's (she was off to Sydney). Mum and Pam came down to see the play and stayed with me. I had five days of meetings with Steve La Hood and Sue Wilson, Pip Campbell (once) and Brian Bell (for ten minutes) about the TV series (now called *Bert and Maisy*). I have a terrible feeling that they are forcing me in the direction of a too-complex series – and what I was originally striving for was something as simple as possible.

At the end of the week I went up to Dannevirke with Mum and Pam and spent the night with the rest of the Lords – during the week I had dined with Jack and Lorelle too. I finally got back to Dunedin on Sunday 15th quite drained and frustrated. Had a week in which to typeset *Bert and Maisy* for OUP, write a monologue for Stephanie Millar for Drama School, update *CW* and to do Episode One of the TV. Managed to get everything done, which was a great relief. Typesetting the play was a good idea as it clued me in to the characters again. Also had dinner with Michael Wooliscroft and friends and went to *Stretchmarks* at the Fortune with Rowena Cullen and Claire Matthewson. This was not a good idea as the play is about broken marriages etc. On the 22nd Gilbert arrived from NY, his luggage had also gone missing but, thank God, turned up the next day. I showed him round

Hanging about outdoors. MS-1907/11/058, Hocken Collections

the Peninsula, including Wickliffe Bay – which I learned earlier that week had been sold to a friend of the estate for $7000, which was enough to make me weep. That night we had a barbecue and Karen came round for a drink, as did Roger Hall, who was off to Britain a few days later for *Love Off the Shelf*. Sadly Gilbert brought no news of great career breakthroughs in the States (a day or two before I had learned that the Old Globe were not going to do *CW*, which had disheartened me, and also a letter from ACT in San Francisco saying they weren't interested either – no wonder I am so depressed).

I drove Gilbert to Queenstown and Nugget Point, which he adored (more than the drive up, which he found bleak). We flew to Milford Sound, did the gondola and also the jet boat. The following day we went through the Haast and up to Hokitika. Gilbert can be very negative, which frustrates. Nothing is ever quite right and he seems to be waiting for the world to do him in the eye. It made it quite hard work trying to keep everything bubbling along.

From Hokitika we crossed Arthur's Pass (shrouded in cloud) and down through the plains to Christchurch, where we stayed at Noah's [Hotel] (and I eavesdropped on Billy Joel talking to his crew). That afternoon we punted down the Avon with Simon Taylor at the helm (Gilbert adored that) and in the evening had dinner with Ianthe, Simon, Tanya and Dominic – Tony being up north.*

The next day (Friday 27th) we drove up the Kaikoura coast and dashed onto the ferry, arriving in Wellington at about 5pm. Pleasant crossing. Picked up another rental and checked into the Michael Fowler Hotel, which is ridiculous – black exterior, monochrome interior, elaborate electronic security except I was given a key which could open any door. That night we went to CW, which was marginally better than I remembered but only marginally. Gilbert was reasonably polite about it. The next day we went out to Pukerua Bay and lunched with Tony Taylor, who was staying at Davina [Whitehouse]'s place.

Sunday 29th we drove to Taupo, stopping for lunch with Mike Nicolaidi and Michael Houstoun (Feilding). Monday we drove to Auckland via Huka, Rotorua, Hamurana, Hamilton. That night Dad was in good form. I agreed to take Mum to Sydney to see the tall ships arrive for the Bicentennial in January.

The best thing about October was the arrival and installation of the coal range and cooking my first meals on it. Great fun if somewhat messy. Love it when the water cylinder bubbles away. Also had a couple of lengthy meetings with John O'Shea and Barry Barclay about *Te Rua*. I really don't like Barry's treatment and find something wrong at the core. When I have problems I am told I'm not seeing things from a Maori POV. I came up with a solution (the lead character being an international Maori opera star) and this was rejected. I have no desire to work on other people's projects.

---

*   **Tony Taylor**'s wife Ianthe, sons Simon and Dominic, and Simon's then wife Tanya Fraser. The family moved to Christchurch after Taylor's time as artistic director at the Fortune Theatre in 1984 and early 1985. Taylor guest-directed several productions at the Court Theatre, as well as working elsewhere in New Zealand.

8 December 1987

Have just updated November and forgot to mention I picked up the new IBM PC in the few days I was in Dunedin and also a couple of books – one on Wordstar and one on MS-DOS systems – and am trying to learn more about the computer world.

On December 1st I drove Gilbert round the city after a meeting with Judy Lessing, who was in town seeing her mother. Then I took him out to the airport and he flew off to Sydney and I to Wellington. That night I went to *CW*, which was an agonizing experience for me – it is now painful to look at, though I try and be chipper when I see the cast. The production has no brio. I had redone the final scene and it was agreed they would try it the next night. I am so enormously frustrated about this play and my career I could scream out loud. I've just had enough and want to throw something through a window.

Spoke to Colin McColl while in Wellington and learned he is not producing *The Affair* in April after all. For no reason I could clearly understand other than he's changed his mind – but he did tell me there are many factors that must be taken into consideration. Obviously my availability isn't one of them. It wouldn't surprise me if he didn't do the play. This has added to my frustrations.

I had an intense lunch with Stuart [Devenie], who wants to direct *China Wars* at the Fortune next year (I think it would be good).

10 December 1987

Have got the new IBM PC system up and running. Spent a couple of hours yesterday over at the Computer Services Centre transferring my NEC disks to IBM ones and am now switched on. Am running out diary etc on the old system and feel very efficient. Have not quite gotten used to the new keyboard, which seems tighter than the NEC, and the cursor keys will take time to master. Oh for my Atari mouse.

Mum called and we are on for our trip to Sydney in January and for Dannevirke for Christmas.

The coal range at 3 Titan Street. MS-1907/008/001,
Hocken Collections

16 December 1987

Have completed Episode Two [of *Bert and Maisy*] and sent it off to
Wellington, thank God. Sue and Steve both seem happy with it. Now have to
write Episode Three, which I am being tardy about starting.

Have got the house business sorted out for next year – have to meet
with Bruce Aitken tomorrow and make him power of attorney etc so it can
all take care of itself. The tenants seem happy. Finally Jon Waite is making
progress on the airing cupboard and tomorrow he'll do the bench in the
kitchen. One day it'll look great.

20 December 1987

A very difficult week. Had a lot of trouble with Episode Three of *B&M*, which
I have just finished. Found I was parodying my writing. Got to about page
20 and had to start again. But every day was a drag and it didn't feel right.

Finally it started coming right on Friday and today (Sunday) it's all done. Had to constantly revise the outline to get the flow right. It is amazing how long it takes to set things up. First half has eight long scenes and the second half 18 short ones. Fly up to Wellington tomorrow for meetings – was meant to be there today but it was getting too tight and making me too nervous. On Tuesday I'll go to Dannevirke and stay there through Christmas – plan to get back here either 26th or 27th: ideally would like to have Episode Four done before New Year – if I can get psyched up on it I'll be fine.

The work progresses on the house. Have been without a kitchen since Wednesday but presume it will come soon. Electricians came on Friday and put in new outlets for the fridge and other kitchen stuff and repaired the stove as well. Can't wait to get the bill for that. The weather has been dreadful but usually becomes fine in the early evening, which is a little late. Managed to get gifts for the tea ladies and the phone ladies and the English Dept. secretary. Had a meeting with Bruce Aitken and gave him Power of Attorney to handle the house and just about everything else in my life. Friday night went to a party and fell into the arms of a young man, which I didn't intend to do but I suppose it was good for me. He is a lawyer and apparently comes from a wealthy family but he won't reveal his last name. Claims to have been seduced at the age of 12 by a man working on his parents' farm and to have continued having an affair with this man for several years, during which the said man managed to get great globs of money from him. Interesting. Heard during the week that Centrepoint will do *Bert and Maisy* in July when I can't be around for it.

28 December 1987

Last Monday morning I flew up to Wellington with Episode Three and had an afternoon meeting with Steve and Sue about it. Their response was very positive and we had some general chatting about the shape of 4 and 5. Bruce Allpress* is not available for Ted Perrett, George Henare is for Tommy Trout. That evening I went to a party at Alan and Val's new Thorndon Quay office and showroom space – a great space and an elegant party with great

---

* **Bruce Allpress** (1930–2020), New Zealand actor.

food and wine but I wasn't in the mood and would rather have been in bed. Tuesday I went out to Avalon again and had a meeting with Sue Wilson in which we talked through episodes four and five and that was helpful. Then I did the last of the Christmas shopping and went up to Waddell-Knudsens' for drinks, which was quite pleasant. Had a chat with Barry Barclay, who seems to understand why I don't want to do *Te Rua*. Neville Carson, somewhat drunk, said he had read and loved *The Affair* and they all seem to want to do it at Circa if Downstage doesn't.*

Wednesday I took the train to Dannevirke, a journey made tedious by the ghetto blaster of the threatening youth behind me and the motoring up and down the aisle of a remote-controlled car. Was met at the station by Mum, Rich and Hilary. All quite pleasant and jolly at the house. Dad looked frail but obviously enjoyed being surrounded by family. Jack and Lorelle arrived on Christmas Eve and Bert came over on Christmas Day. Presents galore. I got a planter and a cast-iron kettle for the house, which I had to lug back down the country (but am pleased to have). The conversation managed to retrace familiar territory to the point it seemed stultifying. Dad talked about the economy and business and banking. Jack Lord uttered several anti-Maori sentiments. Dad said there wouldn't be major trouble – that the decent Maoris would stop it (as soon as they get over this 'thing' about speaking their own language they will be fine). I said as little as possible. Lorelle lamented the shocking state of NZ cricket teams. A lot of ignorant spiders were weaving webs not realizing they were trapping themselves. My brother said the Maori revolution would come in 1991. It was interesting to hear Jack Lord recall an incident 20 or 30 (or maybe even more) years ago in which, apparently, my father thought the name of a racehorse was a Maori word when it was not. This was used as absolute proof that Dad knows nothing about the Maori language. It was implicit in Jack's statement that Dad couldn't have learned a thing over the intervening 20 or 30 years and perhaps Jack believes that. Perhaps he hasn't learned anything in the last 30 years. The more I think about it the more sense that makes. His attitudes certainly haven't changed, they've merely become more deeply

---

*   **Neville Carson**, New Zealand lawyer, actors' agent and film producer, and a member of Circa Council.

entrenched. However, we survived the event. Boxing Day I returned to Wellington leaving Dad not 100%. Flew back to Dunedin yesterday morning. Today I hope to get into Episode Four, which I'd love to have in the mail to Wellington by the end of the week.

29 December 1987

This morning Roger is back at work and it is good to chat about the frustrations of the craft and business as well as catching up on his London gossip and the shows he saw. *Love Off The Shelf* seems to be going well. Last night had a barbecue with the Bests and played cricket on the Selwyn College tennis court, then watched dreadful television and fell asleep. Minor back pain throughout the night. This morning a jar of redcurrant jelly appeared in my letter box courtesy of Jon Waite. Made quite a lot of progress yesterday on Episode Four – a detailed scene breakdown – and a slightly less detailed breakdown of 5. Today I'll start the hard part.

30 December 1987

Quite good progress on Episode Four yesterday – got through the first three scenes, which I looked at last night and revised this morning. This afternoon I hope to get a little further and with luck will have broken the back of the beast by tomorrow night. Yesterday I received royalties from *China Wars* – $1440, which paid off the overdraft. Today I received $902 from Air New Zealand for lost baggage – so now just have to clear off the Visa and Amex accounts, pay the plumber and sundry other bills and I can get out of NZ squeaky clean.

Recipe for salmon: butter greaseproof paper to wrap round and over the fish. Place in a dish lined with paper – grease side up. Knob of butter, pepper, salt. Pour over ¼ cup of vinegar. Seal greaseproof paper. Put in cold oven, heat to 300F. Cook half an hour and turn off. Leave till cold. Don't open till cold.

• • •

1988–1989

On the field. MS-1907/011/077, Hocken Collections

2 January 1988

Much to my relief I completed Episode Four of *Bert and Maisy* on the last day of December 1987. For some reason I had set myself this deadline and, much as I thought, I feel as if I am 'over the hump' and that the next three episodes will be plain sailing. Of course having said that I fully expect to run into major difficulties. Want to get Episode Five done before the holiday weekend ends. Spent New Year's Eve in the office and then went to Karen's to see the year in. New Year's Day was gorgeous and I puttered round the house: managed to tidy out my shed and do laundry – the shed looks as if someone is in control of it again. Then came to work for an hour or so to proof Episode Four and copy it. Had been very high on it the day before but went off it a little during reading but it does have a wonderful feeling and build and the problems I have with it can be dealt with – mainly focussing and trimming the first half. During the evening I had a little barbecue, played with my garden, ripped the shelves out of the kitchen and painted the new under-the-counter shelves in the kitchen as well as all the pale green in the living room and bathroom and the result is delightful – also painted the floor of the airing cupboard and the hearth of the fireplace. The only major painting job now is the kitchen, which I will start tonight. Jon Waite will put up new shelves this week. The plumber is also coming to fix taps and a few minor leaks – I might get him to raise the height of the bathroom sink, which is way too low. I'm going to be sorry to leave the house.

Found myself wondering, yesterday, why I am even thinking of going back to the States. It doesn't seem as if I am going to have a career there. Well shall see. I'm enjoying having Maida (Rowena Cullen's dog) to stay – a Springer Spaniel, she is very intelligent and bright.

11 January 1988

Finished Episode Five and got it up to Wellington by January 6th and have been in a state of relaxation ever since. Steve La Hood returned from vacation and seemed to enjoy 4 and 5 and he and Sue arrive here on Wednesday for a day and a half of meetings. I have suggested that Sue come back later in January, by which time I will have done 6 and 7 and then we can work through the whole series and iron out inconsistencies before we present the first drafts to directors, designers et al. This has meant cancelling the trip to Sydney but I can do that later and Mum seems quite relieved as Dad isn't too well. Kathy O'Shea will come down in the last week of January and we will drive back to Wellington together in my new vehicle – a 1969 Morris Minor 1000 Van which I saw and bought on Friday and which I take possession of today. I just have to go and arrange the insurance etc. Having the van will allow me to travel to and from Avalon while I am living in Wellington without the bother of going to the Courier van. Yeah.

Spoke to Ethan the other day and was delighted to learn that Becky is going to live in Albany with his parents – as a matter of fact she will be there by now. Have also suggested to Ethan that we co-sign the apartment, which will give him a better home in NY. He seems quite gung-ho about that. My vision of the future has been too black and white. Ethan has suggested that I try and spend time evenly in both places and I think he is right. I can go back to the States with a few projects to work on and try to get stuff happening there and pop back here if it doesn't. One must try and keep one's spirits up and the possibilities coming. Don't shut off. Friday I went to dinner at Marc Metzger's flat with Karen, David and Rex Simpson – most pleasant. Then Karen and I chatted far too late. Friday morning I'd done a long TV interview for Cathy Fitzgerald – Rowena did the questions. It will make a 40-minute doco for the archives. Thursday the Hocken came and took away 27 boxes of papers – poor things. Evidently they are inundated at the present with many of the government departments that have been disbanded tossing all their papers in the Hocken's direction. Jon Waite has finally finished off at the house. The place is looking really good with the kitchen shelves appearing most impressive. I bought some fabric on Friday which Karen is making up into curtains to cover over the bottom kitchen cupboard and the window. Have another coat of paint to splash around sundry parts of the house and then all my work is done. Have had some ideas for projects: one, a comedy film about a love affair over ten years as seen against the backdrop of NZ family events. I also thought I could do this as a play but would rather think of it as a screenplay. Then a new play called *Academic Circles* about a visiting lecturer on campus who upsets the ecosystem (and I don't mean acoustics). And I have had some more thoughts about *Boxing Day* – am trying to lighten that idea.

21 January 1988

Perhaps things are moving way too fast. Suddenly January is almost at an end. About a week ago I completed Episode Six and sent it off to Wellington, where everyone seems quite happy with it. Then I had the Creative Writing Summer School to deal with – five days of lectures and workshops. Of course I knew it was going to happen for months but suddenly I seemed to be thrust into it without preparation and not knowing what to expect. The good things were meeting Lauris Edmond again and getting to know her better and also meeting Margaret Mahy, who is a wonderful character and really nice but her sentences go on too long when she speaks.* A minor fault. My public lecture followed that of Prof. Jones (National Identity of NZ Literature), which was really boring and dull, and that of Charles Croot, director of the school, who had lots of diagrams intended to explain the process of writing.† So it was relatively easy for someone as facile as I am to bring smiles to faces.

Strange, I think, how little contact I've had with the writing community in Dunedin since I've been here. Don't know what made me think of that. The workshops were a different kettle of fish. At first I thought I was going to be scuttled by a feisty young female who knew more about anything I mentioned than I did. However, after the first day, things looked up. Lauris and Margaret came round for drinks a couple of times, which was pleasant. The most interesting people were the elderly women writers, whose stories were often cripplingly funny. Prior to the workshop I had discussed my *Academic Circles* idea with Roger Hall and he suggested we do it together, which could have good results for both of us. Now, however, he is having second thoughts. Campbell wants him to do a sequel to *The Share Club*, which he initially rejected but apparently now thinks he can do – with house renovation being the gimmick. I was a bit put out when he told me this today but having thought it through feel much better and am quite glad. It would have been good to have his name to attract audiences but the experience could have been awkward. Possibly that is his thinking too. I think, also, it

---

* **Lauris Edmond** (1924–2000), New Zealand poet and writer who also wrote several plays. **Margaret Mahy** (1936–2012), New Zealand author of children's and young adult books.

† **Charles Croot** (1936–1996), Dunedin teacher, broadcaster and writer. Head of English at Kaikorai Valley High School.

Robert in Dunedin, 1987. MS-2438/223/003, Hocken Collections

will be good if I can leap in and start the play asap. God knows I have enough work to do.

Received a letter from Ray Richards on Monday – apparently Penguin are interested in my idea of a *Bert and Maisy* book.* I love the idea of doing it. I think I should block *Academic Circles* out and start work on it very soon and try to get it ready for a Circa date sometime while I'm in the country. I want to incorporate talking to the audience and fluid setting – juxtapose this with Roger Hall comedy and perhaps a slightly more acerbic ending than he would provide. The weather here has been awful for days with nothing but rain, rain, rain, which has resulted in a leak in my hallway. Jay Funk called yesterday from NYC and is coming out in March so that will be pleasant – he wants me to show him round the country but it will be the fourth trip (Alex, Gil and Kathy – next week) around and I don't know how enthused I am about doing it.

5 February 1988

It is hard to believe that this is the first entry for a month and that it is going to be only a token entry. Obviously things have been busy and the quick picture is that I left Dunedin, drove round the south coast of the South Island, up through Manapouri and Te Anau to Queenstown and on through the Haast, up the West Coast, into Nelson and finally to Picton and Wellington. Olive Oil [the Morris Minor van] behaved very well apart from a broken fuel pump and a puncture. My navigator was Kathy O'Shea, who was great and in good health. In Wellington we spent a couple of days with the senior O'Sheas, during which time I had a good look at Kathy's Raumati home which she is in the process of purchasing – she takes possession at the end of this month and I might well go and stay and write there – Wellington certainly holds no great attraction for me as a place to live. Now I am staying with Michael, Jane and little Richard, which is great fun – the downstairs is half finished (the bedroom is carpeted and painted, my office part is gibbed and needs doing). Most of my time has been working on the TV series. Began with a series of meetings at Avalon with Sue and Steve, which were

---

*   **Ray Richards** (1921–2013), New Zealand literary agent.

highly frustrating and agony to sit through – all the committees' decisions passed on! Then rewrote Episode Seven, which was not at all satisfactory as it was. Following that Sue and I worked through Episode One and I have done a draft of that, which seems to meet with general approval. It took days longer than anticipated and I am meant to be at the end of Episode Four (second draft) by the end of this month but probably won't make it. However, I do feel I'll get to the end of all seven by mid-March, which is the schedule.

During all this we have been casting. Yesterday watched videos of all the auditions and we seemed to settle on several key roles. Wanted to fly up to Auckland and see Mum and Dad last weekend but became too busy. Will try and get up soon. At the end of March Jay arrives for 9 days and I will take time off to drive him around. Also have to write a new scene for *The Affair*, which is being done at Centrepoint (rehearsals start March 15) and I have written to Circa to see if I can direct it there before I go back to the States.

23 April 1988

It's been nearly two months since my last entry and longer since decent entries. *Bert and Maisy* is the reason – five months of writing, rewriting and polishing and now it is in production and I'm unnecessary and relaxing up at Mahurangi with Mum, Dad and Pam. Arrived yesterday after driving up in Olive Oil with Dad. Today lay around reading – an Elmore Leonard, the new book on Mansfield, Belich's book on the NZ Wars, the new Wilde bio and a book on [novelist] B Traven. Haven't had time for a decent read for ages and don't really have now as I should be working on several projects:

A new television series to be produced about next May – have to come up with an outline I can present to Brian Bell next week.

Academic Circles – a new comedy about life in an English Department at a New Zealand university, which I want to finish before going back to the States.

China Wars, which I need to revise for a production by Stuart Devenie at the Globe in June.

A novelized version of the *Bert and Maisy* TV series, which I want to try at least.

A revision of the *Squirrel* play for NY in the fall.

The *Bert and Maisy* set, Circa Theatre, 1986. Photograph by Justine Lord. MS-2438/019/002, Hocken Collections

And there are other ideas too but these are the most pressing.

Must confess to being relatively happy at the moment – I guess I am pleased with my work on the TV series and have enjoyed being busy. Am also enjoying being in NZ and don't think much about returning to the States – though production prospects there do brighten my heart a little – *Country Cops* in Vermont in July. I really don't want to see that play again but hope it works and leads to lots of regional and amateur productions if not to off-Broadway as John Nassivera (producer) wants. So where have I been?

Since arriving in Wellington in early February I spent most of my time at Jane and Michael's with them and baby Richard. Jay arrived just prior to Easter and I rushed him up to Palmerston North to see rehearsals of *The Affair* at Centrepoint and then down to Christchurch and Dunedin. All hurried, but interesting to see the Taylors again – intensity personified – and my Dunedin friends. Claire Matthewson had people round for drinks and we chatted amiably. Back in Wellington I went to the readthrough of the TV series, which I liked, and spent time during the first two weeks checking on the script and a little time watching shooting, which I find boring. Have frustrations galore and guess I will learn from them. The major problem is there isn't enough time to shoot the series properly and so compromises are made all the way through the shooting – this doesn't make sense to me after so much care has gone into the writing. Don't want to moan but I do think I work harder than anyone else involved and that annoys me. Everyone should be working hard. However, the proof will be in the screening. April 16th saw *The Affair* open at Centrepoint and Mum flew down, Rich and Renais came along as did the Svendsens and the O'Sheas. An excellent evening and a good production. So nice for me to feel positive about something, isn't it? The play is very sexy and, I think, rather bleak. Apparently audiences are liking it, which is something. I am directing it in a season opening at Circa on June 9th. After the opening drove Mum to Auckland stopping for a night at the Chateau and then on to Taupo (seeing the Dickies) and Hamilton (the Blakelys). Olive performed well and Mum and I had a good trip. In Auckland haven't seen anyone but have been clearing through papers and sorting out the bits and pieces I left Dunedin with at the end of January. Next weekend I will return to Palmerston North and then on to Wellington to put the cast etc together for the play. Current plans are to return to NY in July.

24 April 1988

The *Sunday Times* came out with a damning review of *The Affair*, which managed to throw me into a depression for an hour or two. I recovered by lying in the sun and then having a nap. The critic begins by commenting how he had praised *Up and Under*, which did poorly with audiences, he then goes on to list the things wrong with my play – including slightness, local references etc. Oh dear. I suppose my upset reaction is due to the review being a surprise – I fully expected a good response and for that probably deserve to be put in my place. Actually as I type this I am feeling better but the thought of wading through years of rejection is too much to contemplate. Now I'm all atwitter about the response to the TV series. Why do I do it? It's all so public. And then there's the 'are they right?' problem, which is always hovering in the background. That which annoys me most is that the critic didn't take the play seriously at all.

30 April 1988

Glorious day. Slight chill, but blue sky and sun. Have just had barbecue lunch with Mum and Dad on the top terrace. Apparently Episode One of *Bert and Maisy* is looking good and everyone seems very pleased with it. Have heard nothing but good comments. Hope they are true. I don't really care, which sounds strange. But feel as if I have done it and now it is gone. But must be positive and enthuse about it to keep spirits up. Last night took Mum and Pam to a NZ Symphony concert with Michael Houstoun playing. Good. Went and had a drink with the two Michaels later on. Tomorrow I leave Auckland and go to Palmerston North, where I see *The Affair*. Monday I'm going to Foxton to meet the Mayor and discuss what he does (background for the tele). Tuesday I have to give a talk at Massey and then head back to Wellington for a Wednesday morning meeting with Jane Vesty for publicity.*

---

* **Jane Vesty**, publicist for Centrepoint Theatre in Palmerston North and at Downstage; managed Jim Belich's Wellington mayoral campaign; later co-founder and CEO of public relations company SweeneyVesty.

6 May 1988

I am currently ensconced in the O'Shea house in Ngaio, having returned from Auckland earlier in the week in order to prepare for *The Affair*. Had an amazing drive down the island in glorious clear weather.

Drove through Taumarunui and past the mountains, then on to Palmerston North, where I saw *The Affair* again. Not bad. It worked in places and not in others. I do want to do some more with the play and made copious notes which I should be putting into practice now. Was supposed to give a lecture at Massey but no one turned up and so I lunched with the English Dept. staff minus John Dawick who wrote the hateful review of the play.* Then down to Wellington.

Stopped off in Foxton and had a meeting with the Mayor, which was interesting and some good local background material should [the television series] *Local Bodies* actually come to life. Last night it occurred to me that I could turn it into a screenplay and spin the series off from it. Have also spoken to Rex Simpson of TV3, apparently the comedy unit are interested in my talent. Perhaps I will hear from them. I kind of doubt it.

20 July 1988

I've been back in the States since Saturday, that is four-and-a-half days. While it seems as if I was never away I am very aware of my cultural schizophrenia. This present reality, so different from New Zealand, seems all I've ever known and yet I know that is not so. Oh dear.

The flight back was incredibly tiring. Mind you, I was exhausted when I got on the plane, having spent several days trying to tie up the scene breakdowns for *Bert and Maisy Two* and having been popping in and out of the hospital to see Dad – who, thank God, was looking better on the last couple of days.

There is great debate in the family over Dad – the immediate family hope he gets well, the wider family keep saying 'wouldn't it be nice if he went in his sleep'. A useless statement as there is nothing we can do about it and it serves to heighten the anxiety for everyone if he doesn't. I have a feeling he

---

* **John Dawick** was in the English Department at Massey University, 1964–95.

might linger on for a number of years, in which case we have got to make the best of it.

Anyway, the flight back! Bounced across the Pacific in a most unseemly fashion – have never known such turbulence but the crew were very efficient and jolly, which put one's fears into perspective. Then a few hours in LA, where I dined with my seating companion, Sue Wood, former president of the National Party – she is the one who fired Muldoon. Most interesting – Tom Scott is doing a TV version of the incident called *1984*.[*]

Arrived in NYC at the crack of dawn and it was spectacular in a sepia heat haze. We flew over Manhattan and out to sea before turning back and landing at Kennedy. Was fairly spaced out for the first 48 hours. Went down to J&R Music World and bought this computer and Wordstar 2000, which is almost beyond me and certainly more able than I need. Have been fiddling for a couple of days and now have enough command of things to start work on a script. Have decided to rewrite *Squirrel* very quickly with some substantial changes. This will be my way of saying goodbye to the script. Haven't had the real inclination to do anything with it for a year and a half but now feel I should leap in. Want to do this before I get caught up with *Bert and Maisy Two*.

New York has been filthy and hot, way too hot and humid. The apartment had been left very clean by Athol Fugard and I have rearranged it twice![†] Have got my office corner set up and have the speaker phone right by the computer so I can talk and type at once.

I have the fortune of seeing Americans once again as strangers and they do seem strange. Watched two actors talking today at William Morris and it seemed so totally false.

This afternoon I bought a new portable stereo which has excellent sound and should keep me happy as I work away. Also bought *Anything Goes* tape and a new Keith Jarrett double cassette.

---

[*]   **Tom Scott**, New Zealand cartoonist, scriptwriter and playwright. The television series about the 1984 snap election became the award-winning two-part miniseries *Fallout* (1994), with Greg McGee as Scott's co-writer.

[†]   **Athol Fugard**, South African playwright, novelist, actor and director.

22 July 1988

Well, hard to believe but I really seem to be making some headway with the computer. Getting sick of having to use two boot disks (DOS and WS2) I tried making my own combination disk yesterday. Spoke to WS people and DOS people and compiled a disk which didn't work. This morning I tried again and added a few files and presto, it is all working. This is good news. It occurs to me that it is only about two years since I got my first computer (the Atari) and was totally bewildered. Now at least I know how to work through problems.

Bridget Armstrong and Maurice Shadbolt have been in town a few days and I've seen them a couple of times.* Nice to get to know them, I like them both a lot. Yesterday we went to the Met and saw the Hockney exhibition, which was excellent though exhausting – it went on and on. Then we walked through the park to my place for coffee and for Maurice to check out this baby.

This afternoon I'm off to Fire Island with Gilbert for the weekend, which should be fun, then on Wednesday or Thursday of next week I'll pop up to Vermont for a few days to check out the production of *Country Cops*. Would be nice to drive up – will try and get Jay or someone to drive me up.

Have been trying to do some work on *Squirrel* – have done some pages of notes which seem excellent and full of sense but I get stymied when I leap into the opening dialogue. It seems flat and uninteresting. Today I am going to reread some of the early drafts and try and get my way back into it all.

25 July 1988

The humidity has dropped considerably and with it the cloud cover and haze. New York looks like a liveable place again. Friday night caught the Islanders bus and went out to the Island with Becky and Gilbert. That night saw Peter Buckley who was 2 sheets to the wind and told me he thinks he's on the way out. I also learned that Robert Boykin is dying and currently in a hospital in the south.

---

*   **Bridget Armstrong**, New Zealand actor, and **Maurice Shadbolt** (1932–2004), New Zealand author and playwright, were married from 1978 until 1992.

27 July 1988

Spoke to Mum last night. Dad is apparently very bad and is failing quite rapidly. He has been moved to the Costley Home (Geriatric) and Mum is trying to get him back to our house so he can die in his own bed. His feet are swelling and the heart hardly pumps but the staff get him up and dressed every day and he walks with a walker. He has been dictating letters to Mum arranging his affairs so he can depart in peace. I am urged not to return.

At the present I am feeling ambivalent about the USA. I feel my friendships here are somewhat lacking. I didn't expect parades on my return but I keep expecting some input from the people I meet, which I'm not getting. So, work. What else is there? Get *Squirrel* done, block out *Academic Circles*, think of a new American play. Write the TV series.

Yesterday went downtown and had my session with Millard Ring and filed for citizenship, then over to the Federal Building and got fingerprinted and photographed. In about 6 months I should have an interview and will either become a citizen or remain a resident for another 4 years and 1 day.

2 August 1988

Swelter! It gets worse. I've never known a summer like it. Thank God for the air conditioner. The air is thick.

Went to Vermont on Thursday and the heat was not much better there. Saw rehearsals of *Country Cops*, which I really liked the look of. Have spoken to Gilbert about getting people to go up and see it and it would be good if something happened.

Having finished checking the galleys of *Cops*, which should be out later this month – two books in print. Yea!

In the meantime I am battling with *Squirrel*, which isn't easy but I seem to be getting somewhere slowly. A different play is emerging with a much stronger central couple – it seems to take ages to do each beat. Want to finish it this week.

Also visited Jack [Hofsiss], who is home from California – he'd been left for the day by [his carer] Maureen – when I saw him he'd been stuck in the one position for 15 hours. But his spirits seem good.

Robert took an oath for US citizenship in New York's Battery Park in July 1989.
Participants read the pledge of allegiance and sang 'The Star-Spangled Banner'.

Last night had dinner with Katharine Brisbane and Philip Parsons – we wandered through the Village and dined at a little French café.* Very good and delightful to see them again.

---

*   **Katharine Brisbane**, journalist known for her theatre criticism, and her husband **Philip Parsons** (1926–1993), director, dramaturg and theatre academic. The couple co-founded Currency Press, Australia's performing arts specialist publisher, in 1971.

5 August 1988

The air conditioner has been on for 48+ hours and I dare say it will stay on until the weather returns to its senses. I have discovered that if I shut the kitchen and bathroom doors the rest of the flat can be cooled down to an acceptable level. I shudder to think what the ConEd bill will be.

Tuesday night I had a quasi date with Jeff, a man I'd met late the previous week. I think the encounter proved I don't really want to date anyone but he is very pleasant.

Called Auckland, Dad is home, which is good I think. At least he isn't surrounded by geriatrics.

Have continued to battle with *Squirrel* when I should probably be working on *B&M2* but do want to get *Squirrel* in circulation again and there is only one way to do that – finish the fucker. Am having fun with the revision and think that it flows and that the centre of the play is clear.

10 August 1988

The heat continues. So does the work. Have been bogged down ten pages into the second act of the revised *Squirrel* for several days but now see a glimmer.

Had a letter from Victoria University Press, which declines to publish anything of mine because they are comedies. John Thomson quite liked *The Affair* but went on to say a lot of other people didn't. I can't deal with it. Made me feel quite inadequate.

Yesterday I threw myself into the scene breakdowns for *B&M2*, inspired in large part by a phone message from Sue Wilson. I managed to get quite a lot done before I spoke to her and should finish the breakdowns today. The show seems to be getting a muted response from the papers and call-ins complain about 'the same old faces'. New Zealand!

11 August 1988

Last night went and saw *Who Killed Roger Rabbit?* at the Ziegfeld with Melvin [Bernhardt] – loved the movie and had a pleasant dinner afterwards and Melvin appeared in an 'up' mood. This afternoon I'm going to the Jersey shore with Jack and Maureen and will return tomorrow. Should be good.

15 August 1988

The trip to the Jersey Shore was a blast. Gravelly, the little village where Maureen's family vacations, is a dirt strip with tiny bungalows on either side and a beach at one end – like something out of *Tobacco Road*. It was unbearably hot and Jack and I sat on the porch with a fan blasting at us as the family and neighbours wandered by. Maureen has six brothers and sisters and they all seemed to be there, her grandmother lives across the street with crazy Uncle Addy with dyed hair, who looked as if he was in the Hoboken Players production of *Pirates of Penzance*. Down the street live cousins and they were always in and out. Maureen was showing off her slimline body and there was much yelling and screaming. Thank God we just stayed the one night – on the weekend there were 19 in the bungalow which could comfortably hold 2.

20 August 1988

Last week picked up my completed tax returns and paid the $500 fee only to find I owed about three thousand in social security tax, which has thrown me back on my financial heels and gotten me a little worried. Instead of having money to live comfortably on I am back in the old poverty squeeze situation but fortunately there will be some money coming through from Vermont and I can pull some out of New Zealand.

In the meantime I have been to Vermont, where the weather was suddenly bearable with little humidity. I found the play [*Country Cops*] overblown and not working as I see it working. In fact I found it hard to sit through, especially the second half. Have tried to analyze what went wrong – after all, the final rehearsal I saw indicated the play was in good shape. I think basically some of the actors don't trust the material – they have to remember it is exotic to the audience and the audience has to be pulled in slowly. Once the audience is 'in' then things can speed up. Lines are also delivered as if they are jokes when they are not jokes.

Then there is a misconception that this is a play about zany John Cleese-type characters, which has been taken too literally I think by Ed Steele playing Sharp. He comes on with such eccentricity that he can't be taken seriously for a moment. I think it is a play about very ordinary people involved in a murder investigation and it should be directed as such.

Jack and Maureen came up and stayed at the Dorset Inn and saw the play Thursday night. They were very nice about it but seemed to appreciate the problems. They didn't think it was as bad as I did. We drove back together yesterday – I handled the car down the Taconic Expressway. Maureen misdirected us and instead of ending up on the Saw Mill we went on some other parkway and then ended up on the Cross Bronx going the wrong way. Eventually turned around and headed back and got off by George Washington Bridge – I was somewhat nervous but managed to survive and guess having done that am now in good enough shape to survive anywhere in Manhattan on the road.

26 August 1988

I'm such a state of depression. Don't know what to do about it. Feel isolated, miserable and a failure. It seems as if I should be facing up to a realization that I have no talent and shouldn't be pretending to do what I do. Hate this feeling. It is heightened by having no friends here – but when I think about it I have no friends in New Zealand either – maybe one or two more.

Have continued to do battle with *Squirrel*. I am a heartbeat away from finishing it and that heartbeat is eluding me. Am going out to Fire Island this afternoon to stay at Gilbert's. Am taking the play with me and also have to do the first episode of *B&M2* and get it in the mail when I come back Tuesday. Gilbert isn't going to be there so I should have some success with getting down to work. As I don't really know anyone out there I shouldn't be too distracted.

Have been getting mail from NZ with reviews and comments about *B&M1*, most of which are petty and negative which irritates me intensely. Dad is selling me the Mini but God knows when I'll pay for it. My finances are in a hell of a state and I realize that writing for NZ from here is financially nuts. Must get some work here.

4 September 1988

I'm writing this up at Melvin's house in Cragsmoor somewhere in New York State – Ulster County – on top of a mountain and covered in cloud at the moment. Came up here yesterday and was driven round the neighborhood, which is charming – older houses, great views and forest. Visited many of Melvin's friends and then walked to Bear Mountain with a great view over the Catskills. Am now set up in the upper lounge of the main house – formerly a painter's studio. Hope to be able to get some work done over the weekend and perhaps to get *Squirrel* near to completion – can't believe I've been stalled at the same place in that play for weeks.

5 September 1988 Labor Day
Last night there were four guests for dinner. Ted, a producer/director who was accompanied by an Irish-American, asthmatic, taxi-driving playwright and Richard, a middle-aged playwright (whose latest is work is under option by Ted) accompanied by his lover, Jacky (a Frenchman). I generally loathed the evening, way too much chat about this play or that, or this star or that, and just too faggy for me to cope with. But I'm sure the guests were charming and I was an asshole.

2 November 1988
One project of the last few weeks has been getting my computer disks from New Zealand converted to Wordstar 2000. Have translated *China Wars* and *The Affair* and have nearly finished *Country Cops*. I have also been working with notes and the Diary disk and have just managed to delete all my letter files from last year, which is probably a good thing as I never knew why I was keeping them and I now established the policy of not keeping letters.

Hope, now that I am adjusted to not going to New Zealand and the frenzy of writing 7 episodes of *Bert and Maisy 2* is over, that I can relax and get back into the pattern of jotting in the diary every day. Certainly much has gone on since I got back to the States and most of it hasn't been recorded. But here we are talking to the diary again.

Work completed since returning to the States: the episodes of *B&M2* mentioned above; two drafts of *Star Crazy*, the revised version of *Squirrel*. I really like the script and hope someone can do it. Have also started on the novelized version of *B&M1* and want to get Chapter One of that finished soon and sent off to see if there are any nibbles. Am about to revise

Happy times in the New York apartment, 1986. MS-1907/005, Hocken Collections

China Wars in preparation for a production at Primary Stages, opening on March 1. Hope to have both these latter projects done by November 13 when I fly off to LA for a week in the hope that I can get some movie work. Wouldn't it be heaven?

John O'Shea arrives in NY tomorrow for a couple of days and I look forward to seeing him. Apparently he has got the funding for *Te Rua*. Hope he doesn't want me to work on it but I'll probably say yes if he does as I need money. *China Wars* got good reviews but poor houses in Christchurch so I'll make no money from that.

22 November 1988

Arrived back on Sunday from a week in LA during which I rushed about trying to find work in films or television or both. I was a little chagrined by the way William Morris treated me. My new agent there – Liz Ramsland – seemed to think I'd popped in for social chitchat and that was all. But in the last few days I managed to get a few appointments and perhaps something will come of the endeavour. It is all so frustrating. I really want a career in the theatre and perhaps that will never happen. But I refuse to give up. Enjoyed driving round LA and didn't have too many gaffes. It certainly makes life easier when you have wheels.

27 November 1988

This is the end of a four-day holiday weekend (Thanksgiving), which I spent extremely quietly. Came up with a delightful idea, I thought, for a movie – *Everything You Ever Wanted to Know About My Hometown*, which takes a week in the life of a 3rd-form high school boy in NZ in 1959 and looks at his family and world. Think it could be really good. Want to get it to Roger Donaldson as it should appeal to his sensibility. Am also trying to gather together ideas for other film and television projects. Gilbert has just dropped Becky off and reports that he likes *Houses and Gardens** and will pass it on to the Lit Dept at William Morris – wouldn't that be swell.

28 November 1988

Last night had dinner with Melvin, who wanted to go to the Mayfair. She seemed pretty potty to me as it is not a very good restaurant right on the other side of town and it was raining cats and dogs. But – and I guessed this – Melvin really wanted to pop into a bar after dining, though why I cannot imagine. Gay bars, any bars, are so tedious. And there was no one anywhere.

3 December 1988

Yesterday met with Rory O'Shea about *Everything You Ever Wanted to Know About My Hometown* and he seemed to like the idea. I have sent off an outline to John O'Shea and hope that Pacific can get the money out of the [New Zealand Film] Commission to get me started – that would be two strong New Zealand projects to keep me going for a while. And today I feel I am going to start the first scene of *Academic Circles* and see where that takes me.

---

*   RL originally used this title to refer to the beginning of a novel based on *Bert and Maisy*; he also used it in a 1989 outline for an 'Aussified version' of the TVNZ series (MS-2441/070, Hocken Collections).

4 December 1988

Spoke to Mum last night and she and Dad had just had a picnic in the garden and the day before a barbecue. Yesterday started *Academic Circles* and managed to do about 16 pages. Can't figure out how I came to start it – I would rather be doing an American play or a *Murphy Brown* episode but I guess the time was right. We shall see how we go today. It would be nice to have a play lined up for production in New Zealand next year. Something new and different.

This morning watched an Australian Wonderworks TV drama *Miracle Down Under*, a sentimental but affecting Christmas tale with a period flavour. Years ago Katharine Brisbane remarked how Aussie films so often look back to the past while NZ films tend to be contemporary. I feel this is because Australians are much happier with their past than Kiwis are. The moral dilemmas of the land wars and the whole treatment of the Maori population prevents the NZer having such a clear-eyed romantic/heroic view of the country's history. The Aboriginal problem in Australia exists on a different scale and very much out of sight.

7 December 1988

Gilbert wants me to take Becky to his house Friday and as a reward he'll take me to the theatre – of course it's gridlock traffic crisis time and I don't know how the hell I'm supposed to get the dog over there.

Academic Circles is now about 20 pages long and there are a couple of good characters, some nice interchanges but no heartbeat – that is really getting me down. Will try and solve it today. Kathy wants me to go to London and I am running out of money.

12 December 1988

This afternoon have a reading of *The Affair*, which will be interesting – to see if it makes any sense in the States and to see if there is any part of it I can use, recycle, here. Have been working on *China Wars*. As I presumed, the first act was a breeze with just a minor adjustment here and there. The opening scene of Act Two I trimmed a lot and then let breathe again. Scene Seven will also be tricky. This rewrite is a bitch. I am torn. Karen's last letter implores me not to touch the script but I know that it is messy. I just want to get it right. A very thin line has to be trodden. I just hate the process. I finally worm my way into a scene, rework it, toss it aside and then have to wait till I feel ready to rework it again and then I have to keep doing it till something stops nagging at me. Swoosie [Kurtz] is going to read the script this week and may do it (I doubt it) but that would be grand.

22 January 1989

The past ten days have been just awful. I have done nothing but lie about and vegetate. Today I attempted to get off on the right foot with a little exercise – 15 minutes on my cross-country ski machine – and I must say it has made me feel a little better. Then I wrote several letters and just sitting at my desk and working always improves my spirits. Now I'm about to stroll along Riverside Park with Mason [Wiley] and as it is a pleasant afternoon my spirits should be improved upon even further. It remains to be seen if I can get anything done when I return home. Of course my humor wasn't improved by the plague mentality which has begun to alter my perception of reality since returning to NYC. It is all too depressing here and one wonders when one's number will come up.

23 January 1989

The malaise seems to have passed – thank goodness. This morning I'm feeling quite bright and enjoyed a 15-minute workout on my ski machine and seem to have solved, in my head at least, the problems with Act One of *Glorious Ruins*.

June 1989

Have been to New Zealand and back, Dad has died, and now I'm in 250 W 85 [the apartment at 250 West 85th Street] for the summer.

• • •

A gap of three months follows the diary entry that records the death of Robert's father, Dick Lord. Robert continued to work on *Glorious Ruins* (a play about tangled relationships in the New York art and museum world) and kept thinking about *Academic Circles* (the story of English Department intrigue set in Dunedin) while embarking on a synopsis and treatment of a new film: *Everything You Ever Wanted to Know About My Hometown*. He received an initial commission from John O'Shea, and the New Zealand Film Commission funded a first draft of the screenplay. Producer Rex Simpson invited Robert to write a 70-page treatment for *The Early Bird Show*, TV3's new children's programme presented by Suzy Cato, and to develop several characters. But Simpson and TV3 decided not to proceed with Robert's characters, and the show, featuring skits, puppets and cartoons sourced from overseas, went ahead without them. Robert was scheduled to write storylines for the popular television series *Gloss*, but the series was abruptly cancelled.

1989–1990

Robert Lord, c. 1989. MS-2438/223/002, Hocken Collections

New York, 2 September 1989

As Amtrak whisks me between Buffalo and Rochester I'm dazzling my fellow travellers with my skill on the laptop which rests happily on the fold-down tray. Actually no one seems to have noticed my sophistication, skill and elegance. They are too busy scoffing their smoked ham and egg on buttermilk biscuit sandwiches and downing Bloody Marys. The occasional jiggle of the train does tend to propel the fingers towards the wrong keys but that is the only problem I've encountered thus far. As was obvious from the scene at the station, the train is fairly ajostle with passengers, a disproportionate number of whom seem to be under the age of 3. At the border the US officials seemed far brusquer than their Canadian counterparts were on Wednesday and several people disappeared. On both legs of my Toronto journey I have noticed that the attendant in the café car on the Canadian sectors has had trouble counting, the first one jotted figures on a napkin, the second used a calculator. The US attendants seem to make all calculations mentally (and, in my experience, accurately). I'm not sure what this means. The Canadian attendants were blond and female. The US attendants Black and of both sexes. Are any of these facts important in trying to make sense of the situation? Is the US education system better? Or do Americans simply have a greater enthusiasm for monetary matters? This is a situation not unlike that I encountered when travelling through the British Isles: in England I was invariably mischarged on shopping sprees and given the wrong change (usually in my favour), in Scotland all accounting was scrupulously accurate.

Went up [to Toronto] on Wednesday, getting there about 8.30pm. On Thursday Margaret [Van Dijk] and I drove to Niagara-on-the-Lake, about 90 minutes away. It is a very beautiful town which is the home of the Shaw Festival, a major summer theatre organization. We saw a matinee of the musical *Nymph Errant* by Cole Porter, which is the show Joey Tillinger and the Long Wharf want me to rewrite. It was interesting to see it staged as it is rarely done.

Friday it rained all day but Maarten [Van Dijk] and I did pop out to the shops for a break and a friend of theirs came for dinner. Today I'm heading home – get back to Grand Central about 9.30. Tomorrow I hope to go out to the Hamptons again and get some time in the sun. It is Labor Weekend – the last weekend of summer – and it would be good to get a final day in the ocean.

15 September 1989

Have finally finished off *Glorious Ruins*. Glad to have it done and am now turning my attention to the *Hometown* screenplay. After much aggravation the first film payment came through, but it was a little sad to see $9,000 dwindle to $4,000 after agency commissions had been removed and the money converted to American. However I am able to pay off a lot of bills, which is pleasant. Am looking forward to my week in London – fly over on the 24th. Have just spent hours on the phone doing my bookings for New Zealand.

I'll be in residence in Auckland until Christmas. I'm storylining the TV series *Gloss* and finishing off a screenplay. It will give me time with Mum, who has been feeling quite lonely since Dad died. I plan to come over to Sydney at least once while back home – probably in mid-November.

Think I am pleased with *Glorious Ruins*. Not an easy play to write – but what play is? NYC is waking from the summer doldrums and the theatre is livening up.

London, 1 October 1989

My week in London has been marred by a strange rash which appeared on my forehead the day after I arrived. At first I thought it was poison ivy. The day before clambering on the British Airways flight (which left ten hours late) I'd been to Jan Paetow's and Larry Crane's wedding, which was celebrated in a tent in their rather large yard in Bogota, New Jersey. Jan's dog, of whom I'm rather fond, had been gamboling in the undergrowth and I imagined I might have picked poison ivy sap off his coat in between dances, drinks and noshing on Mexican food. But apparently this wasn't so. When the rash turned on the aspect of a birthmark it was suggested I go to a doctor, and a small fortune later I was diagnosed as having shingles and armed with a seven-day supply of medication which certainly got rid of it. I feel this is my fault for going to the doctor to have a check-up. As Bert says in *Bert and Maisy*: 'Sure as eggs, if you go to a doctor, he'll find something

Robert's goddaughter Molly O'Shea. MS-1907/011/076,
Hocken Collections

wrong.' So no London theatre-going for me. Mind you there didn't seem too much I wanted to see but had I been in a more conscientious spirit I would have doubtless spent a fortune on tickets. The positive aspect of the ailment was spending time at Kathy [O'Shea]'s flat and getting to know Molly, who becomes my god-daughter tomorrow.

Auckland, 10 October 1989

After an uneventful voyage I am settling into life down under. As yet there is no resolution to the job situation but I imagine I am going to be paid off.

Had a hectic two days in New York during which I discovered that the television show I was going to New Zealand to work on had been cancelled.

Then a busy day in Los Angeles before descending on New Zealand last Saturday morning. On Monday night when I got back to the apartment there was a message to call Janice Finn at TVNZ, who informed me that the next series of *Gloss* has been cancelled and that 'if I didn't want to I didn't have to come down'.* All a little late with the tenants already in the apartment. Apparently TVNZ wants a new production but no one seems to know what. No announcement has been made that *Gloss* has been cancelled and I have been sworn to secrecy. They have suggested I might want to work on the new show but as it has to go into production before April, and as it is two half-hours a week and as no one knows anything about it yet, I feel there isn't enough time and I've been bitten too badly by TVNZ in the past. But we shall see. I would like to get the money and then spend the time here finishing off my *Hometown* script. As usual my life is a great muddle. I have thrown myself into the garden here with abandon and have seeds planted everywhere. Wrote on little plastic stakes what was planted where and then accidentally hosed the writing off. I never knew gardening was so difficult.

I thought the reading of *Glorious Ruins* in New York went very well and am convinced it's my best play. The cast was also enthused, there seems very little which is extraneous and just a few areas that need tightening. Gilbert developed a problem with Laura Esterman, who was reading the central character, and decided he couldn't hear her.† Actually he nodded off. But he has said that now he has an inkling of the style he will read it again. Spare me. I sent a copy to Lynne Meadow myself.‡ Jack Hofsiss, who was supposed to contact Patricia Elliot§ to read the lead and for whom the location of the reading was arranged, went vague on me and claimed not to realize I was in town for so short a period etc and didn't turn up. Fuck him.

---

*   **Janice Finn**, New Zealand actor, writer, director and television producer. She was in the Downstage company in the early 1970s, spent seven years working in Australia and returned to New Zealand in the 1980s.

†   **Laura Esterman**, American theatre, television, radio and film actress.

‡   **Lynne Meadow**, producer, director and teacher, and artistic director of the Manhattan Theatre Club since 1972.

§   **Patricia Elliott** (1938–2015), American theatre, film, soap opera, and television actress.

Though I wish Ms Elliot had read the play as I know Gilbert prefers her to Laura – whom I love.

15 October 1989

I did enjoy my time in London and adored my godchild, Molly. I felt myself becoming overwhelmed by a variety of warm, perhaps even mushy feelings not usually the domain of the middle-aged unmarried. The baptism itself, in a Catholic church in St John's Wood, was a triumph of multiculturality. When we arrived a Maronite Christian wedding was just concluding and petals were being gaily tossed by little bridesmaids in pink. Three children were to be baptised: our very own Molly, who slept through the event (waking briefly for the water on the head part); Anthony Paul, whose entourage seemed to belong to a punk rock band; and Leon LeRoy, a Black child dressed in a white satin sailor suit, whose every move was videotaped by an uncle with a camera implanted in his shoulder. The priest was very jolly and my only regret was the baptismal font itself. I had imagined us gathering round a lavishly carved stone bowl in a sepulchral recess of the church, instead we stood before an aluminium wok resting on a card table in front of the altar. If life was more like my imagination I'm sure we'd all be happier.

Ah, New Zealand. Penguin Books here seem interested in a novel I have outlined (*Private Reserve*) and also in some short stories.* I will do my best to get them underway and finish off my screenplay while I am here.

I feel quite odd at the moment – not quite knowing where I am or why and not too sure what to do about the future. Work, I'm sure, is the only answer, so perhaps I'd better do some.

18 October 1989

After a week of seeing if there was another position for me to fill [at TVNZ] it became apparent that there wasn't. We are now trying to work out a separation agreement and I must say they aren't being terribly friendly and

---

* This novel was never completed; in his 1989 outline, RL described it as 'a social comedy set in Balmoral, a small, upwardly mobile town, in contemporary New Zealand' (MS-1615/010, Hocken Collections).

Robert in the South Island in 1987, photographed by Alex Ely. Alex Ely collection

offered me less than it cost to fly down here. I presume that in a week or two we will have come to some understanding and I will be slightly solvent. In the meantime poverty rules and in order to lift my spirits I am going to Sydney on Friday for a week. My ticket from the States carries on to Australia so it isn't costing me anything and my mother is coming with me, which will be fun for her. I will try and find a little work there but hold out no great hope.

19 October 1989
Went to the hospital here yesterday in order to see about getting a renewal of my various medications only to discover it is not the policy of the authorities here to distribute AZT to anyone who isn't practically already in a coffin. This is most disconcerting. I have contacted my pharmacy in NYC and they are sending another month's supply over. The doctor here suggested I could cut the dosage in half should I run short and he thought this wouldn't have too disastrous a result. By which I gather he means I won't wake up dead. Is this a feasible proposition? In all respects I seem to be remarkably well, chipper and in good spirits.

Sydney, 20 October 1989
Ears seem to be what is lacking at the moment. I find there is no one I can tell my story to. Or maybe I don't want to tell it. It seems an imposition. Something that demands a serious response and I don't know if I want to make that sort of an imposition. Or if I have the right to. This was brought home this afternoon while I was wandering through Newtown with Nick Enright. Over lunch today we discussed my new play *Glorious Ruins*, his new play *Daylight Saving*, which is a huge success here and a primary cause for my visit. We then moved on to more general topics, including AIDS – Nick was in the Sydney company of *As Is* and the recent production here of *The Normal Heart*. He spoke of the number of people he knew who had died, of people who declined to discuss their illness and thereby declined their friends the right to say goodbye. And I just wandered along and said nothing. What can you say? What response do I want? Tears? Sympathy? I don't want any of that. Probably I don't believe it's happening, going to

happen. Maybe being struck by lightning has provided a radical cure. Maybe I don't even have it. And the time? How long? Who knows? There seems little I can do. And I don't even know if the medication I'm taking is correct. I believe it is correct but when I discussed it with a doctor in Auckland last week he was somewhat surprised by the strength of the dosages I've been given and the combination of drugs: Retrovir and Bactrim, both of which he says can deplete the bone marrow as a side effect. It all sounds so unpleasant. I'll visit him in November and have an examination. A complication to this process is the differing policies in the States and the antipodes. The use of AZT as a deterrent, preventative, is now recommended in America but not in New Zealand. Consequently I wasn't able to get a prescription and had to phone the States and have a month's supply mailed to me. And this is hugely expensive and to be paid for by money I don't have. Not an easy situation. Sitting on the plane with my mother, who hates flying more than I do, we talked about my career or lack of it (as Nick said today, a career is really a collection of accidents). And of course my mother worries about what is going to happen to me but in a time frame of ten or twenty years. And I worry what will happen to her if suddenly next year I get some ghastly complaint and fall into the downward spiral. How will she cope with the illness, my homosexuality (which is a bit of a joke anyway – I was never very good at it), and who will look after her? I certainly can't expect her, having nursed my father for the past several years, to do the same for me.

Every time I see Sydney I think the Harbour Bridge has gotten smaller, the truth is everything else is getting a little bit bigger. Today we eased over the Tasman and were met at the airport by cousin Sarah, who looked gorgeous, glamorous, was illegally parked and charmed her way through traffic jams to deposit me at Nick's.* Tonight I'm dining at her house, it is her sister Robin's birthday. Nick is playing Master of Ceremonies at a ball, which sounds a curiously old-fashioned thing to do. I have made my list of calls to make. Have arranged what shows to see. All in all I've been most efficient.

Is this really happening? That's the question.

---

* Sarah Garland's father Ozzie and Bebe Lord's mother Blanche were brother and sister. RL had got to know the Sydney branch of the family after *Bert and Maisy* was staged there.

21 October 1989

This trip to Sydney is rapidly beginning to depress the hell out of me. I am beginning to think of myself as a terminal case, which probably I am. This afternoon Craig Ashley visited and with Nick we discussed New York and names of the departed kept flooding into the conversation. And I smile and chat as if there is nothing wrong with me. What can I say? 'Excuse me, mates, I'm just about to kick the bucket?' It can do them no good to know and I doubt if it can do me much good to tell. It is the inevitability of it that today seems awesome.

Last night I dined at Sarah's Darling Point apartment. There was much shouting and laughter. I took the train back to Newtown and stopped at a pub where 70s disco music was blaring and young men were dancing together. I had forgotten such things happened. The air was soft and gentle as I walked home. I thought of Robert Love, who is contemplating leaving Auckland for London. The other night he said to me: 'There is so much I love in Auckland, the softness of the summer air, the beauty of the Polynesian faces.' Then he sighed and added: 'I don't suppose I'll find that in London.'

On the train a sign read 'Plain Clothes and Uniformed Police Patrol This Train.' To my chagrin I didn't see a polyester suit on a coat hanger wandering the aisles.

I couldn't get to sleep but didn't want to take a pill. I remembered the conversation I'd had with Mother on the flight over, where she expressed her worries about my future (if only she knew) and her own. 'No one minds dying,' she said, 'it's what happens before you die that counts.' She worries that she cannot give me money (I don't want money) because she doesn't know what the future holds for her, what future attention she might need.

I don't want my mother to watch me die. It is so easy to make parents happy. A burp, a smile from a baby can be the source of ecstasy. I wonder if, when a child realizes how easy this is he also realizes how easy it is to hurt. God I'm getting depressed.

There are several projects I must complete: *Nymph Errant*, a new book for the songs from the Cole Porter show for Tillinger and the Long Wharf. *Private Reserve*, which covers many aspects of my year in Dunedin. *Boxing Day*, my family drama, which I'm determined to finish soon. *Hometown*, the screenplay for John O'Shea. *Academic Circles*, my farce about university life. And I want to revise *Glorious Ruins*, *The Travelling Squirrel* and *China Wars*. I also wouldn't mind trying to do one more American play – an update of the lesser Restoration comedy *The Dramatist*. And to finish off my action movie *Lensman*. How much can I get done? And can I get *The Goodbye Book* [this diary in letter form] done too?

22 October 1989

I'm beginning to feel like a failure, which is, now that I feel it and recognize it, how I usually feel when I come to Sydney. I don't think I'm jealous of Nick, I admire him and am glad of his success. I'm jealous of the fact that he is grounded in a place where he can live and work – and it is native to him. My frustrations regarding New York are that I am and always will be an outsider and now I'm an outsider in New Zealand. And even had I remained in New Zealand and never gone to America I couldn't have had the continuous career in the arts that Nick has had here. And now I'm wondering if I shouldn't have settled here in 1974 as I originally intended. But I didn't and so there is no point in even thinking about it. And now this dying business is beginning to sink in and confusing me. Just how big a failure am I? How much have I deluded myself? Will any of the plays ever really have a life?

I still keep going back to *Boxing Day* in my mind and do want to come through to some analysis of it while in Sydney. Last night, sitting in the Playhouse watching Googie Withers and John McCallum in *The Cocktail Hour** – a play about a playwright confronting his parents about a play he has written about them – I kept thinking about *Boxing*. The hard part is to write a character based on yourself. The 'I' character. So in my family drama the 'I' character, the centre, has to be someone other than me. For years

---

* **Georgette Lizette ('Googie') Withers** (1917–2011), English dancer and actress, and her husband **John McCallum** (1918–2010), Australian actor and television producer. The couple had also starred in AR Gurney's 1988 play *The Cocktail Hour* in Brighton (UK) earlier in 1989.

GLORIOUS RUINS
BY ROBERT LORD

The premiere of a new comedy. Directed by SUSAN WILSON
with GINETTE McDONALD, GRANT TILLY, ANNE BUDD
KATHERINE BEASLEY, MARTON CSOKAS
OPENS APRIL 4, 1991, BOOK: OPERA HOUSE, PH 850832
CIRCA THEATRE

in thinking about this play I have been bogged down by the 'I'. If there is to be a parallel with my life then some illness, death must be part of it. Perhaps the 'I' is a daughter. I want the battle between conventional and fundamental morality. I want conventional morality to appear to win but the fundamental to triumph. When the conventional wins we should have: 'We can't finish like this!' The action of the 'I' must appear to have broken the family but we should become aware that there is another force, the greed and rapacity of the sister-in-law with her 'correct' behaviour, which has really destroyed the family. A realization of this can allow for a warm resolution between parents and daughter at the end. I rather like the idea of writing about myself as a daughter. If I am going to die in the near future this is obviously the play I have to finish first. I visited with Ms Withers and Mr McCallum after the show and gave them the *Bert and Maisy* television material. They were extremely charming, offered me a gin, and discussed various options 'if they liked the project'. They felt they would rather do a series in Britain than in Australia – that they would be perceived as Brits easier, that production standards were higher, etc. So now they have the material and I'm glad they've got it. Who knows if and when I'll hear.

This morning I brunched with John Lonie, a television and movie writer, Nick and David X [Marr], who is writing the authorized biography of Patrick White. Charming, witty, well-educated, discussing opera, novels, plays. I felt a tad hickish. I've finally come to realize that wherever I am I'm in the wrong place. I wish I felt a little prouder. Maybe I will tomorrow.

Maarten Van Dijk, speaking of American theatre, always clucks wisely, shakes his head and speaks of the Broadway clause – a mythical precondition that says a play must reaffirm the values of its audience if it is to be a success. This of course is true. Thousands of people are not going to pay thousands of dollars to go to a play which tells them the fundamental values of their lives are false. To Maarten, though, this diminishes the play. I don't think it's got anything to do with plays. I think it's got to do with audiences. A success on a university campus is bound to be a play which affronts the establishment, demands changes and reform, which conscientiously sets out to shock. Which will in fact reaffirm the values of that audience.

I have run aground in New Zealand because I haven't tried to reaffirm the values of the general public (which Roger Hall's plays do so well) or indeed of the avant garde. I don't think of my plays in terms of their audience. My plays have a logic of their own, a world in which they are true, in which the language is consistent. I tend to create a world independent of the audience. Twice this has spilled over: *Well Hung* and *Bert and Maisy* both have strong enough Kiwi roots to speak beyond an opening night. Plays like *Meeting Place* and *Heroes and Butterflies*, both of which I think are good, exist slightly to one side of their audience.

This problem is also true of the American plays. *The Travelling Squirrel* is the one that comes nearest to telling a story the audience shares. I begin to see as I write this what Linda Seger and others refer to as the 'myth' quality in successful dramatic writing (movies): the story on some level needs to be shared by the audience, the audience has to be at one with a character and travel with him or her.[*] I think it is still possible to achieve this in *Squirrel* – I can bring it back. *China Wars* is an elaborate conceit in many respects which works on an intellectual level – I think the problems I've gotten into with that script are when I've tried to make it work on a more human level – the result being a stand-off. I think there is an emotional through-line (Dolly and Ken becoming replenished) but how much an audience can share this I do not know. Will Weiler / Miller / Carrellas ever produce it?[†] Please, God.

It suddenly occurred to me that I feel like Gladys Moncrieff making a farewell tour.[‡] Visiting Kathy in London and seeing Russell and now here in Sydney, where this afternoon I visited Helene and Gil Carroll. I first met Helene before she married Tiri Sotiri, she was Polish Jewish, born in France after the war, he was Greek. A very exotic couple for one of my whitebread background. She remains beautiful with luminescent skin and a delicate sense of humour.

---

[*]   **Linda Seger**, American script consultant and author of books about screenwriting.

[†]   Weiler / Miller / Carrellas, the New York-based general theatrical management firm run by Berenice Weiler, Marilyn S Miller and Barbara Carrellas.

[‡]   **Gladys Moncrieff** (1872–1976), Australian singer who made a lengthy farewell tour of Australia and New Zealand in 1958–59.

After Craig left I wandered up to the pub to pick up a few beers as Roger Oakley and others are coming round and we're going out to dinner.* It occurred to me that I'll never know intimacy again. If I ever knew it. Well, of course I knew it. On a sexual level with Russell and later, briefly, with Jay. But I'm being indulgent. I forget in my self-pity my relationships with Craig, Nick, Karen, Claire, Kathy and so many others in which I reveal myself a modicum. Never too much. Life is better than I have allowed myself to think. There is, though, a panic at the pit of my stomach. What am I going to do? Shame is part of it and yet I don't feel ashamed. I feel my mother will feel shame and that I am the cause of that. This was never the intention. It has occurred to me before that every action leads to a negative conclusion or to a conclusion contrary to that desired. A search for physical love has ended not in happiness and warmth but in isolation and loneliness.

30 October 1989

It is strange being here without Dad but a relief that he's not in the considerable pain that marked his last few years. Mum is coping well I think and last week we went off to Sydney for a few days, which she enjoyed. I had asked her to visit me in the States but she felt it was too soon to leave home – she has been busy working out all her finances and taking control of the things Dad did. Perhaps she will come to America next year or I might spend more time back here. I'm not too sure when I'll get back to Titan Street or, if the job situation stays as it is, if I'll be able to spend extended periods of time in New Zealand.

Auckland has been blanketed by fine rain for most of the day and I've been holed up in the basement attempting to make sense of my life – which is probably a waste of time. Years ago my father wrote to me in New York and pointed out that my career hadn't actually been a roaring success and suggested that I return home and live in what was then 'the recently waterproofed basement'. I wasn't thrilled by the idea and was able to convince myself that success was just around the corner. It is ironic that I'm here now.

---

*   **Roger Oakley**, New Zealand actor who emigrated to Australia in 1978.

A pensive Robert on the beach, c. 1987. MS-1907/005, Hocken Collections

I've spent the weekend getting my letters up to date and my notes in order for the various projects. I've felt vaguely uncomfortable and ill at ease with a nagging feeling that I know nothing about writing and am wasting my time. But what else is there to do?

Last night Mum and I joined a conglomeration of cousins for a barbecue at Sandy Williams' home. Sandy is the eldest of Aunt Pam's daughters. Penny and Jenny, the other two daughters, were also present with their husbands Robert and Garth. Storm, Garth's German shepherd, went walkabout and was found by a neighbour, who was alarmed by the size of the dog's testicles. This provoked a chain of jokes. Robert Buchanan (Penny's husband), normally an exceedingly voluble Scot, was very quiet but had the presence of mind to tend to the barbecue (gas! what is the world coming to). It was a scene of family harmony and as much as I participated I felt outside. Who knows what these pleasant supporters of the National Party will think when they find out what's wrong with me? I presume they'll understand. But there's obviously a question. But the tragedy isn't mine. The tragedy will be Mum's. She will have to survive. And they will have to help her. I hope they do.

What I'm going to do about money I have no idea. On Saturday I received the Amex charge from the pharmacy in NYC for a month's supply of medication. $US779. Oh God. And the previous month's charge hasn't shown up yet. I'm petrified my insurance isn't going to cover this, or that through some machination I will be disqualified. Then I'll really be in the shit. And the added frustration is that I feel as good as I ever have. But part of my mind, all the time, is occupied with the business of the illness and dying. Alternatives appear and disappear like road signs along a highway. Suicide. Returning to NYC. Leaving NYC for good. I certainly don't want my mother to have to nurse me through dying.

The last couple of days in Sydney turned into a whirl of meetings and coffee sessions with Nick and me attacking plot possibilities for the Cole Porter *Nymph Errant* musical. I was a bit confused to read in the *Cocktail Hour* programme that Gurney is working on a madcap 30s musical using unfamiliar Cole Porter songs – sounds dangerously similar.

I've divided my projects up into three categories:

Major Projects (to be tended to immediately): *Hometown* (the screenplay, the first draft of which has to be done by early December), *Boxing Day* (a new play), *The Goodbye Book* (this) and *Private Reserve* (the novel).

Revision Projects (to be done in conjunction with the above, as light relief): *The Travelling Squirrel* (to prepare a script for the Primary Stages production next February), *Glorious Ruins* (to prepare a revised version for the Circa reading at the end of November), *China Wars* (to prepare a final version of that script balancing the Globe script and the NYC script – needed if the 1990 off-Broadway production proceeds).

Future Projects (notes to be taken for): *Lensman* (an American adventure movie I've sketched out), *Nymph Errant* (the Cole Porter project for Long Wharf) and *Academic Circles* (a farce about an English Department at a New Zealand university). Let us pray we get as far as this category.

2 November 1989

I'm in the midst of reading *The Salterton Trilogy* by Robertson Davies and just came across this quote (from *Tempest-Tost* (1951, Clarke Unwin)):

> ... *a man who has been told by his physician that he has a dreadful disease seeks to persuade himself that the doctor was wrong. He feels nothing; he sees nothing amiss; little by little he thinks that there has been a mistaken diagnosis. But one day it strikes, and his agony is worse because he has cajoled himself with thought of escape.*

Life has assumed a huge normality since returning from Sydney and perhaps I'm now in the realm of 'mistaken diagnosis'. Long may it last. Am troubled as I've run out of medication. My phone call to New York some weeks ago should have produced some results – well, it has, I've received the credit card invoice for $US779 but no sign of the drugs. The mail has taken on a new fascination. As to how I will pay the bills I just don't know and I can't think about it. I'm sure if I do dwell on it I'll become paralyzed by panic. I must keep going.

Have been throwing myself furiously into gardening activities here at home and find I'm enjoying it muchly. My main occupation is, of course, working on the screenplay of *Hometown* but every 90 minutes or so I rush outside, grab the clippers and get to work for half an hour. This is actually rather like the way I work in New York except there I don't have a garden and keep inventing household chores. The garden at 40 Macpherson Street is magnificent and a monument to Mum and Dad and the 17 years they spent building it. Mum wrote to me in New York that she no longer enjoyed working in the garden now that she had no one to talk about it with (in his later days Dad couldn't get down into the garden much). I think I'm trying to make up for this and also get the place into a state where all the heavy work needed for a while is done and it will be easier for her to maintain. We are planning on turning the vegetable terrace into an orchid terrace which will look after itself. Perhaps I'm also overcompensating for not taking enough interest in the garden when Dad was alive but I've realized that, for me anyway, gardening is in the doing and as I do it I see more and appreciate more. The trees which have grown since Mum and Dad first moved here have now obscured parts of their view of the water and in addition to other tasks I am cutting tunnels through the trees and ferns, which will allow the water to be glimpsed from the house.

6 November 1989

I should be in a complete panic. The medication ordered over a month ago hasn't arrived from the States although the bill ($800) has. Every day I rush to the letterbox but to no avail. Have already run out of Bactrim but that I think I can get replaced here when I see the doctor at Auckland Hospital on Wednesday. The Retrovir I can't at all for some reason even though I am obviously prepared to pay for it. But I am not in a panic. The worst that can happen is that I die and I'm going to do that quite soon anyway so what the hell. Talk about cavalier. I'm frustrated though and wish the situation could be worked out. Don't know if I should zip back to the States but then where would I get the money to leave there again.

Other problems abound. I'm trying to get an exemption from the tax department for the TVNZ payment and wrote to them on October 17.

Called today and learned they are currently dealing with correspondence from mid-September. Shit. I am sitting here without cash and don't want to borrow from Mum.

Have thought of an idea for a new comedy, *The Nice Guy*, about a man who does everything right and pisses everyone off.

7 November 1989

The medication still hasn't arrived, which is a worry. Spoke to the pharmacist in New York and today will try and track it down through the Post Office here. I can keep going on half rations for another day or so but what happens then I don't know. I'm always waiting on the mail. Money is always in transit, letters en route and everything arrives late. Had an awful day yesterday. Felt tired and depressed. Probably a reaction to not getting any writing done over the weekend – I find if I don't do some every day then I get scratchy.

Have drawn up a list of things that need doing round the house before I go back to the States – want to finish getting all the paths in order and cutting back the trees where needed. Need to build fences in the garden, do some more tree planting and then to tackle the basement and clean out the garbage and tidy it up for Mum. Hope it can all be done.

Continue to think, in the back of my mind, about *The Nice Guy* and the more I think about it the more fun I think it could be. The last thing I need is a new play to write.

It's a very pleasant life here. I enjoy tapping away in the basement and then rushing out and doing a little in the garden. Perhaps I should've done this years ago. But who was to know that a career wouldn't 'take off'? I think Mum enjoys my company and we seem to have an easy relationship and manage to get a lot done. I keep forgetting that she is 76 and shouldn't work so hard. In ordinary circumstances I could expect my mother would die before me, this is now highly unlikely. By being here am I making it harder?

Have just dashed up to the letterbox and again the medication isn't there. Have been calling the Post Office – several calls and everyone politely referring me to someone else and disavowing all responsibility and knowledge. I keep thinking that it can't have gone astray but it obviously seems to have done just that.

8 November 1989

This morning I took myself off somewhat nervously to the Auckland Hospital and a meeting with Dr Mark Thomas, whom I'd spoken to a few weeks ago about getting Retrovir. He was most helpful, as were the hospital staff, and he inspected my body and listened intently to various parts. I don't like to say so but I think he was more thorough than Dr Versace. He also discovered a way in which I can purchase the necessary medication from the hospital at $3 a capsule – Dr Versace was prescribing 10 capsules a day so the expense is considerable. However Dr Thomas said the studies he had read of the use of AZT in HIV positive but not actual AIDS patients had involved some people being given 3 times a day and others 1 and the only difference being those taking 3 caps were more likely to suffer bone marrow deficiency. Ugh! This is all so ghastly. So after discussion we decided I'd be okay to cut back to 1 capsule 5 times a day (still $15). When I returned home I discovered the package of medication from the States sitting in the letter box. This morning I knew it would be there and was dreading that Mum would find it and I'd have to invent some explanation. Fortunately the mail was late. A young man was at the hospital seeing the same doctor, very thin and sickly looking, walking with a cane. Please God, not that. The worst thing about Auckland Hospital is the unpleasing mass of the main building. It sits dull and grey, with a smokestack on the horizon, certainly not looking inviting. On the contrary, looking rather repellent.

Hometown is continuing to frustrate me but I think, hope, I'm coming to terms with it. Got myself in a state yesterday when I couldn't even think about it any longer. It had worn me out. Am scared that will happen in general and that the plays I plan will suddenly seem too tiresome to write. Hope it doesn't happen before I do *Boxing Day*.

Te Puke, 13 November 1989

Here we are in the heart of the Bay of Plenty, in the house of my brother. I have set myself up in the purplish-pink spare bedroom which doubles as

Rich's office and will try and come to grips with *Hometown*, which continues to frustrate me but there is light ahead. A couple of conversations with Sue Wilson and writing a longish letter to her have helped clarify the problem and suggest solutions.

Last week I was sidetracked by writing some sketches for a comedy show for TV3. Sent them five sketches on Friday and hope they find them amusing and that it can lead to some regular work. Three of the pieces were monologues: 'Robin: *Tomorrow*'s Co-Host', based on the character in *The Affair* but much expanded and, as Stephanie Millar is to be on the show, it could work well for her. Might need to be refashioned somewhat. Also sent 'Frank', the rugby player plucked from *The Affair*, and 'Monica Plonk', who turned out to be a rather depressing and selfish individual. On top of this sent two sketches: one about a sharemilker whose favourite book is *The Heart Has Its Reasons* and the other about two Remuera housewives.

Mother and I have done quite a lot of work about the house and have finally sorted through all of Dad's books and have erected and stained the new bookcases. The spare room looks attractive and I'm about to seal off one end of the closet to finish it off. I have also been sorting through all my books left in Auckland since I left and have decided to sell them all. Most of them I'll never read again – especially the university textbooks. Also might as well be organized and ready should I suddenly depart this life.

Bobby and Henry Peake visited. Bobby's mother and Mum's father were brother and sister – other cousins of the same connection are June Blundell and Del Brake. Mother suggested to me that there is a 'streak' in that side of the family. Over morning tea on Sunday, Bobby began talking about friends who have a streak in their family. Mother and I decided on the way to Te Puke that we are all streaked. God knows I am.

As we drove, Mother and I discussed plans for the future, mine. Should she sell the second car or keep it in case I came home, what chairs would I want for my house, and so forth. It's very depressing for I find it impossible to say: 'don't worry, I'm not going to be here.'

14 November 1989

Rich has medication for his gout and is having a blood test today – he went on at length about his pills and his illness, all most amusing. And I'm sitting there not mentioning my own vast armoury of medication.

Auckland, 16 November 1989

Am screaming inside. Suddenly petrified. I don't know what I'm going to do. 'I'm dying. I'm dying. I'm dying' keeps going through my head. I'm scared, not of death but of the intervening period.

22 November 1989

My well-being seems to be intricately connected with how well my writing is going. For the past few days *Hometown* has been clicking into place and I've now completed the first act, have plotted out the first half of the second act and seem to be incorporating all the elements I want and getting a tapestry effect as well – with the interweaving of stories. Settled finally on a voiceover narration from Rod, the 14-year-old from whose point of view we see the film. Had originally wanted to stay clear of this and might in a final draft be able to remove it but don't think so. Today I hope to get well into Act Two.

Heard from the TV3 comedy people about my sketches, which they didn't enjoy and found 'a little sad', which is peculiar. But I have no idea what they're really looking for and they have no real interest in working with me so there we have it. This morning's paper announces the *Early Bird Show* on TV3, on which I did so much work with so much frustration. Ah, well.

Spoke to Dr Thomas, who claims my blood tests are okay, which is a huge relief. I'm beginning to regret returning to NYC in January but realize I have to and it will be fun auditioning for *Squirrel* and getting life squared away there. I should be able to finish off a draft of *Boxing Day*, which I'll start before leaving here, and maybe also work on *Lensman*.

1 January 1990

It's been nearly four weeks since I did any work on this record and I'm not sure why. Work overtook me to a large extent – suddenly *Hometown* had a momentum and rattled into life. I was able to deliver it to Pacific Films on time but was chagrined to learn they no longer seem to have the money ($6,000) which they owe me and I'm about to go back to the USA penniless. A great worry. The screenplay, however, is good and with some tightening up in the first two acts should make a pleasant movie. I finally got the *Gloss* money and was able to pay huge New Zealand and US credit card bills – I'm just sick of not having any money. And having paid the bills there was nothing left.

I received confirmation of being awarded the playwright-in-residence grant at the Fortune but now am in two minds – $12,000 for six months isn't a lot. I still want this American career and should make one more dash for that. Or should I? Confusion. At present I'm reworking *Squirrel* for the umpteenth time in preparation for the Primary Stages production.

Most of my working life this past month has been taken up with *Too Many Cooks*, a television sitcom being produced by Tony Holden of Comedia Productions for TVNZ – they want 14 episodes and it is supposed to go into production in June. Tony employed Anthony McCarten, the wildly successful co-author of *Ladies' Night*, to write the pilot and I have been pulled in at the suggestion of Sue Wilson – script editor – to help devise storylines, to help Anthony come up with a bible etc.* The problem is Anthony is young, inexperienced in television and doesn't really understand the medium and the responsibility to the audience. I hate the project and would love to get out of it but if John O'Shea isn't going to come through with money someone has to and this is the only possibility at this stage. Anthony is also vague in his writing and although *Ladies* is a wild success it isn't because it's a good play, in fact it's an awful creepy-crawly play with some good moments. I've been trying to pull various threads together but so far without success. It is a sitcom without a situation – a seven-member family struggling to get by in the 1990s but with no point of view, nub, whatever you might want to call it. I wish I could extract myself. Basic problem: it's not funny.

---

* **Anthony McCarten**, New Zealand playwright, screenwriter and filmmaker; now best known for award-winning biopics and the 2022 Broadway musical *A Beautiful Noise*, about Neil Diamond.

2 January 1990

My attitude to the illness has been peculiar – I seem to forget about it and then find it nagging at the back of my mind or bouncing round the front of my mind. Am I just going to waste away? Having heard about the months of suffering others have gone through I'm petrified of the same – not so much of dying. And also it is the attitude of family and friends. In the past three months I haven't found anyone I can mention my situation to that it wouldn't be an enormous problem for them to deal with. I constantly feel it's better to keep it to myself. The doctor at Auckland Hospital – Mark Thomas – has been excellent and sympathetic and encouraging. A few weeks back, when Nick Enright was here, I had a few people round for drinks (including Maurice Shadbolt, Liz Greenslade, Ilona Rodgers) and suddenly they were all talking about AIDS and people who'd died and alternative treatments.* I felt quite giddy for a moment and then carried on. When Richard and his family visited for the family reunion Richard made several disparaging comments about homosexuals: I stare at him with blank amazement, how insensitive can he be? Or is he being deliberately cruel? I visit Jack and Lorelle in Wellington and they talk, of course, about their dog Patch whom they adore and the trouble they have had finding a person to trim Patch's coat. Lorelle leapt into a horrifying tale of taking Patch to a dog boutique in Miramar run by a really queer queer. Every three minutes another queer came into the shop. Lorelle couldn't wait to escape. And I look at her and wonder just how stupid she is. At Richard's in Te Puke his sister-in-law gives her husband a tape of Candlelight Piano music which he has asked for. It is by one Carl Doy. The husband makes several rude comments about Doy, who is 'a queer'. It is truly extraordinary. I feel these people have a vicious streak but in good New Zealand fashion manage to camouflage their intentions if not their words. 'Oh, I never thought … he is? … really? Isn't it sad?'

Anyway what this family will do when/if I topple headlong into serious and socially unacceptable illness I do not know. Presumably I will not have to bear the brunt of that – my mother will. And what she will think is another

---

* **Liz Greenslade**, New Zealand researcher and part of 1980s television research company Bluestockings. **Ilona Rodgers**, British-born stage and screen actress who starred as Maxine Redfern in *Gloss*.

problem. I don't really want her going through all the flack. I do try and help her, spend time here, etc. I certainly don't want to get ill and languish in New York. When I go back later in the month I will join the Hemlock Society [an assisted suicide organisation] so I can be prepared if things get too bad. It's strange, I dream about Russell constantly. Ah, that was a mess. Last night we had the Blakelys, Mrs Kellaway and Lady Blundell for dinner – all quite pleasant. Polite. I can't imagine what they really think of me or will think of me. Read in this morning's paper of an AIDS patient being shot by a friend who then shot himself. Received a Christmas card from Mason Wiley, who was off to spend New Year in LA with a dying friend. Reality intrudes.

I feel bad that I haven't done all the jobs I wanted to do while I was here. Really haven't done enough in the garden and have to trim trees on the lower level. But have managed to get the little office downstairs looking good. The room looks great with the bookshelves and tomorrow I'm going to tackle Dad's workshop area. I need to encourage Mum to offload some furniture – there is a lot of stuff in the basement that isn't really useful and just cluttering things up. She is keen on the idea.

5 January 1990

Spoke to John O'Shea today and there is some confusion about *Hometown* – apparently the Film Commission didn't think they had to fund the delivery of the script or something of the sort. Anyway, the six thousand dollars may make an appearance on Tuesday or it may not. I've got to have it, that's all there is to it. And John is being negative about the script – or, to put it in a nicer fashion – not very positive. He uses phrases like 'slight' and says it 'doesn't come off the page'. Etc. I have a terrible feeling it'll all just languish and never happen. In the meantime I have to change my plans and fly down [to Wellington] on Sunday afternoon so I can meet with him, which I'd rather not do. Yesterday I had my ticket updated and promptly lost it and now have to pay another $87. Today I went by the hospital and picked up two weeks' medication at a cost of $190.

• • •

There are no entries for 1990 after that of 5 January. Robert did not resume writing in his diary until early 1991, when he wrote relatively little. He returned to New York in early 1990 to direct a production of *The Travelling Squirrel* at Primary Stages. The *Hometown* movie did not progress to a second draft. Comedia Productions commissioned the television series *Too Many Cooks*, for which Robert wrote six episodes. He returned to New Zealand to work on the production, but it was cancelled. *Glorious Ruins* was staged at Circa in Wellington and later at Dunedin's Fortune Theatre, and Robert took up a six-month playwrights' residency at the Fortune.

In 1991 Robert had returned to live in his Titan Street cottage in Dunedin. He planned to continue working on *Academic Circles* and *The Backbenchers*, but completed neither play. He gave priority to the *Boxing Day* play commissioned by Circa, and a reading was held in June. This play, finally called *Joyful and Triumphant*, was completed and scheduled for production in early 1992. Robert then turned his attention to several film projects. He tried to interest producers in a New Zealand version of *Chicken Kiev*, a screenplay he had written in America the previous year. US-based film director Roger Donaldson took Robert to Cape Canaveral to witness a space shuttle launch and paid him to write a screenplay provisionally titled *Lightning Ridge*. Donaldson also arranged for Robert to write dialogue for a John Keir and Pat Cox movie provisionally titled *The Big Ditch*. Neither *Lightning Ridge* nor *The Big Ditch* was ever made. Robert wrote a radio play called *No Mean Feat*, set in Invercargill, and worked on a detailed plotline for *Private Reserve*, the novel he had been thinking about for a while.

1991

Robert at home in Dunedin in 1991. Private collection

22 March 1991

Outside it's overcast and damp. The first day like this in weeks. We have had an Indian summer. Warm and comfortable. And a time for picnics. Of course it's also been a good time to procrastinate. I finally managed to get the scene breakdown for *Hometown* finished and sent off to Wellington. But since then, although I've looked at *Boxing Day*, I haven't really accomplished much.

There are several projects floating around at the moment. *No Mean Feat*, a shortish play I wrote for radio, could and perhaps should be developed for the stage. *Chicken Kiev*, a screenplay, could also be reworked for the stage. And the aforementioned *Boxing Day*.

The problem with *Boxing Day* has always been plot, or rather the lack thereof. I have wanted to create a play which could take in the whole post-war era, dotting realistic scenes over the past 45 years. But it doesn't seem to be coming out that way. Then I have wanted to make it personal. But personal isn't right either. I don't know what I have to say about my life personally. I find it hard to take myself very seriously but perhaps that is simply a pose – I don't think so.

I find it interesting that people like Tony Taylor and Mervyn Thompson seem to see themselves as the centre of the universe and the intensity of their self-absorption is strong enough to pull others along with them.*
I'm not suggesting that these men are misguided. They have more faith in themselves than I do in myself.

The immediate problem is to complete a draft of *Boxing Day* or whatever I end up calling it. Half the motivation is in order to get the $1500 owed on completion. And I'd like to have a finished New Zealand play anyway. So who am I writing about: who is the centre? It seems to me that I'm writing about Granny Lord and Rose but I have them moved up half a generation.

Another major problem is how to write the play without a cast of thousands. I'd toyed with the idea of a Pete [AR] Gurney *Dining Room* play with lots of scenes and many characters but played by a small group of actors.

---

* **Mervyn Thompson** (1935–1992), New Zealand academic, director and playwright; one of the founders of Christchurch's Court Theatre and also worked as artistic director at Downstage.

HOWICK
LITTLE
THEATRE

presents the
New Zealand
drama by
Robert Lord

DIRECTED BY
SHEILA SUMMERS

8 p.m.

MARCH 5 to 26
Matinée 6 p.m.
Sunday 20 th

Adults $13.50
Senior citizens and
students $10.00

BOOKINGS AT
THE THEATRE
Ph 534 1406

1994

'The Boxing Day play' and 'the Christmas play' became *Joyful and Triumphant*. This is the poster from the Howick Little Theatre production of 1994. MS-1907/031, Hocken Collections

Opposite: A 2016 Circa production of *Joyful and Triumphant* included cast members from the 1992 premiere. From left to right: Jane Waddell, Peter Hambleton, Michelle Amas, Gavin Rutherford, Catherine Downes, Lyndee-Jane Rutherford. Circa Theatre collection

CELEBRATING CIRCA THEATRE'S 40TH BIRTHDAY

JOYFUL & TRIUMPHANT

An incidental epic

written by **ROBERT LORD** | directed by **SUSAN WILSON**

Proudly Supported by **Peter Biggs** CNZM **and Mary Biggs**

circa.co.nz | 801 7992

ⓒ CIRCA

2 April – 7 May

25 March 1991

Have done absolutely nothing for the past several days. Well, not absolutely nothing but certainly no writing. Have bottled fruit, made bread, cooked meals and watched television. I hate these periods of working my way into a project. Life seems negative and heavy on my shoulders. I hope to God it passes soon.

Why am I resisting *Boxing Day*? What is the story? A woman and her mother locked in an unhappy relationship. It seems rather like a thousand other plays. I need to find a level of poetry on which it can work. Or a narrative voice.

28 March 1991

Christchurch. A motel on Carlton Mill Road. I drove up here Monday afternoon to see the radiologist about the growth on my right temple which has been bugging me for the past several months. I should have been getting treatment in Dunedin and it should have started months ago but for a series of delays and evasions which finally revealed the fact that the Dunedin machine was broken. Now I have to come up to Christchurch for twice-daily treatment for 15 working days – and with Easter being on us this spreads out over several weeks. Most annoying and it will mean I have to opt out of Writers' Week – and also a rather nasty reminder of mortality and I'll look bizarre for a while.

Anyway, back to *Boxing Day*. An overbearing mother and a daughter she keeps close by her. A son who has escaped the nest and who is therefore never forgiven by mother or sister. A two-levelled story: front story – Mary, the daughter, has a beau who is, unbeknown to her, married. Mary's mother, Elizabeth, discovers this and gets rid of the beau (Bob). Back story – as a teenager, Mary became pregnant and was forced to adopt out the baby after a trip up north. Her father died shortly after this and Mum has always blamed Mary for his death.

29 March 1991

Back from Christchurch last night. Just under 5 hours in the old Mini, which is hell on the bones, and the mind wanders far and wide and the thoughts flash past like grass on the roadside. Must get some recorded books for the next trip so I can listen to something decent and not the static-laden radio. Spoke to Mum, who is going to delay her trip until after the Christchurch treatment is finished.

Now the thing is to make headway on *Boxing Day* and I'm determined to plot out the action and get some dialogue under my belt before the weekend is over. Oh, do I want it done!

• • •

Overleaf: Tabitha Arthur designed this poster for the 2015 Circa Theatre production of *The Travelling Squirrel*, featuring actors Acushla-Tara Kupe and Paul Waggott. Kupe was also the play's publicist. Circa Theatre collection

UNITED BY LOVE.
DIVIDED BY A SQUIRREL.

THE TRAVELLING SQUiRREL

BY ROBERT LORD
(JOYFUL AND TRIUMPHANT)
DIRECTED BY SUSAN WILSON

NEW ZEALAND PLAYWRIGHTS
PLAYMARKET
AGENT. ADVISOR. BOOKSHOP

5 SEPT – 2 OCT
BOOKINGS
801 7992 www.circa.co.nz

CIRCA
THEATR

CREATIVE WORKS

ROBERT LORD often rewrote his plays, sometimes multiple times, creating many versions of some scripts. He frequently used a working title until he chose a title for production, and he sometimes changed titles for subsequent productions. We indicate as many of these changes as possible in the list below. Lord regarded *Well Hung* to be a different play from *Cop Shop* or *Country Cops*. *It Isn't Cricket* was written for New Zealand audiences, while *The Most Valued Player* retains the same characters and almost the same structure but is written for American audiences. *Bert and Maisy* is the final title for a play that went through many titles and versions: *Family Portrait*, *A Hint of Scandal* and *Unfamiliar Steps*.

We list the first professional staged reading or full professional production of each play. Many plays went through a long process of workshopping and readings by professional actors while Lord lived in the United States.

We also include plays for which we can find no record of a professional rehearsed reading or production (NRPP), although some of these were performed by amateur or student groups. The titles for which we have no confirmed date are listed in the order we estimate them to have been written. The asterisked plays are currently available for production through Playmarket. The others are held for archival purposes at the Hocken Collections or the Alexander Turnbull Library.

Plays for stage

*It Isn't Cricket** (1971), Downstage Theatre, Wellington, rewritten for American
    audiences as *The Most Valued Player* (no date)
*Balance of Payments** (1972, one-act play), Unity Theatre, Wellington
*Meeting Place** (1972), Downstage Theatre, Wellington
*Broken Circle** (no date, one-act play), NRPP
*Friendship Centre** (1973, one-act play), NRPP
Knife (no date, one-act play), NRPP
Nativity (1973, one-act play), Theatre Corporate, Auckland
*Well Hung** (1974), Downstage Theatre, Wellington
*Heroes and Butterflies** (1974), Mercury Theatre, Auckland
*Glitter and Spit** (1975), published in *Act* magazine, NRPP

Dead and Never Called Me Mother (1975), Eugene O'Neill Playwrights
Conference, Connecticut, USA. Developed from the earlier play *The Rough
and the Tumble* (no date)

On a Weekday in Summer (no date), NRPP

I'll Scream If I Want To (1976), Provincetown Playhouse, Provincetown,
Massachusetts, USA

Overture (no date, one-act play), NRPP

Cop Shop (1979), St Lawrence Centre, Toronto, Canada. North American
version of *Well Hung*

*High as a Kite** (1979), Downstage Theatre, Wellington. *The Kite Play* was a
working title. Developed from the radio play *Blood On My Sprigs* (1973) and
the stage play *I'll Scream If I Want To* (1976)

Unfamiliar Steps (1983), Court Theatre, Christchurch; also titled *A Family
Portrait*, *A Hint of Scandal* and finally *Bert and Maisy** (1984), Stables
Theatre, Sydney

*Country Cops** (1985), Circa Theatre, Wellington. Another version of *Well Hung*
and *Cop Shop*

*The Travelling Squirrel** (1986), Long Wharf Theatre, Connecticut, USA. *Roger, the
Travelling Squirrel* was a working title and a later version was titled *Star Crazy*
(1988), NRPP

*China Wars** (1987), Circa Theatre, Wellington

*The Affair** (1987), Globe Theatre, Dunedin

*Glorious Ruins** (1991), Circa Theatre, Wellington

*Joyful and Triumphant** (1992), Circa Theatre, Wellington. *The Christmas Play*
and *The Boxing Day Play* were working titles

*Well Hung** (2011), Auckland Theatre Company: new version edited by
Stephen Sinclair

INCOMPLETE PLAYS

Eliot (no date)

Academic Circles (1991)

The Backbenchers (1991)

ORIGINAL RADIO PLAYS

Moody Tuesday (1972)

Friendship Centre (1972)

Blood On My Sprigs (1973)
The Body in the Park (1973)
Sergei's Strawberry Surprise (1975)
The Body in the Bathtub (1987)
The Garden Affair (1991)

Radio Plays adapted from stage plays
Heroes and Butterflies (1974)
Bert and Maisy (1983)
Joyful and Triumphant (1993)

Unproduced radio plays or adaptations
The Affair
Bert's World
No Mean Feat

Television plays adapted from stage plays
Friendship Centre (1973), NZBC
Joyful and Triumphant (1993), TVNZ

Television series
Episodes of *Ryan's Hope* (1976), ABC, USA
Episodes of *Peppermint Twist* (1986–87), TVNZ
Bert and Maisy (1987), TVNZ

Unproduced television series
Houses and Gardens
Too Many Cooks

Films
The Day We Landed on the Most Perfect Planet in the Universe (1972), Pacific
    Films, NZBC
Pictures (1980), co-written with John O'Shea, Pacific Films

Unproduced films
Everything You Ever Wanted to Know About My Hometown
Chicken Kiev

ACKNOWLEDGEMENTS

PRODUCING A BOOK is a collaborative process, and *Robert Lord Diaries* has involved input from people around the globe. Many of Robert's friends, family members and colleagues came forward to provide some of the biographical details that appear in our notes and to help identify people in photographs. We are grateful to the following for their assistance: Donna Akersten, Sunny Amey, Jim Anglem, Mike Arthur, Craig Ashley, Tim Baigent, Hamish Blennerhassett, Tim Brosnahan, Casey Childs, Sonja Easterbrook-Smith, Karen Elliot, Catherine Fitzgerald, Alex Frame, Roger Hall, John Kelly, Mike Knudsen, Robert La Fosse, Judy Lessing, Reg Livermore, Nathan Lord, Richard Lord, Murray Lynch, Alister McDonald, Garry McDonald, Ginette McDonald, Claire Matthewson, Michael Metzger, Molly O'Shea, Bruce Phillips, Russell Poole, Joyce Reehling, Judy Russell, Ethan Silverman, Simon Taylor, Mary Varnham, Jane Waddell, Michael Weller, Jan Williams, Susan Wilson and Craig Wright.

We would like to thank Russell Craig, Alex Ely and Bobby Miller, who sent us photos of Robert and his friends that appear in the book. Likewise, Steve Dakin's short unpublished memoir, 'Hitching a Ride with Bob', provided rich detail about Robert as a teenager, and we wove elements of this into our introduction.

As always, staff at the Hocken Collections have been unfailingly cheerful and helpful with archival searches and numerous photographic orders.

Jane Parkin is a wonderful editor. She has taken in her stride our many late changes, and her sensitive suggestions have greatly improved the book. Sue Wootton and Mel Stevens at Otago University Press have actively supported the project, and Fiona Moffat has designed a beautiful volume of which Robert would have been proud.

Mercury Theatre's
production of *Bert and
Maisy*, 1986. Left to right:
Alexander van Dam, Ross
Duncan, Maya Dalziel,
David Weatherley,
Alma Woods.

MS-2438/019/001,
Hocken Collections

INDEX

Bold denotes illustrations and captions.

Notes

Where Lord's plays have working/early titles (i.e. *A Hint of Scandal*, *A Family Portrait* and *Unfamiliar Steps* for *Bert and Maisy*; and *Roger the Travelling Squirrel* and *Roger* for *The Travelling Squirrel*), references within the book have been indexed using the final/most common title, i.e. *Bert and Maisy* and *The Travelling Squirrel*.

Where names have been changed, aliases have not been indexed.

Published by Otago University Press
533 Castle Street
Dunedin, New Zealand
university.press@otago.ac.nz
www.oup.nz

First published 2023
Introduction copyright © Chris Brickell, Vanessa Manhire & Nonnita Rees
The moral rights of the authors have been asserted.
The edited diaries of Robert Lord © The Estate of Robert Lord deceased (The Writers Cottage Trust) 2023

ISBN 978-1-99-004858-6

Published with the assistance of Creative New Zealand

Back cover: Robert at Venice Beach, Los Angeles, 10 January 1986.
MS-1907/003/001, Hocken Collections

Endpapers: The set of Bert and Maisy, Circa Theatre, 1986.
Photograph by Justine Lord. MS-2438/019/003, Hocken Collections

Page 3: A 1979 publicity photo of Robert Lord.
MS-2438/223/003, Hocken Collections

Page 5: Robert and his beagle Becky in December 1977.
MS-1907/11/065, Hocken Collections

Pages 6–7: Robert in New York with the Statue of Liberty
in the background. MS-1907/007/001/001, Hocken Collections

Editor: Jane Parkin
Index: Lee Slater
Printed in China through Asia Pacific Offset